Making Sense of the Holocaust

LESSONS FROM CLASSROOM PRACTICE

Making Sense of the Holocaust

LESSONS FROM CLASSROOM PRACTICE

Simone Schweber

Foreword by Gloria Ladson-Billings

Teachers College, Columbia University
New York and London

Chapter 3, "Simulating Survival," by Simone Schweber originally appeared in *Curriculum Inquiry, 33*(2), Summer 2003, pp. 139–188. Reprinted by permission of Blackwell Publishing Ltd.

Published by Teachers College Press, 1234 Amsterdam Avenue, New York, NY 10027

Library of Congress Cataloging-in-Publication Data

Schweber, Simone.
Making sense of the Holocaust : lessons from classroom practice / Simone Schweber ; foreword by Gloria Ladson-Billings.
p. cm.
Includes bibliographical references and index.
ISBN 0-8077-4436-0 (cloth : alk. paper) — ISBN 0-8077-4435-2 (pbk. : alk. paper)
1. Holocaust, Jewish (1939–1945)—Study and teaching—United States.
I. Title.
D804.33.S35 2004
940.53'18'071—dc22 2003067176

ISBN: 0-8077-4435-2 (paper)
ISBN: 0-8077-4436-0 (cloth)

Printed on acid-free paper
Manufactured in the United States of America

11 10 09 08 07 06 05 04 8 7 6 5 4 3 2 1

This book is dedicated to my grandmother,
Dora Schweber (of blessed memory),
whose courage saved whole worlds.

Contents

Foreword

In the mid-1970s I was working at my dream job. I was serving as the social studies/science consultant for one of the eight geographic districts of the School District of Philadelphia. The politics of the position allowed me to ignore everything after the slash and focus solely on the social studies, particularly history. The city was abuzz with its preparation for the nation's bicentennial and teachers throughout the Philadelphia region were searching for resource materials and innovative lessons to teach about the founding of the United States. One of the central office supervisors called me to discuss an idea for a citywide curriculum. In those days, curriculum specialists, teachers, and sometimes community members were responsible for writing curriculum—not textbook publishers or test makers. The supervisor wanted to do a curriculum on the Holocaust.

In 1967 Philadelphia had gone through a radical curriculum shift, brought about by angry African American students. They were tired of the irrelevant, bland curriculum that virtually erased their history and culture from all their school experiences. Their fervent protest was the impetus for the creation of the school district's Office of Afro-American Studies. This office developed many innovative and creative curriculum guides for teachers and ensured that all Philadelphia school students would have access to a fuller understanding of the Black Experience in the Americas.

Initially, I was lukewarm about participation in the Holocaust curriculum. I knew little beyond the military–political history of World War II. I knew that there were concentration camps. I knew that Hitler was a monster. I knew that the United States had hesitated to involve itself in the war in Europe. I knew what most people knew. But I did not know the story from the bottom up. I had never met a Holocaust survivor. I had vague memories of the owner of my corner delicatessen, who had a blue number tattooed on his wrist, but I did not really understand the significance of such a mark. In the process of working on the Holocaust curriculum I got a real education about human suffering. A big component of the curriculum was inclusion of the words of survivors. We included those words through both their writing—stories, poems, songs—and their actual voices, by means of a speakers' bureau component. It was impossible to participate in that curriculum-writing process without making a commitment to it. We emerged with a powerful curriculum project that maintained the specificity of the Holocaust and linked it to the general concerns of worldwide human suffering—historical and contemporary.

The most startling aspect of working on the Holocaust curriculum came as we began community and professional development to launch it. Some in the African American community could not see its relevance to their children's educational experience, but as we helped people understand the connections between this specific horror and the broader dangers of discrimination, racism, hatred, and genocide, more African American community members recognized the value of such a curriculum. Almost always, by the time one of the survivors told her or his story, the constituents endorsed the curriculum. In some areas we encountered reactionary voices that denied that the Holocaust ever occurred. Typically such speakers were rebuked by the audience and paradoxically made our case for us. A more curious group was a group of survivors and children of survivors. A number of them did not want "the whole ugly era dredged up." Why were we talking about this? Why didn't we just let it stay buried in the past? Didn't we understand how painful this was? These reactions were not unlike those of older Blacks who had escaped the humiliation and terror of the Jim Crow South and wanted to live out their lives in the northern cities without any reminders of that horrible past.

It was with this last group that I had my most difficult moments. It was also with this group that I had my own breakthrough. "How would I have ever known of your suffering without this effort?" "How can we prevent this from happening again?" "How can my children learn to respect your children if they do not know the road your children have traveled?" The struggle for the curriculum was in itself a lesson in the promise of democracy. It reminded me of why I had chosen a career in education.

In *Making Sense of the Holocaust: Lessons from Classroom Practice*, author Simone Schweber offers both a caution and a hope. The caution is derived from the examples of classroom teaching in which the Holocaust is constructed as a set of facts about a historical era. This construction is in some ways similar to the current construction of the Iraqi torture and mass killings that are emerging on postwar news coverage. We see the magnitude of the tragedy but we see it through the narrow lenses of our own interests. We assert that we did the right thing in invading Iraq because the cruel dictator had to be stopped. However, the victims of the suffering remain nameless and faceless. There is not even an Anne Frank–like character to serve as a tableau upon which we can play out our emotions and sensibilities about the suffering.

The hope offered in this volume springs from those lessons that allow students to delve deeply into the experience of the Holocaust. Here we see teaching that engages students on multiple levels—intellectual, emotional, and spiritual. This is a hope for a kind of educational experience that transforms learners from passive recipients of knowledge to active, participatory citizens in an increasingly diverse democratic society. When I read about Mr. Zee teaching the students about the concept "universe of obligation," and the problematic of "simulating the Holocaust," I was struck by the daunting challenge of helping students understand and "do something with" the moral discourse of the Holocaust.

In Schweber's description of the Castlemont High School/*Schindler's List* incident I was reminded of my own experience at the opening of Spike Lee's *Malcolm X*. I saw the movie in a downtown Detroit theater that was filled with teenagers. They began laughing and talking, which continued until an imposing African American man began to patrol the theater aisles with a flashlight, warning them that they would be thrown out unless they quieted down. What moral lessons can adolescents absorb? What moral lessons can adolescents who are on the social and economic margins make sense of when their own basic needs are so regularly and systematically ignored?

Making Sense of the Holocaust is simultaneously provocative and poignant. The portraits of the teachers and their practices are vivid and revealing. The students and their responses are predictably unpredictable. We never know what they will say or how they will make sense out of what their teachers attempt to teach them. The book is neither damning nor celebratory. Instead, it is a combination of microscopic and telescopic. It looks at the fine grain of individual teachers in their classrooms, and it also looks at the big picture of the moral overlay that teaching about massive injustice instigates in U.S. schools. This is a powerful mélange of curriculum, pedagogy, and the theories that undergird them.

Gloria Ladson-Billings
University of Wisconsin–Madison, July 2003

Acknowledgments

There are many people to whom I am indebted for helping me envision and complete this book. First among them are the teachers and students who welcomed me into their classrooms, shared their work with me, and allowed me entrance into the private realms of their thoughts. If not for their daring, I would not have been able to do the research on which the book is founded.

I also want to thank members of the Stanford University faculty, whose support took many forms. Lee Shulman consistently pushed me to consider the "big picture," stretching me to see the Holocaust as a case-of rather than an end point. Steven Zipperstein's quiet encouragement and clear enthusiasm buoyed my spirits at particularly low moments, and his keen insights honed my historical thinking and sharpened my writing. I wish to thank Nel Noddings for the graceful way in which she illuminated moral complexities that I had overlooked or underestimated. And to Larry Cuban, I owe more than I can write. His immense integrity and intellectual rigor, the kindness with which he dispenses hard advice, and the ease with which he laughs have helped me become a better teacher, a competent researcher, and, in an attempt to follow his example, a more honorable person.

My two friends and reading group members, Denise Clark Pope and Katherine Simon, were tremendously influential in shaping this work. I thank both of them for their acuity of vision in this project, their relentless editing, and their unflagging emotional support. (I also forgive them for having their wonderful books out well in advance of this one.)

The following people read chapters at one point or another, talked me through them, or both, providing me with invaluable feedback from both within and beyond academic horizons: Michael Apple, Miriam Ben-Peretz, Egon Bitner (of blessed memory), Aryeh Davidson, Ellen Dekker, Barbara Goodman, Carl Grant, Beth Graue, Diana Hess, Esther Landau, Joe Lukinsky, Lisa Malik, Daniel Pekarsky, Tom Popkewitz, Joe Reimer, Eileen Soffer, David Sorkin, Stephanie Stone, Laura Woodlief, Ken Zeichner, and Michael Zeldin. This book couldn't have been completed if not for the hard work of my friends and students Susan Gevelber and

Rebekah Irwin, who cleaned up the manuscript in its (one of its many) final stages.

I need to thank the Wexner Foundation, the Center for Jewish Studies at the University of Wisconsin–Madison, and Michael and Judy Goodman for their generous support of my continuing education. And, for her editorial prowess and supreme patience, I thank my editor at Teachers College Press, Susan Liddicoat.

Finally, I wish to remember my mother (of blessed memory), to thank my father, and to recognize my siblings, who together first nurtured in me a thirst for intellectual challenge and an eye for moral complexity. And for my biggest fans, my spouse and children, I count my blessings daily.

Making Sense of the Holocaust

LESSONS FROM CLASSROOM PRACTICE

Chapter 1

From Inexperience to Education

In one of my first jobs out of college, I worked at a small, nonprofit Holocaust organization that collected books, catered to the needs of local survivors, and provided materials and resources to area teachers. As the education coordinator, I had the job of accompanying to school engagements the few survivors who spoke publicly about their experiences in Nazi-occupied Europe. One of these trips stands out strongly in my memory, not for what happened at the school but for what happened on the way to it.

I was traveling with René Molho (now of blessed memory), a survivor of Auschwitz who came originally from Salonika, Greece. René had lost his entire family in Auschwitz, his brother dying in his arms after having had ruthless medical experiments performed on him. René survived, returned to Salonika, and married someone he had known growing up, a woman who had survived the war in hiding, and who, like him, had lost her entire family. In the hopes of escaping their nightmares, they had eventually moved to the United States, succeeded professionally, and raised an only son who was tragically killed in a car accident years later.

After retiring, René frequently spoke at schools, sometimes more than twice a day, and he always insisted on being the one to drive. On the morning of this memory, we were scheduled to appear at a rural school for a first-period assembly, which meant that we had to leave the city at about 6 A.M. When René arrived to pick me up, I had bought coffee for both of us, in portable, paper cups, what was then a newfangled technology. I don't remember how it happened exactly—probably René was regaling me with jokes—but somewhere along the highway, unused to carry-away lids, René lifted the wrong side of the cup to his lips, spilling scorching hot coffee on his white turtleneck.

The car swerved for just a moment, but it was enough to ignite the sirens of a policeman a few cars behind us, hidden by the heavy traffic. René dutifully pulled over, and the policeman asked to see identification. As the officer walked back to his car to check René's license, I noticed that René was clutching the steering wheel with white-knuckled force and sweating profusely. Men in uniform, he explained to me, always provoked that reaction. He pushed up his sleeves to try to cool down.

As the policeman approached the car window to return René's license, he noticed the blue number on René's forearm. The coolness of his manner dissolved instantly. He seemed to falter as he asked about the tattoo: "Is that what I think it is?" René, always mischievous, replied in thickly accented English, "That depends what you think it is." "Were you in one of those—uh—camps?" "More than one," Rene responded. "Well, Jeez, be careful out there. You didn't live through all that to lose it on the road," the officer exclaimed, patting René's arm gingerly and letting him go without a ticket. René turned his turtleneck around, as he didn't want the students' first impression of a survivor to be of one with a stained shirt. He (carefully) sipped some coffee, joked about Auschwitz finally paying off, and drove to the school.

I recount this memory here because the policeman's reaction epitomizes a response to the Holocaust that I think of as typical for a certain generation of Americans. Regardless of what the officer actually knew about the Holocaust or the concentration camp system, and regardless of whether it was the result of intuition or schooling, he understood enough to know that the number on René's arm signified the endurance of horrors, and he knew enough to react with a sense of wonderment, even awe.

The students René and I encountered in schools, by contrast, had little, if any, connection to the Holocaust and no emotional apparatus through which to apprehend it appropriately. If a family member served in World War II, it was likely a grandparent or great-grandparent, someone whose experience was far enough removed for the emotional ripples to be invisible or at the very least inaccessible. While my visits with survivors to schools were made in the hopes of paving the way to understanding, the students had so little background knowledge of the Holocaust that at times our visits felt fruitless. "Where were the police?" I remember one student asking a survivor. "Why didn't you escape?" was always posed. I think the following events vividly illustrate the ramifications of such inexperience, illuminating the impetus behind my writing this book.

FROM INEXPERIENCE TO EDUCATION

On January 17, 1994, Martin Luther King Jr.'s birthday, a group of mostly Black and Latino students from Castlemont High School in Oakland,

California, went to the movies with their teachers. The students, most from low-income families, were excited at the holiday outing's prospects. They had wanted to see the movie, *House Party 3* (Hudlin & Toney, 1994), a teen comedy about fraternity house shenanigans. Their teacher, Mark Rader, had recommended they see Steven Speilberg's just-released drama, *Schindler's List* (Spielberg, 1993), instead, as a way to honor the memory of Martin Luther King Jr., by learning about another instance of racial discrimination. With a trip to an ice-skating rink promised as a reward, the students agreed to see Rader's choice. The students arrived at the local theater for the matinee showing. They had neither studied the Holocaust nor been alerted to the serious content of the film, its 3-hour length, or its black-and-white format. What happened next ignited a flurry of media coverage and political maneuvering that reverberated for months.

As Christine Spolar of the *Washington Post* (Spolar, 1994) described it:

> About an hour into the matinee at the Grand Lake Theater, a boy shouted as a young Jewish woman was slaughtered on screen. "Oh," he said, "that was cold." Laughter followed. A couple of dozen other moviegoers—some whose family members had died in the Holocaust—besieged the theater manager to complain.
>
> Suddenly, the lights came up in the theater. Owner Allen Michaan walked out and asked for all Castlemont students to go to the lobby. Too many other patrons had complained, he said later, that the students talked and laughed throughout the movie, and, in particular, laughed at murder. As the 73 students walked out, some of the patrons, obviously angry, gave a standing ovation.
>
> No teacher or student expected anything more to happen. In the insular world of Castlemont High, the episode was chalked up as a minor disaster. (p. C1)

The students left the theater and returned to their school. Their trip to the skating rink was canceled. One student, whose reaction was probably not unique, explained her feelings this way: "I tell you, I was disappointed; it was my first time to go ice skating" (p. C4).

A short article about the incident appeared the next day in a local paper, catapulting it into national attention by the week's end. Numerous other newspaper articles, editorials, and letters were published on the topic throughout the country, while radio talk shows and nightly television coverage fanned the flames of controversy. Had the students been anti-Semitic? Were the Jewish patrons at the matinee or the Jewish theater owner racist? Was this yet another eruption of heightened tensions or another proof of soured relations between Blacks and Jews? Or was it a case of "ordinary teenage behavior and adult response" (Spolar,

1994, p. C4)? Had the students' constant exposure to violence both in the media and in their real lives inured them to the seriousness of the Holocaust or to violence in movies? Was the subject matter of the Holocaust inappropriate for a Martin Luther King Day commemoration, considering how little most of these students knew about African American history? Was the movie dull, or were the students' parents to be blamed for never having taught their children proper etiquette? Was it the teacher's fault for not having prepared his students, or did the Jewish audience members overreact, demonizing nervous laughter in a movie theater? Questions like these swirled around the Castlemont students, prompting local and state agencies to intervene.

Within the first week of the article's appearance, both Jewish and Black organizations competed for the privilege of giving workshops and presentations at Castlemont. Over the following few months, the students were taken out of regular classes repeatedly to be taught about the Holocaust, to hear survivors speak, and to be lectured on the Black diaspora, relations between Blacks and Jews, the importance of tolerance, and the functioning of the news media. By 3 days after the incident, the students had received enough media attention to realize the magnitude of their faux pas. At a news conference, a self-possessed student council president, Kandi Stewart, issued an apology on behalf of all the students who had attended the show. For this she earned then-governor Pete Wilson's praise, for having transformed a blunder at a movie theater into an opportunity to educate. (At a later ceremony held at the Simon Wiesenthal Museum of Tolerance in Los Angeles, Wilson presented Castlemont High School with a Courage to Care Award in recognition of their quick recovery under the spotlight.)

Almost 3 months later, on April 11, without the teachers having been notified ahead of time, Wilson and director Steven Spielberg visited Castlemont. The two had chosen Castlemont as the site at which to unveil a statewide, and what would become a nationwide, effort to educate youth about the Holocaust using *Schindler's List*. Wilson's reception at the school was chilly. Kandi Stewart articulated widespread resentment against him in the region, saying to his face, "I see your visit as a failing governor's publicity stunt that enables you to portray yourself as a caring politician" (Rosenthal, 1994, p. A3). Spielberg, by contrast, was warmly embraced. Despite a handful of Black Muslim demonstrators protesting his visit by "carrying placards asking 'how a Zionist Jew could teach them about racism and oppression'" (p. A3), the students within the auditorium snapped photographs and listened eagerly. When Spielberg began his remarks by telling the students that as a teenager, he had been thrown out of a screening of the movie *Ben Hur* (Wallace & Tunberg, 1959) for talking too much, he won a standing ovation.

The *Schindler's List* Project, the program Wilson and Spielberg launched that day, consisted of Spielberg's paying the costs of showing the film to high school students at private screenings in movie theaters across the state. Wilson announced that starting that week, 16,000 students would thus learn about the Holocaust. As one newspaper columnist wrote, "That means the Castlemont students will finally get to see the rest of [*Schindler's List*]" (Laughter at Film, 1994, p. B11). According to Wilson, the point of the project was to help people "understand the potential evil of prejudice and hatred—and serve as a springboard to teach the lessons of all racial, religious and ethnic tolerance, and promote the notion that one person can make a difference" (Rosenthal, 1994, p. A3). In later months, following the worldwide, colossal financial success of the film, Spielberg expanded the project to include distributing videotaped copies of the film at no charge to high schools all over the country. With the rest of the approximately $100 million netted from *Schindler's List*, Spielberg established the Survivors of the Shoah Foundation, an organization dedicated to educating about the Holocaust through the production of documentary films and the collection of survivors' oral histories.

In retrospect, the Castlemont High incident was revealing in a variety of ways, not least of which that it exposed the ease with which the American press and public racialize conflict. Of special significance for this book, though, is the historical moment it highlights. By the mid-1990s, in contrast to earlier periods, wide consensus had crystallized around the Holocaust as a topic of educational import. The opening of the U.S. Holocaust Memorial Museum in Washington, D.C., the success of *Schindler's List*, and the 50th anniversaries of many key historical events such as the D-Day landing, the Warsaw Ghetto uprising, the liberation of the concentration camps, and the end of the war, all raised the visibility of the Holocaust in American public discourse, a trend that has continued. As Peter Novick (1999) writes, more than "fifty years after the fact and thousands of miles from its site—the Holocaust has come to loom . . . large in our culture" (p. 1). Whether a catalyst or by-product of this trend, there was consensus among a much larger public that Holocaust education in American public schools, once mainly the concern of Holocaust survivors and Jewish groups, was important. Indeed, many U.S. states (17 at last count; Feinberg & Totten, 2001) now mandate Holocaust education in some form, and it is more likely than not that a student graduating from an American public high school will encounter the Holocaust as part of the school curriculum. In this book I carefully analyze a few of those encounters and how they worked morally in the hopes of improving teaching, and ultimately learning, about the Holocaust.

TEACHING MORALITY

Underpinning the consensus around its import is the widespread belief that education about the Holocaust, by virtue of its subject matter alone, is a venue for instilling moral values. The U.S. Holocaust Memorial Museum's *Guidelines for Teaching About the Holocaust* (Parsons & Totten, 1994), for example, opens with the claim that "the history of the Holocaust represents one of the most effective, and most extensively documented subjects for a pedagogical examination of basic moral issues" (p. 1). This orientation is not unusual. Having examined many published Holocaust curricula, I have yet to see one that does not hold the inculcation of moral values as a central and defining mission. Similar goals motivate the *Schindler's List* Project—that prejudice and hatred potentially wreak havoc; that racial, religious, and ethnic tolerance are crucial; and that "one person can make a difference." Other moral lessons the Holocaust is often assumed to convey include understanding the importance of maintaining the sanctity of all human life, questioning authority, opposing unjust laws, eschewing indifference to the suffering of others, fostering the rights of the individual, safeguarding the rights of minorities, and considering the potential consequences of racism and totalitarianism. Since the Holocaust is widely held to contain lessons for all human beings, it is considered especially relevant subject matter for that subset whose moral compasses are thought to be undergoing fine-tuning for future use: adolescents. Because the Holocaust has become, in the words of one cultural critic, "a master moral paradigm in American consciousness" (Loshitzky, 1997, p. 8), education about the Holocaust is often perceived as a perfect venue for moral education.

Perhaps because of these widely held assumptions, Castlemont teacher Mark Rader fell prey to a common misconception about this moral content. He assumed that the importance of the Holocaust would be as self-evident to his students as it no doubt was for himself and for the police officer who stopped René on the highway. He assumed that the Holocaust's moral lessons would not require formal teaching and that its resonance with American history would be plain. He presumed, in other words, that the film itself would suffice in teaching students about the Holocaust. While the Castlemont High incident points up the limits of using movies as education, it also implies something crucial about Holocaust education itself: while a film such as *Schindler's List* may serve as cinematic support for such an endeavor, it cannot replace it. I do not believe, in other words, that the Castlemont High School students' reactions were unique. Despite seeming self-evident to previous generations, the moral messages of the Holocaust are no more obvious to contemporary teenagers than the events that constitute it. As Howard Gardner (1999) wrote, "Attaining historical mastery of the Holocaust is not equivalent to understanding its moral dimensions" (p. 183). Both must be taught if either stands a chance of being learned.

REPRESENTATIONAL ISSUES IN HOLOCAUST EDUCATION

While it may not sound inflammatory to suggest that Holocaust history and its concomitant moral lessons should be taught together, this position has been subjected to compelling critiques in the educational literature that has burgeoned since the mid-1990s. These critiques, in turn, elucidate arguments central to Holocaust historiography and Holocaust education.

Historian Deborah Lipstadt (1993) is best known for her influential work on Holocaust denial and for fighting the libel lawsuit spawned in its wake. Holocaust denier David Irving filed the suit against Lipstadt and Penguin Books, (*DJC Irving v. Penguin Books Ltd and Deborah Lipstadt,* 1993), her publisher, claiming that her book had wrongfully defiled his name and injured his reputation and that "far from being a 'Holocaust denier,'" he was a well-accepted historian. Irving filed suit in Britain, since libel laws there place the burden of evidence on the plaintiff rather than the claimant; in other words, in the High Court of Justice, it was not Irving's job to prove that Lipstadt and Penguin Books had harmed his reputation. Instead, it was the job of Lipstadt and Penguin Books to prove that what Lipstadt had written was true. Lipstadt won the case without ever taking the stand. She had refused, on principle, to argue with Holocaust deniers.

As both a noted Holocaust historian and as the plaintiff in that case, Lipstadt is acutely aware of the moral dimensions of Holocaust representations. Yet, according to Lipstadt (1995), education about the Holocaust ought to focus on its particular informational terrain rather than its moral relevance or historic parallels. Rather than promoting that we teach the ways in which the Holocaust is comparable to and distinct from other instances of genocide and other institutions of slavery or how it may resonate with students' own experiences, Lipstadt argues for teaching about the Holocaust in a more insular fashion. "I teach the particulars," Lipstadt (1995) has written about her own college-level courses, continuing, "I let the students apply them to their own universe, [and] they never fail to do so" (p. 26). For Lipstadt, it is not the job of the teacher, even at the secondary level, to instruct students morally but to provide information from which they "must draw their own comparisons" (p. 26), presumably both to their own lives and to other histories.

To support her argument, Lipstadt (1995) cites evidence from her college-level courses wherein students drew generalized moral lessons from the particular information she provided:

> Watching Claude Lanzmann's epic documentary *Shoah* (Lanzmann, 1985) in my . . . class, the students did not learn only about the Holocaust. As they listened to contemporary Poles decry the fate of the Jews and then, using imagery from the New Testament, seamlessly slip into explanations of why this was really the Jews' fault, the student sitting next to me groaned, "Blaming the victim. Again."
>
> . . . For me, the most moving responses came from the Christian students in the class who spoke about the challenge of reconciling what they consider to be a religion of love with the history of contempt which they now recognized as intrinsic to it. I did not have to spell this out. They did so on their own. (p. 26)

While Lipstadt acknowledges the contested nature of moral lessons, advocating that teachers avoid the thorny morass of moral instruction altogether, what her stance discounts is the inevitability of moral tutelage inherent in any educational enterprise. After all, moral messages are embedded in the very information that she, or any teacher, chooses to teach; in the example above, Lipstadt chose the particular sequence from Lanzmann's 9½-hour film to show in class. Teachers don't have to say to their students, "What do you think we should learn from the Holocaust?" or, "How does this apply to your own lives?" in order to engage the moral lessons of the Holocaust. Through both content selection and curriculum sequence, teachers already convey deeply moral notions. While Lipstadt may be advocating that teachers not explicitly state their moral agendas for student learning, ultimately those agendas are already embedded in what and how they teach. Teaching is ultimately and inescapably morally loaded, as is that which gets taught, regardless of teachers' explicit intentions (Hansen, 1993; Jackson, Boostrom, & Hansen, 1993; Purpel & Ryan, 1983; Simon, 2001; Tom, 1984). If representations of the Holocaust that are constructed in classrooms are inevitably morally loaded, they are also morally loaded in particular ways.

Lipstadt's curricular admonitions grow out of her critiques of Facing History and Ourselves (FHAO) (Stern-Strom, 1982), one of the major Holocaust education organizations in the United States and one whose curricular approach is dedicatedly comparative. What Lipstadt categorizes as "fast and loose" comparisons, though, Melinda Fine (1993a) considers to be the strength of FHAO, its ability to

> guide students back and forth between a historical case study [the Holocaust] and reflection on the causes and consequences of present-day prejudice, intolerance, violence and racism. (pp. 771)

In support of FHAO, Fine documents the ways in which students at an inner-city high school, through study of the Holocaust, are enabled to "reflect critically on their own attitudes, biases, and behaviors" (pp. 774–775). For Fine and others, (Heller & Hawkins, 1994; Weinstein, 1997), FHAO's power, then, is precisely its relevance, the ways in which the curriculum helps students articulate social dynamics that endure across situations, across history. The disagreement over whether such connections should be made explicitly in classrooms is part of a larger historiographical debate over the nature of the Holocaust itself.

The debate originated in what might be considered the early period of Holocaust historiography and centers on whether the Holocaust is unique or universal as an event in history. Briefly, those who argue for the Holocaust's uniqueness tend to claim that the Holocaust was so atrocious as to be unintelligible, unknowable, and profoundly unrepresentable except to those who experienced it directly. The theologian Arthur Cohen (1974), for example, refers to the Holocaust as a "tremendum" that exceeds a single human's capacity for imagination. The memoirist Elie Wiesel (1990) claims that "only those who lived it in their flesh and in their minds can possibly transform their experience into knowledge," while those who didn't, "despite their best intentions, can never do so" (p. 166). Others who maintain the Holocaust's uniqueness emphasize the ways in which it was historically unprecedented, highlighting, as examples, the "Promethean ambition" of Nazi ideology; the "machine-like, bureaucratic, regulated character" of the killing process (Marrus, 1987, p. 22); the fact that "perpetrators conducted this genocide for no ostensible material, territorial, or political gain" (Lipstadt, 1995, p. 26); or the gas chambers themselves (Kren & Rappoport, 1994). (For fuller treatments of the unique-universal debates, see also Bauer, 2001; Clendinnen, 1999.)

In educational arenas, those who assert the uniqueness of the Holocaust recommend strategies and materials to mark its difference in the curriculum. Thus, Deborah Lipstadt (1995), while recognizing that the act of drawing comparisons can be educative, nonetheless advocates teaching about the Holocaust in curricular isolation, implying a kind of incomparability to the event. And Sam Totten, one of the most prolific writers on Holocaust education (Totten, 1988, 2000, 2001; Totten & Feinberg, 2001), cautions teachers not to use literature "that treats the Holocaust as simply another event in history or another story to be told, without fully acknowledging [the Holocaust's] specialness" (Totten, 1988, p. 211). Chaim Schatzker (1982), writing about Israeli contexts, bemoans instruction about the Holocaust that is rational, informationally driven rather than commemorative and emotionally engaging, worrying that "there is a danger that it will be dwarfed, diminished and will lose its unique significance . . . instead of making students sensitive to the abnormalities of the Holocaust" (p. 80).

On the other side of this historiographical divide are those who argue for the universality of the Holocaust by objecting to the terms of the debate itself. For these authors (Bauer, 2001; Clendinnen, 1999; Marrus, 1987; Novick, 1999), all historical events are both unique and universal: unique in the constellations of events that produce, propel, and constitute them, and yet universal in their implications, or at least potentially so. No event lies outside history, nor could it. And all human suffering that is not our own bodily or psychic suffering is indecipherable and unbreachable to our selves, whether en masse or individual, whether mass produced with an assembly-line efficiency (as in the concentration camps) or whimsically effected by the randomness of chance (as in the loss of a child to a freak accident). To apprehend the suffering of another, whatever its form, is always and unavoidably constrained by impossibilities, not uniquely so when considering those who lived through or died during the Holocaust.

In turn, these universalists claim that the Holocaust is no more or less representable than other large events in history. With sympathy and straightforwardness, Holocaust historian Yehudah Bauer (2001) explains:

> True, the depth of pain and suffering of Holocaust victims is difficult to describe, and writers, artists, poets, dramatists and philosophers will forever grapple with the problem of articulating it—and as far as this is concerned, the Holocaust is certainly not unique, because "indescribable" human suffering is forever there and is forever being described. (p. 7)

Bauer is careful to qualify that "this does not mean that the explanation [for the Holocaust or indeed its description] is easy" (p. 8), only that the events themselves are fundamentally explicable, and hence, fundamentally representable, despite the considerable obstacles involved in both endeavors.

A few of the issues swirling around Holocaust education thus become not whether the Holocaust is representable, but how to represent it; not whether it is unique or universal, but in which ways it is each; not whether to teach its moral content, but how to teach it; and finally, not whether to explicate the moral lessons of the Holocaust, but which moral lessons to embed and in what ways.

THE FOCUS OF THIS BOOK

I first became interested in studying the moral dimensions of Holocaust education while visiting schools with Holocaust survivors such as René. I arranged the visits carefully, always trying to make sure that they occurred at the conclusion of a Holocaust unit or course. Usually, I would present a slide show overview of Holocaust history (meant to serve as a reminder of what students had hopefully covered in greater depth), and the survivor would then speak about his or her life in Nazi-dominated Europe. We would end by providing ample time for student questions.

In my first few months on the job, I was continually surprised by the questions students asked survivors: "Why didn't you run away?" "Why didn't you fight back?" The sentiment you-must-have-done-something-to-deserve-that-treatment was also sometimes expressed, if not stated outright. Although I didn't know it at the time, these were questions asked so typically of survivors that the Italian writer Primo Levi (1989) described them as "obligatory" (p. 151). The survivors were used to these kinds of questions, and most answered them patiently, gently explaining as much as possible to try to bridge the gulf in historical imagination. I, however, the daughter of a European refugee, would get upset. I remember marveling at the naïveté exhibited by adolescents who thought themselves invulnerable to victimization, able to resist brutality, or more important, impervious to the social forces that enable people to brutalize and dehumanize others in the first place. Not surprisingly, I became interested in what the students I was meeting had learned before we visited.

That curiosity eventually propelled the study that became this book. In order to get a sense of what was being taught and learned about the Holocaust, I chose to study very experienced teachers who were teaching in public high schools with diverse student bodies. Essentially, I wanted to know how students with no particular connection to the Holocaust, like those at Castlemont High, could learn about the Holocaust in a way that was historically informative, personally relevant, and morally powerful. My assumption was that by studying teachers who had been teaching about the Holocaust for a long time and who came highly recommended, I might be able to provide models of expertise for others venturing into this largely uncharted territory.

Three questions guided my investigation:

- How do experienced high school teachers teach about the Holocaust?
- What moral messages do they convey implicitly and communicate explicitly?
- And, most important, what do their students learn?

As may already be apparent, in this book I consider moral issues as those that in some way affect the well-being of persons through their interrelationships. My definition follows Katherine Simon's (2001), who defines moral issues as those that "have to do with how human beings should act (or should have acted) in situations that involve the well-being of oneself, of other human beings, of other living things, or of the earth" (pp. 6–7). Thus, moral issues may address conflicts involving right and wrong, justice and injustice, or right conduct in a given situation. They may also address specific orientations; I consider democratic values, for instance, to be a subcategory of moral values, at least in the sense that they clearly indicate a sensibility about human relations.

In addition to actual experience and hypothetically lived situations, the category of the moral here also includes the realm of the symbolic. Issues of narrative and representation have crucial implications for human perception and, in turn, human action, such that ultimately they, too, are morally laden. For example, whether a teacher referred to perpetrators of genocide during World War II as "Nazis" or as "Germans," as "people" or as "madmen," is a question of curricular representation that has moral consequences. Clearly, the choice may influence students' perceptions of this atrocity and potentially shape their attitudes toward present-day Germans. While some may balk at the breadth of my usage of the term *moral*, my hope is that they will perceive my findings as useful nevertheless.

In my study, I examined Holocaust curricula as they were originally designed by curriculum writers and then adapted for use by the teachers; how those adaptations were in turn transformed by classroom interaction; and finally what the students understood or learned from the curriculum they experienced. While all the phases of the process are educationally important, in this book I focus primarily on the last two transformations, paying close attention to the enacted curriculum (that which happened in the course or unit) and the experienced curricula (that which the students learned from or despite their studies).

In brief, I focus on four experienced high school teachers who welcomed me into their classrooms as they taught about the Holocaust and talked with me about their intentions for and reflections on their courses. All the teachers taught in large, public high schools with diverse populations of students and few, if any, Jewish students. From each class, I interviewed a select group of students who were ethnically, racially, and religiously diverse and who represented a range of previous academic performance in school. I wanted to track the students' reactions to the material they were learning:

- What did they think was interesting?
- Did they ever consider the material outside school?
- How did they understand Nazism?
- What information did they know or had they learned?
- What areas had they missed, overlooked, not been taught, or not understood?

I tried to evaluate the target students' informational learning as well as what moral sense they made of it. In addition, I surveyed all the students in each class before and after their Holocaust units were completed, trying to assess what they had known already and what was new or interesting to them.

I want to point out that I observed their classes in the aftermath of the widely publicized Castlemont High incident described above, a time of heightened awareness nationwide about the importance of teaching students about the Holocaust. It is important to note, too, that it was a time unmarred by terrorist attacks on American soil, a time when young students had yet to experience directly a sense of national vulnerability, one that arguably might help them understand the Holocaust. The general mood of the American public toward Israel has changed since the time of these observations as well. Most U.S. citizens were more optimistic about the prospects for a peaceful resolution to the Israeli-Palestinian conflict then, making them more predisposed to be interested in Holocaust history than they may be now, especially in urban school districts.

In the chapters that follow, I try to capture in prose the experiential qualities of the Holocaust courses I observed over 2 years and my interpretations of them (Eisner, 1991). What did it mean, for instance, that one course began with extensive revelations about the teacher's life and another unit began with an overview of Holocaust history? What was the significance of one Holocaust unit's ending on rescue and another's ending with the end of World War II? What were the moral implications of those course narratives, and what were the pedagogical trade-offs involved (Cuban, 2001)? Most important, I try to establish what it was that the students had (and had not) learned about the Holocaust from their classroom experiences and their homes.

In the following section of this chapter, I provide a brief analysis of one course to serve as a contrast to those presented in detail in Chapters 2–4. Unlike those that follow, this case highlights the problematic consequences of teaching about the Holocaust primarily by lecturing.

MR. JEFFERSON'S FACT RACE

Mr. Jefferson[1] was the kind of social studies teacher whom most students encounter at some point in their high school careers, the kind whose teaching is so familiar as to be parodied in popular film and educational research (Wilson & Wineburg, 1991). A White, middle-class man somewhere in his mid-60s, he wore a jacket and tie to school each day. He had taught history and government at Hilltop High School for more than 30 years when I observed him, and he had lectured almost exclusively for most of that time.

He was a speedy lecturer. Regardless of the topic, Mr. Jefferson knew what he wanted to say, and he needed no notes to guide him. Historical names, dates, events, and even statistics tumbled out of him rapid-fire and well organized. His speech didn't slow even when he was writing on the chalkboard or cueing up a video. Watching him lecture, I was reminded of shiny pennies flowing out of a mint; each coin—symbolizing a historical fact—was discrete but generated too quickly to be beheld as such. Mr. Jefferson simply wanted to convey more information than a typical 50-minute period could accommodate. His students' job was to try to keep up, as they scribbled down the notes he dictated.

Over the course of 3 weeks, Mr. Jefferson covered an impressive amount of information, loosely organized around 5 governing questions that he wrote on the chalkboard:

1. What was [the Holocaust]? What happened?
2. How did it happen?
3. Why did it happen?
4. Of what significance is it?
5. And what do we do with the information we have?

---

[1] All the teacher, school, and student names in this book have been changed to protect the identities of the participants. I encouraged the teachers and students to choose their own false names; sometimes this resulted in humorous selections.

His lecture topics included Jewish life in Europe before the Holocaust, the history of anti-Semitism, the rise of the Nazi Party, anti-Jewish legislation in Germany, the bureaucratic organization and rise of the Nazi state, landmarks in World War II history, the ghettoization of Jews, the concentration camp system and social-psychological research used to explain perpetrator behavior. He closed the unit with a clear list of moral messages, among them "Racism continues (We must be on our guard)," and "Fascism/ethnic cleansing is not dead!" The unit test assessed students' recall of the information he had covered, testing them even on the list of lessons to be learned.

My interviews with Mr. Jefferson's students before and after the unit revealed that they had learned Mr. Jefferson's information. The focus students could recite what countries were involved in World War II, how Hitler rose to power, and how European Jews were treated in various time periods, for example. Even the student Mr. Jefferson identified as the least academically inclined of the group, a young Latina woman named Elizabeth Miranda, could answer such questions easily. Another student, a Hindu American named Vince, was even moved to make new behavioral decisions in light of the lecture on social psychology. Having heard about the Kitty Genovese story, Stanley Milgram's experiments on obedience, Solomon Asch's studies of conformity, and Philip Zimbardo's prison simulation, Vince reported near the end of the school year:

> [When my teacher] was giving those examples on that research that they did up in Stanford, I think, or something like that . . . well, that affected me in like, if somebody tells me something to do, I'm going to think twice now to make sure I'm doing the right thing or not, if I'm hurting somebody or if I'm not or something like that. Like a while back, a couple of my friends, they were sort of like messing around. They were like capping on each other and stuff like that, and I was thinking, "Should I get involved 'cause everybody's all doing it?" Should I get involved or will this like lead to something else if I say something that might offend somebody? So, I was like, no, I don't think I'll get involved.

Vince told me that, before hearing Mr. Jefferson's lecture, it was likely he would have joined his friends in rounds of teasing and pummeling. While the content of Mr. Jefferson's lecture clearly wielded a positive moral impact on Vince, its format allowed morally problematic assumptions to persist in other students.

In the one departure from lecturing, Mr. Jefferson had his students read aloud a play set somewhere in the late 1930s wherein a German

Christian family discusses whether to hide the German Jewish family who has sought their help. The Christian family, mired in indecision, solicits their pastor's advice, who informs them not to provide shelter, since the Jews are forever "Christ-killers." Mr. Jefferson had had the students read the play as a crystallization of Church-based, anti-Semitic teachings that paved the way for Nazi atrocities to occur.

During interviews with me, though, Elizabeth Miranda expressed opinions similar to the ones the pastor espoused in the play. When asked why she thought the Holocaust happened, Elizabeth Miranda talked about destiny and cited the Christian teaching, now widely repudiated, that Jews are perpetually culpable for the crucifixion of Jesus. As she explained, "In my eyes, I look at it and I go 'why was it supposed to happen?' It was written, just like it's destiny, you know?" She elaborated:

> The past was already written. They couldn't change it. They said that the Son of God was going to die so that's the way it was supposed to be. You know, well I'm Catholic. But after I think about it, it was our fault for killing the Jews, but it was their fault for killing Jesus. . . . It was already written.

What Elizabeth Miranda had heard in the pastor's remarks affirmed what she had already believed about the determinism of history. When I pushed her further, asking whether she thought it was fair to blame Jews for the death of Jesus, she tempered her answer somewhat. "Well not really," she said, "because it wasn't their fault that they killed Christ is what I think"; it was simply their divine role to fulfill historically. In short, Elizabeth Miranda considered the murder of Jews during the Holocaust, if not excusable, at least explainable by their perpetual and collective culpability for the crucifixion of Jesus.

Researchers of the teaching and learning of history have been aware for some time that students and teachers bring various features of their family heritage, background knowledge, and personal disposition to the classroom that then shape what they learn in it (Epstein, 1998; Gourevitch, 1995; Grant, 2001; Ladson-Billings, 1995; Seixas, 1993b; VanSledright, 1992). Yet few studies (Grant, 2001, p. 83) have focused on the relationship between teachers' practices and such predispositions. In this case, Mr. Jefferson's pedagogical reliance on lecture submerged Elizabeth Miranda's religious interpretation of the Holocaust. That Mr. Jefferson simply lectured about the play allowed her interpretation to remain undetected, invisible, unmined, entrenched. Mr. Jefferson's lecture format allowed Elizabeth Miranda to hear confirmation of her beliefs in the reading of the play. In contrast to the Christian students in Deborah Lipstadt's classes, Elizabeth Miranda, it might be argued, needed more than Lipstadt was advocating against; she not only needed the lessons "spelled out," she also needed them to be discussed.

By virtue of Mr. Jefferson's lecture format, too, the information he disseminated seemed tidy, orderly even. In his chronological narration of the Holocaust, each event described in summary form, Mr. Jefferson unintentionally conveyed an inevitability to Holocaust history, the sense that "history is a chronicle of what happened, and that it had to happen in [a] fixed way" (Grant, 2001). No other options existed, "occluding" the role of individual human agency in the unfolding of historical events (Wineburg, 2001). In Mr. Jefferson's narration of history, individuals' decisions, for the most part, did not make up the stuff of history. Inadvertently, then, Mr. Jefferson's lecture format supported Elizabeth Miranda's understanding of history as "destiny," as events fated to happen whether because of the forces of history or as a result of the direction of God.

In Mr. Jefferson's content—specifically the narrative shape of his content—the Holocaust bore testament to America's greatness. By ending his unit with an account of American soldiers liberating the concentration camps rather than with the dropping of the atomic bombs on Hiroshima and Nagasaki or with the difficulties Jews faced in trying to immigrate to the United States, Mr. Jefferson presented the United States as heroic. World War II and the Holocaust, to him, were "America's finest hour."

In Mr. Jefferson's hands, too, the category of the moral seemed subsumed into the informational. Rather than choosing historical facts over moral messages—as Lipstadt urges—Mr. Jefferson transmitted both as forms of information. He seemed, in other words, to consider moral messages as yet another form of factual knowledge to be "transmitted" to students, imbibed by them, and then tested. Moral content was not presented as involving issues to be engaged, questions to be debated, or ideas about which reasonable people can disagree, but as dicta. Disappointingly, in his Holocaust unit, Mr. Jefferson had treated moral issues just as he had covered historical information; both were stripped of their inherent richness and complexity.

In sum, through the Holocaust, Mr. Jefferson represented history as destined or inevitable, the United States as morally triumphant, and the moral and informational as intellectually and emotionally unchallenging. While there are lessons to be learned from the Holocaust, important lessons even, his lecture format flattened out their moral texture. Metaphorically, Mr. Jefferson razed complex moral/historical terrain so that his students might traverse it easily, in the process distorting the Holocaust itself. By contrast, the teachers whose courses I describe in the rest of this book brought thorny moral issues to life for their students, using them to illuminate barbarously complex historical terrain.

Chapters 2–4 each has a focus on an individual teacher's class. I begin each chapter by providing background on the school setting and the teacher and then portray what happened in the Holocaust course or unit. I supply much detail in these sections, often in the form of excerpted transcripts, in the hope of conveying a sense of what it was like to be present in each classroom. The final part of each chapter consists of my analytical interpretation of the descriptive section that precedes it, though it's worth noting that my perspective shapes the first section of these chapters, too. Within my reflections, I identify patterns of the teachers' pedagogies and content coverage, speculating about their accompanying moral messages and reporting on students' reactions and learning. In the final chapter of the book, I look for patterns across sites, drawing conclusions about the teaching of the Holocaust and its lessons.

My hope is that this book will provide some answers and raise some questions regarding what models to emulate, what pitfalls to avoid, and mainly, what issues to consider in the important work of Holocaust education and of history education more broadly. It is my conviction that the in-depth study of one tragedy's teaching may help guide the path to teaching about other tragedies, no matter how dissimilar. As René Molho surely knew and the Castlemont High School students came to understand, the lessons of the Holocaust are necessarily complex, neither easily taught nor easily learned, and neither awe nor inexperience can help navigate them. My hope for this work, then, is that it will spark conversations among educators and researchers to help us all better understand the history and moral legacies of the past.

Chapter 2

Facing Ourselves But Not History

Maplewood High School (MHS) is a suburban, public high school, nestled in the rolling foothills of Southern California. During part of the year, early mornings blanket the school with a light dusting of mist, and the hills are shrouded in green. At these times, the concrete buildings of MHS, hugging the ground and surrounded by a high, wire fence, seem oddly incongruous with the lush environment. The rest of the year, though, the sun blazes, and the grayness of the campus buildings seems appropriate, as if the intensity of the light had leeched out their original colors over time. Regardless of the season, when the bells ring, releasing students in swarms for brunch, lunch, or class changes, the campus comes alive. Girls in tiny skirts and 3-inch platform heels walk alongside boys in ballooning pants and $120-dollar-a-pair high-top sneakers, regardless of the weather. Some girls go "grunge," and some boys dress down, and many reveal pierced body parts. All wear their hair long. As the first morning bell rings, the students pour in from the student parking lot, every spot of which is reserved. By the time the late bell has rung, only a few stragglers on the main campus or heading out to the trailers are still visible. The group of three trailers, housing six classrooms each, extends outside the chain-link fence, testimony to the community's population growth.

The student population at Maplewood is very diverse; more than 56 first languages are spoken among the 2,400 students who attend. Almost 70% of the student body is made up of ethnic, racial, or cultural minority groups; 30% of the students are White. More specifically, the year I observed, 31% of the students were White; 28% Asian; 17% Hispanic; 17% Filipino; 6% Black; and 1% Native American. These percentages are deceptive, however, as many of the students who attend Maplewood escape easy ethnic categorization and have been forced to choose, or have had chosen for them, a single ethnic identification. In the class I observed, for instance, almost one quarter of the students were biracial: Black and Asian, Black and White, Vietnamese and White, and so on.

Partly as a result of this great diversity, the faculty and staff at MHS are dedicated to cultivating intergroup tolerance among the students and faculty. A group called Teachers for Tolerance meets regularly to discuss ways to make and keep the campus "open-minded" about diversity. Also, efforts have been made on the administrative level to increase minority representation in faculty and staff hires. The outdoor cafeteria walls are adorned with murals that proclaim: "It takes different colors to make a rainbow," "There is no one way," and, "Tolerate difference." Nonetheless there are frequent fights on campus. One of the security guards told me that when school is in session, he breaks up at least one fight per week. Although not always racially or ethnically motivated, these incidents of violence add a particular urgency to the goals of the school.

MR. ZEE

Mr. Zeeman has taught at Maplewood for more than 15 years, and he is widely recognized as an expert teacher. He has been showered with teaching awards and promotions. In the middle of the semester in which I observed him, he was bestowed with the district's Best Teacher Award. A short, muscular man, he has coached the swim teams at MHS for more than 10 years, and one wall of his class reflects his pride at that accomplishment. Gleaming groups of fit, tan, scantily suited swimmers smile out of their year's large-format glossy photo. Walking with Mr. Zeeman through campus, I note that he seems to know all the faculty, all the staff, and most of the students by name, no small accomplishment in a campus of this size. As he recognizes each face, he waves and smiles, hollering out a friendly word. The students and other staff members smile and wave back, often calling out the nickname by which he is known here: Mr. Zee. It doesn't take long to realize that Mr. Zee feels at home on the campus of this school.

Mr. Zee has gained a reputation both on and off campus not only for his charismatic personality, but also for the course that he teaches on the Holocaust: a nontracked, full-semester history elective that he fought to have offered at MHS. The course, titled Facing History and Ourselves (FHAO), is designed and distributed for a fee by the national organization of the same name. Established in 1977, it is one of the oldest Holocaust education organizations in the United States, and as such carries considerable name recognition (Fine, 1995). Mr. Zee worked for FHAO for a brief stint, and he actively promotes the organization, working it into even casual conversations. He is a great salesman for the program, as he believes in it deeply.

In our interviews, Mr. Zee spoke fluidly, never hesitating, never unsure of himself. He was adept at discussing his philosophies of education. Moreover, his points about FHAO, the organization and his course, were clothed in the latest educational jargon; he referred to his class as a "learning community," to his practices as "student centered," and to his assessment strategies as "authentic" and "portfolio based." During our discussions, I imagined Mr. Zee taking me on a cruise down a well-traveled river, where he knew every twist and turn our conversation would take, but like a professional tour guide, never revealed his boredom, answering every question earnestly and politely. It is no surprise that after years of teaching, Mr. Zee was recruited to work for the Maplewood District Office to help train novice teachers and provide continuing professional development opportunities for experienced ones. The year that I observed, Mr. Zee's work time was divided between his teaching commitments and his district obligations. He taught only two courses at MPH, which, that semester, were two sections of FHAO.

Mr. Zee's courses were among the most popular in the school. As a guidance counselor mentioned to me, all his courses were overenrolled, FHAO in particular. Although guidance counselors often recommended that students take the course, especially in cases where they felt students would benefit from its message, most students chose the course themselves. "I heard that this course like changes your life," one student explained when I asked why she had signed up. Other students' enthusiasm was similarly generated by word of mouth, from other students, teachers, and the principal. "It's the most important curriculum that occurs at this school," the principal explained when asked to describe the class. "The kinds of dialogue that never occur in real society," he elaborated, "occur in this class." He concluded the interview by telling me that if he could, he would require that FHAO be taken by all the students in the school.

MR. ZEE'S GOALS

When asked during our first interview how he got interested in using FHAO, Mr. Zee explained the ways in which the curriculum met his priorities for student learning:

> I think to really have an impact on the way people think, rather than, not only on how they feel, but how they think *and* feel, you have to have a lotta hooks to hang ideas on, you have to have a whole new vocabulary. You have to have a lot of information in

> your head; you do have to know, you know, when the Nazis came to power, what the American eugenics movement was, or who Father Coughlin was. . . . You have to have some chronology, but you have to have a lotta hooks to hang all that stuff on, or you won't be able to make meaning from it. And this program [FHAO] does that.
>
> If someone just said, . . . what's this curriculum about? It is an antiracism and anti-bias curriculum; it is about developing a language about human relations; it is about a specific history, or a couple of, more than one specific history, and how insights from the rigorous study of that history might play out in people's own thinking in their classrooms, in their family lives, in their communities; it's about participatory citizenship; it's about taking responsibility; it's about a lot of things that rarely get spoken about above the level of a generality, and it's great to be able to have these kinds of conversations and to have kids have these conversations with each other, and then to have a way to help them construct meaning out of it all. . . .
>
> And it's tough to do. You walk a real fine line between the particular and the universal messages and implications of the history. . . . And, um, that's difficult—you sort of sculpt the curriculum on a daily basis; it's not a programmed, by-the-numbers kind of curriculum.

Mr. Zee's dedication to the FHAO curriculum revolves around what he perceives to be its attributes: the curriculum's balanced orientation toward Holocaust history as both particular and universalistic, its outright embracing of complexity in generating questions and providing answers, its attempts to engage students emotionally without sacrificing intellectual rigor, its focus on the moral, and its dedication to what Mr. Zee calls "conceptual hooks." The challenge of achieving these goals, according to Mr. Zee, justifies his fluid process of curricular adaptation.

PROGRESSION OF THE COURSE

I began observing one section of Mr. Zee's course at the end of January 1996, the beginning of MHS's second semester. Mr. Zee's class met for 55 minutes, from 8:44 to 9:41 A.M., 5 days a week. In the class were mostly juniors and seniors, as well as a handful of sophomores. Almost immediately, I started to understand its widespread appeal, much of which stemmed from Mr. Zee himself. Animated and easygoing, he gave the students the impression that their lives mattered to him.

Although he knew many already, Mr. Zee had learned the 30 students' names by the end of the first class session, and he seemed to know something about each student. He had also implicitly and explicitly delineated some of the differences that students could come to expect between his course and others. When the students walked in the door, they were allowed to sit in any of the chairs arranged in a semicircle, which evoked audible expressions of "Cool" and "Dang." During the school's amplified announcements, Mr. Zee circulated among the students, looking at their semester schedules, asking after parents and family members. Just after the announcements, he related to the students a personal anecdote, the first of a vast number that would liberally pepper his course. He revealed that he had had trouble passing algebra in college, and that "math is tough" for him. "It carries over to the checkbook in our house today," he told his students, eliciting chuckles. In these few interactions, Mr. Zee was establishing his classroom as what he called a "comfort zone," a place where traditionally formalized and hierarchical relations would become more personable and egalitarian.

Not only would the cultural norms of this class be nontraditional, Mr. Zee implied with his casual behavior, but the content would be, too. "You know a lot of times, history classes are dull; history gets filled up with facts, and it stops being interesting," he remarked, following with the promise, "Not in this class!" The familiarity of his tone implied that he, unlike other teachers, understood the students' desires. What was interesting to them, he was projecting, was what interested him. Almost invisibly, and in a very short amount of class time, Mr. Zee positioned himself as being both interested in the students themselves and knowledgeable about their presumed likes and dislikes.

The rest of that first week, Mr. Zee defined some key terms: *individual identity, group identity, universe of obligation,* and *barriers*. He also described the students' homework, which like so much else in the class, he claimed was special, or different from other teachers' assignments. The students were assigned to hand in one portfolio entry per week. These were assignments of any length for which students could choose the topic and format of their work. To combat confusion over the nature of their assignment and to inspire them as to its possibilities, on the 4th day of class, Mr. Zee showed examples of former students' entries that he had kept over the years: posters, pictures, collages, audiotapes, videotapes, sculptures, poems, and essays. While showing these, Mr. Zee slipped into storytelling.

A previous student's work was hanging on the wall; it read, "PGE CURE," a mnemonic device to recall the following word series: *Plague, Germs, Education; Critical Thinking, Us, Race and religion, Empathic imagination.* To guide students through its meaning, Mr. Zee explained the first word in the acronym, positioning racism as a plague and exploring the effects of having contracted another such "plague" himself. The anecdote that he related as illustrative of the plague was not, however, one that dealt with racism but, rather, concerned scapegoating or violence more generally:

> I would say that the day in my life when I participated in the beating at age 19 of a fellow soldier who couldn't carry his own load was a day I got that plague! It's true that the guy was a pain in the butt; it's true that he wasn't very likable; it's true that if we had fought together in a war, I woulda been killed 'cause he was just plain dumb. Nonetheless, that doesn't excuse what we did to him. Before that, I thought that the plague of conformity was a disease I had antibodies for. I thought that because I was raised in a religious home, I was raised in a tolerant home. . . .
>
> Before that, I thought I couldn't do that to another person. I was raised in a place where you were taught to welcome the stranger. It took the army exactly 2 months to transform me from the person I like to think of myself as to my worst self. And I'm not proud of that. I have to live with the knowledge every day of my life that there's at least one person walking around this earth who doesn't see me like you do, but like a member of a mob, an angry member of a group that beat him and used him as a—[the raised pitch of Mr. Zee's final word and the following 2-second pause indicate that he's waiting for student input, but none greets him] goat. A goat. It's almost a tradition for groups to mistreat nonmembers of the group. We all have stories. Well, there's a portfolio entry.

Mr. Zee's main goal in telling this brief story was to demonstrate for the students what might constitute a successful portfolio entry drawn from his own life, the implication being, of course, that the students could create portfolio entries out of stories from their lives, too.

After recounting this army experience, Mr. Zee described someone he once met, a "reformed White supremacist" whose body was still generously tattooed with supremacist messages. As a hate monger, this man had committed countless acts of violence against perceived enemies. Although the man was reformed, the tattoos had kept him from getting a job and earning a living outside his organization. As Mr. Zee described it, a Jewish doctor and Holocaust survivor aided the man, removing all his tattoos at no charge. "I bet he could tell you a lot about what caused his plague," Mr. Zee said, connecting the story to the portfolio piece he had shown earlier.

A master storyteller, Mr. Zee filled the class with anecdotes like these. He described such vignettes easily, as if the stories just spilled out of him, barely provoked. In addition to the vast repertoire of stories in his head, he had a crate of videotapes in his closet and a pile of audiotapes in his desk drawer. A VCR resided in the closet, and a tape-recorder sat on his desk, allowing him to draw on these storehouses at any time.

It was never clear to me that Mr. Zee knew what he would be doing in the class before he did it; the "sculpted" curriculum's shape was constantly in motion. With the masterful eye of an experienced teacher, Mr. Zee gauged the pulse of the class with invisible precision, and his flexible planning (or nonplanning) allowed him to choose an activity to suit the moment. When student attention waned, for example, Mr. Zee would pull out a video or take an informal poll, sometimes asking students to do something zany just to perk them up. In short, there was a looseness about the architecture of Mr. Zee's lessons, a sense that anything could come next, that helped make his course engaging to students.

Mr. Zee explained to me that what may look unprofessional from the outside, as though he was "winging it," was actually all intentional. His strategies for engaging the students, his comparisons to other classes, his personal stories and informal polls, served a purpose:

> In the first few weeks what I want is to build up the capacity of the class to be totally engaged so that there are no quiet spots that are quiet for the wrong reasons, that there's no one who feels like what they say won't be acknowledged or even honored, and . . . we have to set that tone right away. You have to make sure that people feel like their voice is an important aspect of this course.

In other words, the surveys he took and stories he told were equal-access engagement tools. All students in his nontracked class, whether they were college bound or not, could participate if all that was required of them was to voice their opinions or listen to stories.

The students rarely took notes, wrote in class, or read anything longer than a page. Aside from the weekly portfolio entries, they had very little homework to complete. The few readings assigned were drawn mostly from their FHAO resource book, whose excerpts rarely exceeded three pages. On the whole, the students were expected to occasionally watch a videotape, listen to an audiotape, or read a short piece, but mostly to listen to Mr. Zee's stories. It was clearly important for Mr. Zee not to present any stumbling blocks to his heterogeneously grouped students, especially during the first phase of the course.

The course included four distinct phases overall. In the first, Mr. Zee introduced students to his expectations, his style, his stories, and his vocabulary about human behavior. He considered it a time of community building, where everyone could become comfortable enough to express his or her voice openly. The second phase of the course focused on the concept of identity, and in it the students revealed themselves to their peers and Mr. Zee. In the third phase of the course, Mr. Zee intended for students to apply the case study of the Holocaust to the vocabulary about human behavior he had taught them in the first phases. In the fourth and final phase, the students viewed role models for what Mr. Zee called "participatory citizenship" but in another venue might be called real-life heroes.

Phase I: Community Building

The introductory phase of Mr. Zee's course lasted 6 weeks and 2 days, approximately one third of the semester. As mentioned above, in it, Mr. Zee told numerous personal stories, presented a range of media, began building a sense of community among his students and introduced them to vocabulary that would punctuate the entire course. Thematically, all the activities in this phase were linked by issues of identity formation and human behavior, though the connections were loosely drawn.

My impressions of this phase of the course are powerful, and yet it is oddly difficult for me to summarize them. Mr. Zee's teaching style, especially in the first few weeks, was fluid; the stories, activities, videos, in-class readings, and discussions flowed seamlessly, as if occurring haphazardly or, at least, ordered inconsequentially. The image that for me metaphorically captures Mr. Zee's teaching in this phase is of an artist who meticulously designed each card in a deck some time ago and now shuffles the pack randomly each day, playing whatever happens to turn up. The suit that dominated the pack, however, was storytelling.

Mr. Zee told stories such as the ones above, and whether they were brief or elaborate, they were masterfully presented. Throughout the semester, but especially concentrated in the first 6 weeks, Mr. Zee wove tales about his own life, about his parents and extended family members, about his wife and children, and about numerous encounters with strangers, friends, and even past lovers. Below, I quote at some length one story from the 2nd week of class, as it illuminates Mr. Zee's storytelling prowess.

As he spun this tale, he used his entire body to enliven it. When, for example, he described his grandmother's posture, he extended himself to his full height, puffing out his chest like a blowfish; and when he described her greeting patterns, he walked around the small stage area at the front of the class, waving deliriously to imagined passers-by.

> My grandmother . . . lived to be in her late 70s. She lived in Pinemont, near Lake Virginia, in a not what I would call upper-middle-class neighborhood, very sort of full of apartment houses in her area, kind of a tough neighborhood. My grandmother was in the habit every morning for 45 years, from when she was in her 30s to when she was in her 70s, of walking around Lake Virginia. 3.2 miles. She walked around Lake Virginia every day, unless it was hailing or the rain was so heavy that it made it impossible to do it. Even in the rain, she had this big umbrella. She was a little, heavy-set lady who carried an umbrella and a cane. She had a purse over her shoulder, and it was one of those sort of big suitcase-like purses, grandmother purses that carry the whole world in it. . . .
>
> And she was very, she was a very sort of straight person. She had great posture, my grandmother. She looked at the world from a height of 5 feet tall. She looked at the world from that height, and she saw it on her own terms. She wasn't haughty, or full of pride, she just looked at people as if "I'm me and you're you and we can do what we need to do." She was very matter of fact. . . .
>
> And I know a lot of this because for about 2½ years, I lived with her in her apartment, and especially on weekends, I stayed there. For a little bit of that time, my mother was ill. My mother had tuberculosis, and my grandmother was in charge of us for a certain amount of time. So, I got to know my grandmother very well. . . .
>
> Anyway, she'd walk around Lake Virginia, and for 45 years she did that. And I used to walk with her. On Saturdays and Sundays, I'd walk with her. On Saturdays I would stay there all day and on Sundays, I'd walk with her, and she'd take me to Sunday school and pick me up. . . . And you know, when I walked with her, here's what she did. As she was walking around the lake, she'd pass somebody, and she would always ALWAYS—I never saw her pass somebody by without saying hello. That's just the way she was. She'd be walking and she'd pass somebody walking the other way, and she'd be: "Good morning!" and she's walking,

"How are you today?!" and she's walking, "Beautiful day, isn't it?" She's walking. . . . Lots of contacts with lots of different kinds of people.

Lake Virginia, in the 1950s, which is when this was happening, the late 50s, was a very—wasn't segregated in the slightest even though it was pre–civil rights movement in this country. It wasn't segregated; neither were the schools that I went to segregated. This was California; it [was] on a different kind of time scale than a lot of other places. That doesn't mean there wasn't an amazing amount of racism, it just means that in the institutions, it didn't look like Georgia or Louisiana or Mississippi.

So, we'd walk around the lake, and I'd say that half the people we would see and say hello to were of different races than we were. My grandmother therefore had . . . five pleasant contacts per trip around the lake, five pleasant "Good morning"s, "How are you today," "Fine, thank you," "Have a good day," those kind of things. That's a lot of contact with people. And half of them, I would say fully half of them were with young African American males. . . . I remember quite amazingly some of the faces of some of the people she would greet, and you know some of them would call her by her nickname, 'cause they'd been seeing her for a long time walking around the lake. They called her Nana.

[The students are quietly listening at this point. Some are leaning in toward the stage area, with their chins cupped in their hands; some have heads lowered onto their desks, but are clearly listening; others sit, attentively waiting for the plot to thicken.]

Everybody called her Nana. She was everybody's Nana. And she was open to the world, this woman. Open to the world. So, why then—she had one bad experience, in her early 70s, one bad experience, and after that, she had a hard time seeing people in the same way she had before. She was knocked down; someone tried to take her purse. One bad experience, out of, I don't know how many—if it were three contacts a day for 15 years, or 45 years, that's a heck of a lot of contacts, but one out of thousands was enough. [Mr. Zee pauses briefly.]

Now I don't say this with any degree of pride. To awaken whatever little, dormant kind of racism was within my grandmother, that one experience was enough to let it come out, and it lasted till the end of her life. It didn't take a negative form like name-calling, . . . but . . . she would make some judgments and sometimes around the dinner table, she would make some judgments in the way that she would refer to people, and I don't mean

> that she would say things that would get her in trouble or get her smacked in the jaw by someone who didn't like it. It didn't happen that way, but you could tell that there was a racial edge to her after one experience. [Mr. Zee paused for a full 2 seconds here, letting the point sink in.] What do you think about this?

At this moment, I think it's surprising that Mr. Zee hasn't explicitly reported on the races of the purse snatcher and his grandmother; I infer from the locale of Lake Virginia, a now mostly Black neighborhood, that the perpetrator was an African American, and I assume from Mr. Zee's ethnicity that his grandmother was White. I wonder, though, whether the students have made the same assumptions or whether this aspect of the story confuses them. I also find it puzzling that in a class purported to confront racial issues head-on, Mr. Zee has shied away from doing so. The students don't immediately respond to Mr. Zee's question, though he waits a full 5 seconds before prompting them again.

> What's your response to this? Understandable? No? Don't think so? [Without pausing this time, Mr. Zee calls on a student by name.] Atlas, what do you think of this? What does it make you think about when you hear this story? What comes to your mind?
>
> [Atlas responds:] Just how one bad experience can ruin the whole picture.
>
> [Mr. Zee continues:] Yah it's really interesting. One bad experience can ruin the whole picture. Interesting way of putting it. I wonder how many of us have had bad experiences that have sometimes ruined our experiences. Anybody willing to admit to that? That one bad experience might have poisoned the well a little bit? I have, I have to fight that.

Almost paradoxically by admitting this shortcoming, Mr. Zee holds himself up as a role model for students. Even he, a seemingly open-minded and tolerant teacher, has this flaw, and he knows he has to "fight that." He wants the students to do the same. Shortly thereafter, Mr. Zee explicitly shares one moral of his story:

> Here's what I'd like you to think about. I'd like you to think about the fact that distance can be created by many, in many different ways. My grandmother had distance created between her and her image of an entire group of people because of one negative experience out of thousands of experiences. It was able to create distance. The fear that she experienced became synonymous with the dis-

> tance that she created in her mind between her and a whole group of people. It wasn't about them; it was about her. The distance that gets created is sometimes created by ourselves.
>
> To recognize the human face of somebody, the specific human qualities, personhood, the individuality of people, is a big step towards getting rid of collective prejudices. You can't identify a whole group so easily and label it, when you've broken it down to individual actors. You can't. That's why I told you the story about my grandmother. Her basic personality was to be friendly to everyone, but she never really got to know anyone so well enough that it would offset the fear that she felt after one experience. That's a hard idea. . . . Let's at least be in general more open to people. Maybe they all have stories like this.

With these comments, Mr. Zee's extended story abruptly ended, punctuated by a string of moral lessons: "Let's . . . be . . . more open to people" and in that way avoid creating "distance" between people and between groups, which is sometimes or often created "by ourselves."

While slightly longer than most of Mr. Zee's stories, this one was nonetheless representative of others he told both in terms of the effectiveness of its performative telling and the blatancy of its intended lessons. Like most of his other stories, too, this one exposed Mr. Zee's personal history to his students. Rather than constructing psychological distance between students and teacher, Mr. Zee put his students at ease by revealing himself to them. I am convinced that part of the distinctiveness of his classroom evolved from this willingness to share his life with his students. Thus while I was often surprised by the choice of morals for many of his stories, I was nonetheless impressed with the high level of trust he was able to foster among students by telling them about his life.

One of the students whose reactions to the course I followed remarked, unprompted, on just this aspect of Mr. Zee's teaching. Roberto, a Mexican American senior who had just enrolled at MHS that year, explained:

> Other teachers, like, I might be good friends with them, but I don't know anything about them. Mr. Zee, he tells us stuff about himself, his family, stuff around him, when he was young, what he did, and what happened, and he got personal. That's why he's my favorite teacher. . . . He's like the teacher who really respects his students, and is really there for his students. . . . He's like the best teacher I've ever had.

While Mr. Zee's collegiality, conveyed through his stories, won Roberto's trust, Mr. Zee's moral messages, also conveyed through his stories, seemed not to reach Roberto. More than 2½ months after its telling, Roberto remembered the grandmother story; "Oh yah, she was like walking around for so many years and she got mugged one time?" he asked me by way of confirmation. He even remembered details from the story. And yet, he had no idea why Mr. Zee might have told the story or what it was he was meant to learn from it. When I asked as much, he replied:

> Even though you might know somebody, I don't know. I understand what [Mr. Zee] means by saying hello to everybody, 'cause in my little town, everybody, we say hello to everyone even if we don't know each other. Maybe she didn't feel safe anymore or something? I remember it [the story], but I don't have a clue [why he told it].

Bob, another one of the students I followed, was similarly enthusiastic about Mr. Zee and the class, but somewhat less befuddled than Roberto about this story, though the message Bob took from the story whitewashed it, ignoring its antiracist orientation. A White football player with hair dyed jet black, Bob characterized himself as an "artist who just wants to have fun." Mr. Zee was the reason Bob had signed up to take FHAO. "You can trust him; he'd understand you very well," Bob told me about Mr. Zee, explaining, "He's always outgoing; he's always happy . . . always willing to listen, always willing to help." He had gotten to know Mr. Zee when enrolled in Mr. Zee's English course the year before and had heard him tell his grandmother's story already once in that context. As Bob told me, he thus "had a pretty good idea what it was about when I heard it again." To him, Mr. Zee had probably told it (again) "'cause, the way he places himself as a understanding guy, but I guess to also show that the people he's close to are not perfect." Bob continued by describing Mr. Zee's grandmother: "I mean, after she was mugged, she didn't trust anyone; I guess he wanted to show how things get to people, how personal experiences can change a really good person to nontrusting."

Rene, a poised, African American student, had understood Mr. Zee's intended message. She told me that she had been so impressed with the story that she had shared it with her mother. "My mom was mugged by a White guy," she explained, "and she didn't hate him afterwards, I mean she didn't hate White guys afterwards." For Rene, her mother's and Mr. Zee's stories reinforced the moral that "you shouldn't just hate all people, I guess, just 'cause one person does something to you, you shouldn't just hate all people, the whole race." Like Roberto and Bob, Rene was a big fan of Mr. Zee in part because of his storytelling. "[He] makes it fun, likes to get into it, [and the stories] make it even better, to know somebody that's went through something." Whether with the intended impact or not, Mr. Zee's stories consistently engaged his students.

When asked to talk about his extensive storytelling, Mr. Zee described his own natural proclivity toward narrative and its utility in both building community and evoking student voice:

> First of all, [storytelling is] something I'm very comfortable with; it's something that I do in general, not just with students but with people in my life, because I think that once you make connections with people, you find out that they have baggage just like you have baggage, or they have stories just like you have stories; they're interesting people even when you didn't think [so]. . . .
>
> It's sort of the first step in breaking down the distance between people. The most obvious kind of distance is an authoritarian sort of distance, an authority distance—you're the teacher and they're the students. You have power; they don't have power. Well, when they find out that you've been hurt or you've been saddened by things or you've been made very happy or you have feelings, well, you have experiences that make you not very different from them, or you have experiences that make you very different from them—you tend to get more voice later. I find that the more I invest in story, the more they are willing to invest in story later on. . . . Stories are central to understanding and constructing meaning; it's the prism through which I look at my entire life.

For Mr. Zee, stories thus served as an engagement tool, a "distance" eliminator, a vehicle for meaning making, and, as was obvious from the story about his Nana, a provider of moral lessons, whether they reached the students or not.

For Mr. Zee, storytelling was a crucial component of community building, which was a first step in the accomplishment of his curricular goals; only when a community was built would students express their voices. In other words, only when students felt comfortable with one another and with Mr. Zee would they be able to delve into the tough issues in his course content. Community building, in Mr. Zee's philosophy, was thus instrumental, a necessary condition for learning to take place.

I mark the end of the community-building phase of the course by describing a pivotal moment in class relations. Throughout the activities of the first phase, the students had remained cordial with one another despite occasional differences of opinion. They were getting to know Mr. Zee, and they rarely overstepped the bounds of polite classroom conversation. There was one exception, though, that burst forth after a video on race relations. Importantly, this was not the first material concerning racism that the students had confronted. In the 5 weeks preceding the video, Mr. Zee had shown other videos, of, for example, a Ku Klux Klan indoctrination or discriminatory landlords' practices, and, as in his grandmother's story, racism had appeared as a theme in his personal stories.

In the middle of the 6th week, Mr. Zee showed a video on East St. Louis and Belleville, adjoining towns whose populations were mostly Black and mostly White, respectively. The all-White newspaper staff in Belleville had investigated their all-White police department's ticketing behavior and found a pattern of institutionalized racism. Furthermore, residents of Belleville had erected a wrought-iron gate on the one road connecting the two towns, which concretized the attitudes rampant there. After the video was over, only a few minutes remained of class time when a brush fire of responses erupted, ignited by a remark by Mari, a White senior in the class.

"It's not like that everywhere," she protested, continuing, "I mean I'm not saying that it doesn't happen anywhere. It's true in *that* area, but, I mean, you don't really see stuff like that happening here." Several students called out simultaneously, clearly angered by this remark. Penny, a Black student in the class, hurled her retort above the din, "How would you know?" Mr. Zee pounded on the table, trying to corral students' attention. "I mean, you may be Black here, but you don't get pulled over for it!" Mari exclaimed.

In trying to restore formal classroom order, Mr. Zee imposed an interpretation of Mari's remark that seemed more hopeful than realistic: "There's no hostility in what she just said. It's a perspective that explains many things about the way we work together." Mr. Zee then designated it Penny's turn to speak, and the rage evident in her voice indicated that she, too, interpreted Mari's remarks differently from how Mr. Zee would have liked. Although Penny began slowly, the pitch and speed of her remarks increased as she talked:

> First of all, no, things like that don't happen like that always, everywhere, to that extreme, but I know a lot of times, when a lot of my friends—they're Black males, they go driving down the street, a White cop will pull them over for nothing. And that's just right

next door in the city of San Martine. People don't go to that city. And maybe, Mari, maybe you don't see it because you're not Black. But *me*, as a Black woman, I see things like that. I see things happening to my uncles, my cousins, you know. But you're White. You know what I'm saying? You don't get that whole perspective of everything, because people think that the White race is superior. Even now, people still think and people—they don't understand. That makes me so angry! Man. I—I gotta calm down right now.

Penny's voice is charged. She is practically yelling at Mari when she retreats into quiet. Several students clamor to speak as she stops.

Mari: It makes me angry that people—it makes me angry, too! But look, it makes me angry that people—[Mari's voice is lost amidst multivoice squabbling, but it rises up out of the hubbub, resisting what she heard as Penny's claim that Whites are necessarily supremacists.] Come on! I mean, it seems—I'm not saying that you guys think that all White people are like that. But, I mean, in a way that's sort of what you're saying. That when you see, like—
Penny: That is not—
Mari: Any White person walking down the street, you're gonna be all, "Oh, she's White, I'm not talking to her—"
Penny: No, I don't! I don't do that—

Here again, the conversation erupts seemingly from all sides of the room, overtaking individual speakers' voices. The pace is fast, the emotional intensity is thick, and it's clear that every student has his or her ears peeled for what will happen next. Dondrea, Penny, Charles, and Peaches, four of the seven African Americans in the class, sit together on a regular basis in the front-left corner of the room. Much of the class discussion bubbles up from that area at this time:

Penny: No, like, Mari, I don't know you, so I'm not going to judge you, OK? I'm not gonna . . . disrespect you, because that's not the way I was raised. Some White people are like that, but just as a general public, you know what I'm saying?
Dondrea: It's just like that with all different races. Asians don't like Blacks; Blacks don't like Jews; it's all like that.
Penny: I know it is, but me, as a female, I haven't experienced any real hostility towards any other race. And that's just true. That's just how I am.
Charles: We still judge people on the basis of race, though.

Mr. Zee interjects here, positioning these issues to be addressed in future classes as a way to calm the intensity of the present. "We're gonna move, we're gonna move into that," he assures students, but is soon overpowered by Mari, the flow of the argument washing over him.

Mari: I've experienced things where people are, you know, like, put me down or made fun of me *because* I'm White, you know? I mean, I've experienced it, too.

Mr. Zee: Does it raise hostility in you?

Mari: No. Because, I mean, I'm not going to judge everybody, you know, the whole entire race for, you know, what one person did to me. I'm not like that.

[Several students interrupt simultaneously.]

Mr. Zee: Okay, hold it. Just a minute. First of all, I wanna make really clear. This needs to be made really clear, because I don't want anybody to leave here with hurt feelings. It's OK to be critical. It's OK to feel tension. It's not OK to be hurt over it. This is a community where we need to be able to talk about these things. I did not hear Penny say, or anybody yet say, that her anger is a general aim at all White people. I hear her say she has those feelings in her head, and that she has to deal with them—and I heard her say that she has to regulate.

The bell rang as Mr. Zee closed the conversation. There was, though, an unusual, fleeting pause before the clamor of moving desks and shuffling knapsacks. "Now we're getting into it," Mr. Zee commented to me in the subsequent quiet of the room. Later, he explained that he had feared Mari would "catch hell" on campus for voicing such opinions. Mari had faced many of these issues recently as a White young woman dating an African American young man. (By the end of the course, Mari would be pregnant with their baby and facing her family's disapproval.) Despite his concerns, Mr. Zee considered the emotional intensity of the conversation a small victory. To him, it served as proof that his community-building efforts had worked; that students could voice such opinions meant that they had come to trust one another enough to argue about the deep racial issues plaguing them and U.S. society in general.

Erin, the fourth student I followed in this case, was a very shy White Mormon, who, as was typical for her, had remained silent throughout the interaction. She had been engaged, though. To her, the conversation testified to the uniqueness of Mr. Zee's teaching. "I was glad that they could talk like that," Erin said about Penny and Mari, explaining, "'Cause in classes usually, that would not happen." "In other classes," she clarified, "it would appear to be that they were fighting or something and the teacher would break it up."

The following day, Mr. Zee explained that he had heard in the previous day's discussion "pain from every corner: pain of identity, pain about the way people see [others], pain about the way people see them." What he considered to be the moral lessons of that pain followed:

> I'm interested in having everybody understand that there is pain out there for everybody. To universalize pain is not a good goal—you know it's not like, "Take Facing History and you'll feel really bad." That's not what I want necessarily to happen, but I do want you to understand that everybody has mountains to climb; everybody has experiences to deal with; everybody has images that they're expected to conform to; everybody has expectations laid on them; everybody has, to some degree or other, pain; and one of the problems that we have is that it's really hard to sense other people's pain. It's really hard to do that. How do we figure out how to give ourselves access [Mr. Zee writes the word *access* on the board] to another group's or another individual's experience or pain? 'Cause if we don't have that experience or we've never felt that pain in the same way, it's pretty hard to do.

Without pausing, Mr. Zee turned the floor over to Penny, who stood up at her desk and, in a wavering voice, apologized to a stunned class:

> I would like to make a apology to the class in case I offended or insulted anybody yesterday in what I was talking about. I just wanted y'all to know that it was a personal opinion, and it's just how I feel, and if you know me, then you know that I'm not a, I'm not, I'm not a racist. If it doesn't come out, I know how to control myself. And if I offended anybody, I apologize to the group.

The students clapped spontaneously when Penny sat down. Mr. Zee ended the class with a brief "free-write" time for the students to reflect on what had transpired.

Phase II: The Identity Phase

The second phase of Mr. Zee's course was named for student presentations called Identity Projects, which dominated the following 4 weeks. Each day, students took turns presenting some aspect of their identities to the rest of the class. The overall goal, in his words, "was [for each student] to build a small, little window into someone else's life." Mr. Zee hoped that once students saw one another as individuals, they would be less prone to stereotyping one anothers' groups. Each student was thus assigned to make a formal presentation to the class, but as was typical of Mr. Zee's assignments, that presentation could take almost any form.

Every student did an Identity Project during this phase, and most class sessions included three presentations. On the 1st day, four students presented. Before they began, Mr. Zee was careful to set up rituals that would accord each presenter respect. The students were instructed, for example, to applaud both before and after each presentation. They were warned not to have books out on their desks or to fall asleep, or Mr. Zee would see them after class. In a sterner-than-usual tone of voice, he elaborated his expectations for students' behavior in class:

> Each project is approximately 3 to 5 minutes long, and the goal is this—here's what happened last period. The first person who had their Identity Project is someone you may know, and I'm not going to tell you her name. This is someone who might seem to you to be securely among the "haves" rather than the "have-nots"; this person has lots of friendships, socially seems very well adjusted. She's got good grades, and she's going to college next year.
>
> Well, she brought in a candle for her Identity Project, a beautiful candle, ornate on the outside, and she talked about how she was like this candle. People saw her from the outside, and there, she seems pretty, smart, to have a lot going for her, but the inside is more like it. On the inside, she's burning, and she explained why. She talked about the generational pain of having been abused as a child and having dealt with it and how she's still dealing with it. The pain has a legacy, which is that sometimes she's afraid of being with a man and what that will be like. So, afterwards, people were shocked, shocked that this was someone they thought they knew and didn't know at all. The point is that pain is universal; struggle is universal; and sometimes the people right next to you have a real nobility in getting through.

To a hushed audience, Juan spoke first. A slight but sturdily built Mexican American, Juan walked to the front of the room and sat down at a desk facing his peers. In halting, accented English, he described how he had been living alone for the past 3 months after having been kicked out of his home at Christmas. "I started drinking alcohol and smoking a lot of weed, and my dad just kicked me out," he explained. "I probably have enough money for 2 months, and after that, I don't know what I'm gonna do." His voice quavered only a little as he spoke, betraying hints of fear nonetheless. His presentation went by quickly, and he stopped abruptly, marking the end by asking his peers, "You guys have any questions?" After a short pause, Juan himself broke the ice by saying about his Identity Project, "I think mine went hella fast." The other students in the class chuckled and asked Juan a variety of questions: "How old are you?" "Is pride more important to you than being with your family?" "Does your ma help out?" Juan answered politely, and Mr. Zee closed the conversation, asking Papoo if she was ready for her turn. The students applauded for Juan as he returned to his seat and applauded again as Papoo rose to take Juan's place facing the class.

Papoo was a tall, soft-spoken Filipino student who had prepared a written script to read from. Although she was grateful for all the things her sister had helped her through in life, she explained that she resented her sister, too. "Throughout my life," she explained, "I've lived in [her] shadow." That feeling had ended for her at a religious retreat recently when she was "binded with cloth." Her sister, a minister, had "unbound" Papoo, but in the interim, she had felt "touched by the rush." She had asked for forgiveness from her sister and then felt saved by Jesus Christ. She finished her presentation by asking everyone in the class to close their eyes "and reflect on who makes your way" while she played a tape recording of her uncle singing a Christian hymn. Like Papoo's sister (and brother), her uncle was a minister at her church. His mellifluous voice was accompanied by soft jazz piano as it praised God and Jesus in a song called "He Will Make a Way." Papoo sat down after it was over, whispering to a friend nearby, "I was afraid I was gonna cry."

Atlas's project, which followed Papoo's, changed the tone of the room considerably. Atlas, a boyish-faced White student with a wry smile and a self-deprecating sense of humor, had brought in samples of his major collections: minicars, minitrucks, and full-sized, realistic-looking plastic guns. "I'm a packrat for novelties," he said as he began laying out his collections on the floor, commenting on each cherished toy. "My dog ate this one, you can see," he said, pointing out the teeth marks on one minicar. "I was pissed," he explained. When he had finished with the cars and trucks, Atlas took out the guns—toys that would not have been allowed on campus had he been searched. About the MIG and Ouzi replicas, he announced, "There was a big controversy over these 'cause kids were getting killed, so you can't find them anymore." The students passed around the plastic guns, joking about their potential uses on campus. "What'd you say about my mother?" someone enunciated slowly, imitating Arnold Schwarzenegger in conversation with a school administrator.

Over the following few weeks, the rest of the students took their turns, and an amazing array of student talents, hardships, hobbies, and strengths were conveyed through storytelling, video, art, dance, and music. Aija, a tall young man, who at no other time during the semester spoke in class, rapped a poem about his identity as an African American male. José told a heartbreaking story of his father's leaving their large family penniless, ending his project by pulling up his T-shirt to reveal a tattoo of his father's name spanning his back. Roberto read original love poems he had written in both English and Spanish, earning him an offer from Rene to accompany her to the school prom. Umesh, an Indian American young man, talked about his pride at knowing his heritage and showed a video of an all-male Hindu dance performed in traditional dress. Colette, a mature, quiet young White woman, talked about a personal ordeal she and her brother had suffered at the hands of her mother's cocaine addiction. Vyn Huan, a recent immigrant from North Vietnam, discussed her escape by rowboat and showed photographs of friends in the Philippine camp in which she was detained. Peaches, an outspoken young Black woman with a reputation for fierceness, described taking care of a toddler every day after school. Erin quietly showed some old photographs and stuffed animals that were close to her heart. Bob created a minigallery in the classroom, covering the walls with pen-and-ink drawings. Rene tearfully recounted the car accident that had killed her aunt and cousin.

Key terminology lessons and overt "processing" interlaced these student presentations much as it had during the introductory phase of the course. In the following excerpt, for example, Mr. Zee discusses the Identity Projects in order to teach the concept of empathy:

> Because this course is an anti-bias course, it's about being able to look at someone and not see them just on the surface. It's about saying, "Hmmm, not only is that person different than I thought, but it means that when I look at entire collectives of people, they are different than I thought." And that opens things up. It also means that when we say, "I hadn't heard her pain before, and now I hear it," maybe it means, "I haven't heard a whole people's pain before, and I might be able to open up to that." So that's the intention of the projects. . . . It's about empathy . . . being able to put yourself in other people's shoes; that's what it's about.

In Mr. Zee's experience, the Identity phase is the most emotionally charged one for students and the most memorable. In line with these expectations, all four students I interviewed—Bob, Erin, Rene, and Roberto—reported being very impressed by the Identity Projects. Bob had been shocked by Jose's story because it had resonated with his own troubled childhood. Bob had been abused by his father, his mother had left the family, and he had been placed in the custody of the state for a period of years. Hearing Jose's longing for a father's presence had given Bob new respect for Jose, even if it didn't prompt him to actually speak to Jose.

Erin had been stunned by the presentation given by Colette (the young woman whose mother had become a cocaine dealer). Erin and Colette had sat together in a number of classes over the years, and yet Erin had never known this about Colette. As a result of the projects, Erin explained,

> I'm starting to look at people more personally now and realize they're not just a face or how they look. They do things other than school, they have a life, and everybody's a lot more similar than they seem to be.

Rene had also been stunned by Colette's project, having thought that because she was White, Colette had "the perfect family." Rene had ended up somewhat embarrassed about her own Identity Project; she hadn't realized that talking about the deaths of her family members that had occurred more than a year earlier would still provoke her to cry. Nonetheless, seeing the other students' Identity Projects had caused her to reevaluate her assumptions and transform her reported behavior, as she explained:

> Yah, like when I'd hear Asian people talking, I'd go "szoo szoo szoo," but not anymore. I was "What are they saying?" 'cause I'd go get my nails done, and you know, nail shops are usually Asian owned, and I was wondering if they were talking about me or something, so that's what kinda made me mad, so I would try to repeat them. ["How did that change?" I asked.]
>
> 'Cause you can hear it. Just hearing other people and what they have to say. Like that Indian guy, you know. I used to think that Indian guys didn't wear deodorant, that there's one custom and they don't believe in that kind of stuff, or bathing once a month and they have their hair wrapped up, you know. I used to always make fun of them. Listening to him [Umesh], I understand now that all people aren't like that. It's just hearing it from somebody.

Unlike Erin's and Rene's experiences of their own Identity Projects, Roberto claimed not to have been nervous at all about his and to have been proud of the way it went. He bragged about his Identity Project, saying that "it was the bomb." Like the other students I interviewed, though, Roberto was moved both emotionally and intellectually by his peers' projects. Juan's Identity Project in particular had affected him. "Like before, I had him [in] a class, and I looked at him, like, 'Nah, whatever,' . . . and this class, it changed my point of view toward him." In light of learning about Juan's independent living status, Roberto felt sorry for him. Roberto told me that after the Identity Projects concluded, he "looked at . . . [all] the people in this class . . . a different way than before." "Now that I got to know them more, I know their pasts and what's going on in their lives," which accounted for why he no longer "judge[d] them as much." Roberto had been so moved by the Identity Projects, in fact, that he dwelled on his point, telling a story similar to Rene's:

> Before I would be like, "Oooh, look at her or look at him, why's he wearing that?" or "Why's she wearing that little skirt?" But see I really don't know her. Other people might see her as if she's a little whore or something, but deep inside, they don't know her. They just make judgments to what she wears and stuff.

To Roberto, Mr. Zee's class could "break that down," or squelch students' tendencies to stereotype, but only if "you really get into it." As Mr. Zee had predicted, this phase of the course affected the students I interviewed and, judging from the unanimity of their responses, had probably affected the other students in the class similarly.

The students' presentations ended on April 8, the week after Easter break. I demarcate the end of this phase, though, with the Identity Project of a visiting speaker on April 10, the middle of the 10th week of the course. On that day, a survivor of the Holocaust spoke to the students for an extended 2-hour period. Louis had been a child in France during World War II and had never spoken of the traumas he suffered at that time. Like those of many first-time speakers, his story seemed to tear out of his body in involuntary fits and starts, and each time he pedaled closer to his childhood experiences, he veered off into a related but less emotionally charged topic. The students listened politely to Louis's shifting tacks, overlooking his inability to tell his story. Louis seemed to apologize to the students at one point, saying, "I am a grandfather," having failed to divulge what he had come to reveal.

The Identity Projects were finished; they had provided students with glimpses into one another's worlds, illuminating their values, hardships, humor, and a range of differences associated with race, class, culture, ethnicity, religion, family structure, language, nationality, country of origin, grade, age, gender, and historical moment.

Phase III: The Holocaust as a Case Study

> It's gonna be sort of a downward swipe when we start looking more at history than we are at individual lives. We're gonna start looking more at history, more at collective stuff, [and there will be] more traditional work for a while. And some of you are gonna think, "Cool, it's about time." And others of you are gonna think, "It was better when we didn't have to do this kinda stuff." The end result has gotta be . . . on the same level as the first 6 weeks, where you're involved, you're curious, but you're also academic.

With these words, Mr. Zee began the third phase of the course, warning students about becoming "academic," a state he opposed to being "involved and curious." He had assigned a short, sophisticated reading on the historical roots of anti-Semitism to coincide with the school's Easter break, during which many of his students, he told me, would be going to church. When the course met again after the break, the students reviewed the reading, sharing their reactions first with their peers and then with the whole class. Peaches, it turned out, had never been exposed to the idea that the history of the Christian Church was not uniformly positive. "I think it's all lies," she proclaimed loudly, wrapping her head in her arms and resting them on her desk as if to block out all forthcoming information. Other students, though equally uninformed about church history, were less skeptical about the content of the handouts, expressing simple surprise. "I thought it was interesting that there was a guy named Martin Luther who fought against Jews when Martin Luther King fought for African Americans' rights," one student shared. Mari remarked that she hadn't known that anti-Semitism started with Jews being called "Christ-killers"; she had thought that it started with the "whole World War II thing."

Given that almost the entirety of this class session focused students' attention on an idea central to this history—that anti-Semitism predated Nazi Germany—it seemed to me that Mr. Zee was beginning his promised rigorous study of the Holocaust. The class, however, turned out to be unusual not only in comparison to what preceded it, but to what followed it. Although Mr. Zee did incorporate more Holocaust-related content, the third phase looked much like the first. Mr. Zee continued to tell stories from his life. He recycled through some key vocabulary, adding a few new phrases, and he showed videos. While the Holocaust was often a topic in these activities or came up in the surrounding discussions, it was more often peripheral than central. Rarely, in other words, was the Holocaust discussed in terms of the historical events that constitute it; rather, it was almost always talked about in class as "the Holocaust"—a single, whole entity. Thus it formed a thematic link between Mr. Zee's activities or served as historical backdrop to his stories, even while often left unexamined.

In the 2nd week of this phase, for example, a reporter visited Mr. Zee's 1st-period class, and assuming that students understood the composition of the Holocaust, she had asked the students whether "it could happen here." Explaining the reporter's visit as a catalyst, Mr. Zee posed the same question to his 2nd-period students, the class I observed, asking them to write an answer to the question silently before they discussed it aloud. As the students scratched out their answers, Mr. Zee wrote guiding questions on the board under the heading "Things to consider: Could 'It' happen Here?":

1. What is "it"?
2. What would something *include* before a "comparison" would *fit* enough to say Yes!

Mr. Zee opened the discussion by using a format he called a tag team. A group of four students revealed their ideas to the whole class and then tagged four others to do the same.

What was striking to me about this activity was that the range of students' answers displayed how little prepared many were to draw careful comparisons. Atlas, in the first group "tagged" by Mr. Zee, said, "I don't think it could happen. . . . Back then it was unprecedented; now people have jobs studying history and they know what to look for." Rene, in the second group tagged, disagreed. "I think it could happen—'cause who says we're not livin' in a Holocaust now? Just look at all the homicides and suicides!" In this format, Mr. Zee's students talked *about* the Holocaust without ever having discussed what constitutes it. In reading about historical anti-Semitism, they had discussed one reason for the Holocaust, but they had yet to read about or discuss what had happened *during* the Holocaust. Rene considered the Holocaust to include "homicides and suicides," in part because she was never exposed to the concept of genocide, and Atlas had not learned enough about "it" to know in what ways the Holocaust was unprecedented and in what ways it was not.

In a later class session, Mr. Zee summarized Simon Wiesenthal's book *The Sunflower* (1977), and while the story informed some students about historical events that make up the Holocaust, it did so only indirectly. Wiesenthal, while a concentration camp inmate, had been called to the bedside of a dying SS man seeking absolution. Mr. Zee recounted the story in florid detail, soliciting students' thoughts on what they thought they would have done had they been in Wiesenthal's position. The students shared their opinions, some arguing for smothering the SS man with a pillow, others justifying the importance of forgiveness. The comments launched Mr. Zee into a long digression about the concepts of heaven and hell in Judaism and Christianity, about the possibilities of viewing life optimistically or pessimistically, and even about the notion of rejoicing over capital punishment. Eventually, Penny interjected, "Didn't you have like some family die [in the Holocaust]?" "Oh yeah," Mr. Zee responded. "[So] what would you do?" she asked.

Rather than directly either answering or refraining from answering it, Mr. Zee used Penny's question to reflect aloud on how his prejudices reflected the legacies of his experiences. He illustrated this theme with a short story about a former neighbor whom he distrusted, an elderly Lithuanian whom he suspected of being a "Nazi bastard." This story carried him swiftly into another about serving in the National Guard and being stereotyped as wealthy because of his Jewish last name. Some of the students had heard these tales before and "phased out" as he spoke, eyes staring into the distance or heads resting on their desks. By the time Mr. Zee had finished talking, Penny either no longer remembered her original prompt or simply didn't pursue its answer.

Near the end of this phase, in the 15th week of the course, Mr. Zee held class in the swimming pool. As he envisioned it, the day would be a lesson in false constructs, societally molded conceptions of beauty or normalcy. As Mr. Zee related to me, he wanted Pool Day to have lasting moral impact:

> We're not just going swimming on Thursday. There is a reason to do what we're doing. It is something they will, semesters from now, be able to articulate something about cultural expectations and how they shape human behavior, and they may be able to do it on two fronts. One, on a simple, individual front has to do with their own body consciousness, or their own experience of what it felt like to be in a swimsuit or in the shower room in front of other people. But on the other hand, that's a vocabulary that serves them well when they think of the unfolding of many different kinds of histories.
>
> And I think that there are academicians in the world that would decry this and think of it as a terrible trivializing of what

> we're talking about, but I would submit that you have to look at what the end result is meant to be. If it's meant to be not just something cognitive, not just something they can remember the flow of history by date and time and place and people, but if it's meant to have some impact on their own personal ethic, if it's meant to have some impact on their ability to articulate their own decision makings, either individually or collectively, or nationally, for that matter, then I don't see a better way to engage them than by massaging the tension on a daily basis between what's universal and what's particular, what's in their own experience and what's in historical experience. And that's really in a nutshell, the philosophy of my entire approach to Facing History or any other segment of a course I might teach.

Despite Mr. Zee's lofty goals to have students consider their own body images as well as societally constructed norms, Pool Day looked (from the outside of the pool) like simple fun. About one third of the students brought their suits to class and spent part or all of class time splashing about in the pool. The other students sat on the ground or on folding chairs poolside, using the time to gab or catch up on assignments. Mr. Zee himself jumped in, swam a few laps, and tossed a basketball around. As Roberto recalled only a few weeks later, the experience was "cool" and "fun." "I just liked talking to my friends," he told me. Roberto did suspect that there was some reason that Mr. Zee had held class in the pool, but he thought he had missed it. As he told me, "There had to be a catch somewhere, but I didn't catch it." Having arrived late to class, he wrongly assumed that Mr. Zee had communicated the point earlier. "When I got there," he said, "everyone was just fooling around." Bob, who had attended the entirety of the class, didn't consider Pool Day to be any more significant than, in his words, "a free for all." Rene had no idea why class was held in the pool; she was just disappointed at having forgotten her suit that day.

Mr. Zee's warnings, then, that this phase of the course would be heavily academic, an intensive examination into the case study of the Holocaust, went unfulfilled. The students, though they heard about the Holocaust on a regular basis, never learned what events constitute it. In our second interview, Erin expressed dismay at this state of affairs. Although she still liked Mr. Zee's course, she felt "lost":

> I like it [the course], but it seems like, I thought we were going to be more into the history by now, I mean, maybe he is, and he's moving too slow or too fast, but most of the time it's a lot of dis-

cussions, and to me, it doesn't seem like we're really into actual events. I mean, he said he's gonna try to stay away from the time line thing, but for me, I'd appreciate it if we went over the facts of what happened more. I don't know, I'm kinda lost at this point in the class. . . . He's a great teacher. He's a good teacher, but I'm used to teachers that just lay down what they're gonna do more than just kinda have fun with the whole class and like discuss and everything, so I'm not really used to him as a teacher, but I think he's really good.

[Here I asked Erin to elaborate what she meant by "having fun."] It seems like that's what happens a lot of times, we end up going off the subject or just talking about whatever. I mean that's good, but I still feel like we don't know that much about what happened during the war and the Holocaust. And, that's one of the big reasons why I took the class.

When asked to rank her learning about the Holocaust from Mr. Zee's class on a scale of 1–10, 1 being least and 10 being the most, Erin told me disappointedly that she thought she had learned, "probably a 5 or a 6." Elaborating, she explained,

I think it's just the way I learn. I'm more of a factual person. I get kinda lost when we just talk about discussions. . . . I haven't really learned about, I don't even remember if we discussed like how many countries took over, or what the time period was, but we did learn about the number of Jews that were killed and like how affected their lives were. And that's all I can think of.

Bob, too, felt frustrated with the lack of focus on Holocaust history. When I asked him during our second interview how he felt about the class, he told me, "I still like it, but there're some things, like we don't move in any which direction often." Class is composed of "usually just a lecture or a story," he continued. "I don't know, if we moved more directly into the Holocaust instead of just stories, personal stories, maybe that would grab the class's attention." Because Mr. Zee neglected to directly confront Holocaust history, Bob implied that he felt lacking in the "bigger picture":

I think we can get right into it and learn more, but we kinda stayed back, looking at individuals, which is all right, but that wouldn't help me if I was talking to someone about it. They wouldn't understand, like, "Why are you talking about someone's

> personal story?" unless after they knew the general idea of what happened to everyone.

Although he ranked himself as having an understanding of Holocaust history equivalent to a 9½ out of a possible 10, and he could answer my questions about Holocaust history easily, he ascribed having learned the information he knew to the content covered in his World History course, not to Mr. Zee's classes.

Roberto, too, it turned out, had learned little in the way of Holocaust history from Mr. Zee, though he ranked himself as having learned the equivalent of a "10." Unlike Bob, however, he had not had the benefits of more traditionally structured history courses. When I asked him what he thought he still hadn't learned about the Holocaust, he responded with very basic questions about Holocaust history:

> The thing that I wish I knew was, I just have questions. Like how come the Jewish people let themselves go and not try to fight? And, um, why did the Nazis pick the Jews? Is it 'cause they knew they'd have more control over them than anybody around them, or is it because of their appearance? Hitler wasn't blond, he didn't have blue eyes, wasn't he even . . . um, Polish was it? Or, Romania? [I tell Roberto here that Hitler was from Vienna, Austria.] He was Australian, he wasn't German. How come all those German people felt—didn't he say he didn't like people other than Nazis or something? [Roberto asks this question very earnestly. "Yes," I answer.] Well, were the Polands, were they Nazis too? Didn't they take over Italy too?

Later in the interview, when I asked Roberto specific questions, his answers evidenced his complete confusion. When I asked him to explain how Hitler had risen to power, for example, Roberto responded, "I don't know—wasn't he a politician?—I don't know." When asked how he would define the Holocaust, Roberto answered that it was "a terrible mass murder, a big event, something that should have never happened [that] changed a lot of people's lives; it's just like horrible." When I pushed him for some specifics—years, locations or events—he had no facts at his disposal. "I don't know; I don't think it should ever have happened," was his response. While Roberto had gained pedestrian knowledge of the Holocaust, Mr. Zee's class had done little to advance in him a more sophisticated understanding of its events, instilling in him instead the false sense that he had one.

Rene, too, had tremendous difficulty answering my questions, though she felt she had learned "a lot" between her American History, World History, and Facing History courses, all of which she felt had covered that historical terrain. When I asked her how Hitler rose to power, Rene struggled to answer. "I remember he was a nobody, then he—oh, man, I can't describe this," she told me, exasperated at being asked. "OK, I can remember he was in jail and he wrote that book," she said, seeming proud to have remembered something. "So, then everybody just started reading the book, and then they started believing in Hitler and thought that he was just gonna change everything," she guessed. Asked to recount an example of Nazi anti-Jewish legislation, Rene replied, slightly ashamed, "Jeez, I can't think. No, not off the head." She was able to list only four countries that fought in World War II: Germany, Italy, Japan, and Great Britain. And when asked to define the Holocaust, she had such difficulty that she ended up claiming the term resisted definition. "You can't really just give a definition, 'The Holocaust was such-and-such such-and-such,'" Rene said, "'cause there's just more to it; you can't just give it a word." Rene was a solid A-student; she had rarely missed class and always paid attention.

Rather than having the students delve into a systematic investigation during this phase, Mr. Zee had presented the Holocaust via stories and handouts that touched on some of its aspects. As with the activities of the first phase, Mr. Zee's Holocaust-related content seemed to arise in no particular order, with no particular structure, but rather when Mr. Zee's memory was triggered to tell a story about it or when he happened to pull out a worksheet on it. In other words, the Holocaust circulated as a frequent topic in this phase, but was never itemized, examined, or explored. Perhaps because in his own words, Mr. Zee "hate[d] . . . time lines," he similarly eschewed organizational structure of any kind, preferring instead to let topics rise and fall, appear and disappear, in his "sculpted," more organic way. Unfortunately, judging from the students' remarks—Erin's about a lack of knowledge, Bob's about his frustration with it, and Roberto's and Rene's displays—it became clear to me that Mr. Zee's orientation left most if not all, of his students, lacking basic information about the Holocaust. Mr. Zee, in his devotion to storytelling and in his efforts to investigate the period's complicated moral dimensions, had not given his students any facts.

Phase IV: Participatory Citizenship

For the final 2 weeks of the semester, Mr. Zee introduced the students to people whom he hoped would serve as role models for them. Through videotaped testimonies and documentaries, these contemporary figures told stories from their lives, mostly stories of heroism. Although Mr. Zee continued to share recollections from his own life, tell stories with some historical content, and introduce new vocabulary, this new phase was dedicated mostly to students' viewing and Mr. Zee's discussing these impressive people. Mr. Zee titled this phase of the course "participatory citizenship," one of the official FHAO goals.

This section of the course was loaded with video clips provided by FHAO. The students saw no fewer than 10 testimonies in as many days, each ranging in length from 4 to 25 minutes. Among the role models were a rescuer who had shot a local policeman in order to save her Jewish charges during the Holocaust, a human rights activist who had brokered a truce between feuding gangs in Los Angeles, and a refugee of the Khmer Rouge's child army who had returned to Cambodia to try to help other formerly coerced soldiers. The students saw so many testimonies in such a short time, in fact, that at one point, they confused the heroic activities of the individuals, mistaking the Holocaust rescuer with a battered women's advocate. "Too many videos in a week," one student muttered by way of explanation when Mr. Zee had clarified the misunderstanding.

In addition to their viewing role models' activities, a course requirement that students contribute 15 hours of community service introduced them experientially to participatory citizenship. Mr. Zee assigned the written work to accompany their social action with a typically dictated moral message:

> General info: Write a 4–6-page, computer-typed or typed paper. . . . *Be sure that your paper has as its thesis the ideas that everyone matters, and that negative traditions can be fought*—and that means that the rest of us have little excuse for not doing the right thing.

Perhaps as a consequence of the assignment parameters, Erin, whose project involved helping take care of children with Down's syndrome, described her experience in language similar to Mr. Zee's:

> They [the children] were funny. A lot of people ridicule them and make fun of them, and I think that's just horrible, 'cause they can't help the way they are. They're human beings just like us [only] they're mentally retarded. . . . I see them more personally now. Having [Mr. Zee] make it a requirement has made me think about, you know, I need to contribute more to society. . . . Sometimes, I won't do anything unless I have to. I've never really done things for the community, except for a few things here and there.

To fulfill their community service requirements, Roberto took a CPR course, Bob continued working at the student-run recycling center on campus, and Rene volunteered at a battered women's shelter. According to the closing survey I administered, 90% of the students echoed Erin's sentiments, considering the assignment to have been worthwhile.

In the final few days of the course, Mr. Zee's activities were appropriately summative. One day, for example, he had small student groups brainstorm at least one "Big Idea" they had learned from FHAO. Each group, its members befuddled at first, eventually came up with one, such that the class generated an impressive list later reworded by Mr. Zee as

- Ignorance and the lack of education results in the continuation of deep-rooted negative traditions.
- Identity is not based on simple facts such as looks, race, gender, and religion, but on complex facts such as experiences, attitudes, and life circumstances.
- People are like blades of grass; they cover up a large area but they are each individuals.
- An individual has the power to change things.

The second-to-last day of class, Mr. Zee also showed one final videotape, a documentary called *Not in Our Town*, about the outpouring of communal support shown to local Native American and Jewish victims of hate crimes in Billings, Montana.

Finally, on June 12, the students took a 2-hour test, which Mr. Zee creatively called their "final experience." As he had from the beginning, Mr. Zee was emphasizing the nontraditional nature of his course. The test had three parts. In the first, students were assigned to a small group, and each group was given one Big Idea to discuss for a few minutes. (The students had seen the full list the day before, over the objections of some who had wanted the final to be more challenging.) The small groups took turns sharing their ideas with the rest of the class. Some groups listed stories Mr. Zee had told that were related to their group's idea; one group performed a short skit. Then the raucous room descended into quiet as each student wrote a journal entry on one of the ideas presented.

In the second part of the "experience," the students circulated around the classroom, examining pictures Mr. Zee had duplicated from an exhibition catalog on Anne Frank and mounted on the walls. The photographs were surrounded by explanatory text blocks, and the students were asked to choose three images as a "basis for a short writing to illustrate what [they] know, what [they] think, and how [they] feel."

As I circulated among the students, I heard Atlas saying to Penny about the black-hatted Jews depicted in one photograph, "There's the Amish, right there." He was not joking. Later, Penny asked Mr. Zee how the Nazis got work, and a third student didn't understand the caption explaining that the Germans "willingly gave up democracy." Nonetheless, the students wrote quietly and diligently about the images they had viewed.

In the third part of the experience, Mr. Zee showed a brief videotape on the architect Maya Lin, designer of the Vietnam Veterans' Memorial in Washington, DC. Because no time remained, however, the students did not have to write their thoughts on what they had seen in this videotape. Instead, they were dismissed from Facing History and Ourselves to their summer vacations.

REFLECTIONS

Mr. Zee's course had clear successes, among them the high engagement level of his nontracked students, the palpable sense of community he fostered through the sharing of personal stories, the unusually broad range of topics he touched on, and the opportunities he gave students to consider morally complex issues. For all these reasons and because of Mr. Zee himself, the students considered his class to have been a positive experience overall. All 30 students circled Yes on the second survey when asked just a few days before their final experience whether they had liked the course. Moreover, all but one answered affirmatively that they would recommend the course to friends, and the one student who hadn't, wrote in, "Don't know—they might not like it." The students had considered the course to be different from their other classes at MHS, just as Mr. Zee had consistently encouraged them to think. Given the "extraordinary sameness of instructional practices" that characterize high schools, according to John Goodlad (1984, p. 246), Mr. Zee's having provided students with an atypical school experience, it might be argued, represents a significant accomplishment in itself.

In addition, it appears that Mr. Zee did influence many of his students' senses of morality and understandings of human behavior, another significant accomplishment, although one harder to assess. The students' self-reports, nevertheless, attest to the influence of Mr. Zee's class. As Bob summarized:

> To me that class was more of a personal learning—I think it's for myself to understand myself to help people and what kinda things

> people do to each other; I keep it in my mind all the time . . . so I can be more aware about how these things could happen and what I could do to not be a Nazi or something else, but to be more open to ideas and stuff like that. . . . I feel I'm learning how to respect people more, actually.

Bob told me, too, that as a result of this class, he was more likely to intercede when he heard "people saying racial slurs or ethnic jokes." Whereas in the past he "would have gone along with it, and 'ha ha ha, OK,'" now he "stand[s] up . . . a little more." Erin told me that though she was too shy to intercede on behalf of others, the course had at least provided her with a role model of what that might look like. Moreover, Erin had felt support for some of her own ideas through the class discussions. At home, she felt her parents had "been racist against" her boyfriend, who was Filipino and Chinese, and they had wanted her to stop seeing him. FHAO, she said, had helped her decide to remain involved with her boyfriend. Roberto explained, "I used to stereotype people; now I don't as much anymore." Rene, too, had curtailed her stereotyping and had started to love learning "just how to interact with other people, other races, and to get a better understanding of them." These reactions, not atypical for FHAO courses (Fine, 1993a, 1995; Heller & Hawkins, 1994; Shultz, Barr, & Selman, 2001; Weinstein, 1997), reflect the fulfillment of Mr. Zee's goals that his course instill "anti-bias, antiracist" orientations in his students.

Such impressive changes in the texture of students' thinking were a result of Mr. Zee's innovative adaptation (Ben-Peretz, 1990) of the FHAO curriculum. As the official curriculum suggests, Mr. Zee had devoted much class time to building students' vocabulary on decision-making processes and exposing them to the domain of the moral. As the curriculum also recommends, he had presented students with role models of altruistic behavior, himself included. He had also provided students with glimpses of some of his less impressive decisions, filling himself out as a truly human "work in progress."

The Identity Projects allowed the students to do the same, albeit with less floor time. As such, the assignment was risky; Mr. Zee essentially invited students to raise issues and share experiences that posed inevitable teaching challenges. The mishandling of that kind of personal information by other students, if not by Mr. Zee, was clearly a risk with possibly disastrous consequences. One could easily imagine teachers shying away from such an activity for just this reason. From the students' points of view, the Identity Projects also involved risks. The students had to decide which part of themselves to make public, having had little experience to help them imagine the consequences. Perhaps as a result of these very real risks, the Identity Projects both broke down the barriers between students and developed among them a strong sense of community. With Mr. Zee's running commentary of lessons to be drawn from them, the Identity Projects provided students with a powerful learning opportunity enjoyed by all. Not a part of the official FHAO curriculum, this phase of the course had been designed by Mr. Zee himself.

It is not surprising, given this consistent emphasis on the moral, that much of what students reported learning from the course was moral in nature. When asked on the second survey, "What do you think are the most important things you've learned in this course?" the majority, 80%, of students' answers were morally inflected, indicating perhaps that the bulk of what they considered themselves to have learned was conceptual rather than concrete, moral rather than informational. Their written-in answers included "Make a difference in the world"; "Fight prejudice"; "Learned about human behavior"; and "I liked learning about myself and others." Most of the students, 90% in fact, indicated agreement with the statement "My attitudes towards other people have changed because of this class." One student wrote in his survey that he had learned a lesson that I suspect Mr. Zee would consider quite an accomplishment: "Everyone is an individual." In brief, Mr. Zee's students had responded very positively to his course, to his teaching, and to his highly morally laden content.

That content, both implicit and explicit, usually concerned the role of individuals in making decisions and taking action. With the laudable goal of empowering his students, Mr. Zee had regularly focused on the behavior of individuals, the roles of their decisions in shaping experience, and conversely the roles of their experiences in making decisions. Usually, though, Mr. Zee focused so exclusively on individuals that he neglected the larger forces of history that inevitably influence their decisions.

In the story he told about his grandmother, for example, Mr. Zee had concluded by saying, "The distance that gets created is sometimes created by ourselves." As was typical for Mr. Zee, this moral centers on the role of the individual, in this case, his grandmother and her part in forging "distance" in the wake of having been robbed. Obviously critical of the choice he implies she made, Mr. Zee conveys a moral that is stripped of the story's larger racialized context. In his choice of morals, Mr. Zee put "one bad experience" at the forefront of lots of walking rather than putting thousands of stereotyped images and a history of racism into the background of her reaction. Although there was a moral in Mr. Zee's grandmother story that could help students forge the connections between the insidiousness of racism in U.S. history, of anti-Semitism in Holocaust history, and of prejudice and intolerance today, the moral Mr. Zee chose—that we "sometimes" fashion distance ourselves—did not foster these connections. Frequently, Mr. Zee's depiction of individuals' decisions were similarly presented as if separable from the social contexts or historical moments in which they were made.

The moral meanings of his stories, however, were typically more complicated than the explicit lessons he imputed to them. In the story about his beating of a fellow soldier, for example, he explicitly stated in conclusion that it's "almost a tradition for groups to mistreat nonmembers." While not justifying his behavior, this statement positions it as a quasi-historical *group* phenomenon, in some small way mitigating his responsibility as an individual. Probably not intentionally, his use of the metaphor of disease to open this story functions similarly. By framing his collaboration in a group beating as his having contracted a "plague," or disease, he is in some small way again implying that his behavior was unavoidable or caused by forces outside himself.

The simple moral implied in his statement is that groups *shouldn't* mistreat nonmembers, which in turn implies that students should beware of group dynamics. As he told students, because he was a "member of a mob" in this one instance, he now suffers lifelong guilt for his actions. An additional moral dimension at the level of the story content thus involves the human potential for cruelty.

The fact that a teacher, Mr. Zee in particular, told the story, however, framed this message. If even Mr. Zee, an institutionalized role model, a man who in his own words was "brought up . . . [to] welcome the stranger," could perpetrate such cruelty, then, Mr. Zee implied, anyone can. On the levels of both content and context, students were meant to beware of the circumstances under which people are transformed into our "worst sel[ves]." Also at this level of the storytelling context was an implied model of propriety. In telling this story, he was actually modeling for the students how to tell these kinds of stories appropriately, how to reconfigure inappropriate acts, how to "story" them with regret. In confessing his misdeed this way, presenting it as a true-to-life parable, meant to instruct, appropriately emoted, the story told in this context becomes redemptive.

For this seemingly simple 3-minute tale, then, like the longer story about Mr. Zee's grandmother, there are many, admittedly related but nonetheless distinct and occasionally competing, moral messages, both on the level of content and in the realm of context. How then can one decide on the primacy of any one moral message in a story? Does Mr. Zee's explicitly stated moral take precedence over the implicit ones?

In the story that followed the beating story, the protagonist was an ex-neo-Nazi, and the hero, a Jewish doctor who removes his White-supremacist tattoos. What was the moral for that story? Mr. Zee concluded his tale about the ex-Nazi with the statement "I bet he could tell you a lot about what caused his plague." By using the term *plague* again, Mr. Zee was emphasizing the message that students need to beware of the plague certainly, though what that plague meant exactly was unclear. Perhaps for Mr. Zee's purposes, whether plague refers to group mentality, racism, or hatred in general is unimportant. The point may be simply to inoculate students against all three. But in the context of having just told the army beating story, this story is situated as its complement. If the message of the first story in this class was that everyone is capable of evil under certain circumstances, then the message of this story seems to be that people are also capable of reform (for the ex-supremacist) or of generosity (for the Jewish doctor). In short, the two stories' textual proximity highlights the particular message that the behavior of individuals spans a wide range of possibilities. Less than a minute later in the class, Mr. Zee stated as much. "My human behavior" he explained, ranges from the "angelic" to the "beastly." While Mr. Zee's stories therefore touched on the group dynamics involved in complex situations, the ultimate morals of the stories tended to crystallize into lessons about individuals as such.

In the majority of his stories, Mr. Zee was the moral center, the hero willing to stand up against racism and fight intolerance. In one story, for example, Mr. Zee spat in the face of a bully twice his size; in another, he reported the racist comments of a checkout clerk to her supervisor; in a third, he refused to let an uncle into his house unless the uncle desisted from using racist language; in another, Mr. Zee stopped an elderly man from beating his wife with a stick. Thus Mr. Zee's stories modeled for students a value system that encourages interceding and the capabilities to do so. He was showing them not only that it is important to fight racism and brutality, but also that they too could stand up and take action against all forms of oppression. Mr. Zee, after all, presented himself as a "regular guy," with failings and strengths, "a work in progress." One message of Mr. Zee's positioning himself as the main character of his stories, then, was that he, a "regular guy," and thus they, "regular students," could be heroes. These stories, as well as activities such as the Identity Projects, while meant to empower individual students, nonetheless focused almost exclusively on individuals stripped of the larger contexts of their decision making and action taking.

This emphasis on the role of the individual is in part a strategy to universalize the Holocaust, to make its lessons widely applicable across situations, a reflection of the universalistic orientation of the FHAO curriculum. Deborah Lipstadt (1995) has soundly critiqued such an orientation, arguing that "this approach . . . elides the differences between the Holocaust and all manner of inhumanities and injustices" (p. 26).

The appeal of this theme is also, arguably, very American. Americans tend to like to believe that we shape our own destinies, that we act as individuals, that we can overcome any limitations. In one of the most comprehensive renderings of the toll this ideology extracts, Bellah, Madsen, Sullivan, Swidler, and Tipton (1985) write:

> American cultural traditions define personality, achievement, and the purpose of human life in ways that leave the individual suspended in glorious, but terrifying isolation. These are limitations of our culture, of the categories and ways of thinking we have inherited, not limitations of individuals . . . who inhabit this culture. (p. 6)

Mr. Zee's emphasis on the theme of the individual was so complete, however, that it impeded focusing on the historicity of the Holocaust. The theme of the individual as a moral being—or of the individual acting individually—doesn't lend itself to explaining mass phenomena, the issues involved in group behavior. Thus, his paradigm not only obscures explanation of the perpetrators' behavior, it especially mystifies excuses for the behavior of the victims.

The disjuncture that results is highlighted in an accusatory remark that Peaches made toward the end of the course: "I still don't understand how y'all let yourselves be gassed like that." Ultimately, Mr. Zee's dedication to the goal of empowering students precluded their gaining a complete understanding of the Holocaust; the American ideal of individualism, no matter how attractive as ideology, is limited as an explanatory framework for Holocaust history.

As with the emphasis on individualism, the structure of Mr. Zee's course seemed particularly American as well. Mr. Zee ended with a study of participatory citizenship, profiles of people who made a difference in the world. Thus, even though he explicitly referred in class to the Holocaust as a tragedy, he concluded the course with an uplifting, empowering unit on rescue during the Holocaust and resistance to injustice in the contemporary United States. This conclusion, while morally inspiring in its content, was intellectually questionable by virtue of its placement, implying a redemptive ending to a tragic event. In other words, the structure of the course implied a kind of happy ending or at least a substantial silver lining.

In an essay on Anne Frank's diary, Bruno Bettelheim (1960) claims that the admiration bestowed on Anne, the Franks, and the diary result from a common desire to deny the harsh realities of history. In his discussion of the "Americanization of the Holocaust," Alvin Rosenfeld (1995) agrees, stating that it is an "American tendency to downplay or deny the dark and brutal sides of life and to place a preponderant emphasis on the saving power of . . . collective deeds of redemption" (p. 36). Many subsequent writers have concurred (Loshitzky, 1997; Novick, 1999; Ozick, 1996). I would argue that Mr. Zee, by mitigating the tragedy of the Holocaust in the structure of his unit, fell prey to the same kind of human impulse against which these writers warned.

In Mr. Zee's consistently talking about the Holocaust without his leading his students to discover what it was, the Holocaust became iconic in his classroom, discussed as a symbol rather than understood as events. Although I was very impressed that Mr. Zee taught students about the history of anti-Semitism, something I have rarely seen done in other public high school classrooms and a topic that is frequently overlooked (Dawidowicz, 1992; Short, 1995), I was disappointed that so little other factual terrain about the Holocaust was covered. In our first interview, Mr. Zee had told me that when he saw the FHAO curriculum, he

> was looking for a program that would be developmentally sound, not commemorative, but educational, not only particular in its vision of what the history means or who it has implications for, but very universal in that regard, so that we can make meaning out of it and for our own lives without trivializing it or bastardizing it in any way, without reducing it to the level of generality.

And yet my impression of Mr. Zee's class was that this was exactly what he had done to the Holocaust by so frequently treating it as if it were an entity already known among his students. Mr. Zee had told me during our first interview that, though students "have to know" a variety of information, they also need "a lotta hooks to hang ideas on." In his enacted curriculum, however, the "hooks" were more important to Mr. Zee than was committing chronology to memory, so much so that discussion of these conceptual hooks, in the form of building a vocabulary about human behavior, supplanted *any* chronology or almost any information being taught at all. In the closing survey I administered, only 11, or a little over a third of the class, could identify the Nuremberg Laws, and only 8 could define the term *Kristallnacht*, or Night of the Broken Glass.

An embedded lesson that Mr. Zee thus seemed to teach students was that it is possible to make judgments without information; it is possible to decide what Simon Wiesenthal should have done with regard to the bandaged SS soldier, for instance, without knowing what the SS was or what Wiesenthal had endured at their hands. Likewise, it is possible to consider whether the Holocaust or its variant could (or has) reoccurred without first knowing what "it" was. Mr. Zee's determination to be antiacademic, to be experiential, for his course to be different from traditional ones and more easily accessible led to an alarming paucity of factual information.

Although it is important not to overgeneralize from scant evidence, it seems possible that even Mr. Zee's terminology of human behavior was lost on the majority of students; only two students, for example, could identify the term *altruism*, though Mr. Zee had lectured about it just 1 week before their completing my second survey. Mr. Zee's delivery model of student learning, the idea that the students would internalize his chosen vocabulary of human behavior by hearing stories about it or seeing the terms occasionally written on the board, was, finally, not very effective.

It's worth noting that Mr. Zee did not teach his students Holocaust history for lack of information or for lack of resources. Mr. Zee himself was exceedingly knowledgeable about the Holocaust, and the FHAO resource book that each student received consisted wholly of detailed and informative readings. But Mr. Zee rarely assigned readings from the text, and he never insisted on their completion. There were no in-class activities, discussions, quizzes, or evaluations based on the readings. Students could use the readings for their portfolio entries, which Mr. Zee suggested at times, but that choice was purely optional. Not surprisingly, then, when asked on the second survey, "Approximately how much of the assigned reading did you do for the class?" more than three quarters of the students checked "Some of it" or "Little of it." Only one student checked "All of it." Given the constraints of working part time; fulfilling other, more demanding course requirements; playing sports; or participating in extracurricular activities, the majority of students did not read the assigned readings, because it was not required for their full participation in his class. Because Mr. Zee did not cover information about the Holocaust during class time and because most of the students did not read their textbooks, they learned about Holocaust-related issues without actually studying the Holocaust.

The danger in this kind of approach is that the students left Mr. Zee's course with the misguided impression that they had in fact learned a lot about the Holocaust. They had heard Mr. Zee tell numerous stories related to the Holocaust; they had heard him talk about Holocaust survivors; they had textbooks filled with information about the Holocaust (even if they didn't read them); and they had taken a "final experience," almost half of which was dedicated to writing about images from the Holocaust. In short, they were surrounded by indications that their elective history course had been about the Holocaust. As testament to their misguided sense of their own knowledge base, 73.3% of the students agreed with the statement on the second survey "If I were to meet a Holocaust denier, I could prove to him that the Holocaust did happen," a task that would presumably require students to possess substantial and specific Holocaust information.

Ironically, Mr. Zee's course had all the components that could allow students to explore Holocaust history deeply: few time constraints; a psychologically insightful, knowledgeable, and engaging teacher with a willingness to discuss difficult moral issues and spend time developing a strong sense of community in his classroom; and a solid curriculum resource and many fascinating materials about Holocaust history. With even slight modifications, Mr. Zee could have taught his students much more Holocaust information, while still hanging it on the conceptual hooks he so valued.

The ultimate irony of Mr. Zee's course is that, while it didn't teach students very much Holocaust history per se, in some sense perverting the goals of the informationally loaded official curriculum, it did seem to instill in them the moral lessons most people want conveyed to students from rigorous study of that history—that racism is abhorrent, that interceding on behalf of the unjustly oppressed is necessary, and that even a single person can make a difference in the world. Mr. Zee's course seemed to accomplish the hard goal of instilling in students the tenets of antiracism without teaching them the seemingly more straightforward content of Holocaust history. Although he had engaged and inspired his students in nontraditional ways, teaching them to "face himself and themselves," Mr. Zee had not taught them to "face" Holocaust history.

Chapter 3

Simulating Survival

I first heard about Katie Bess's teaching of the Holocaust from a former student of hers who had become a student of mine. The student, a young Jewish girl entering 10th grade at the time, told me that it was the "coolest" class she had ever taken. The 9th-graders taking the class "played Jews," and the 10th-graders who had taken the class the year before came back to play "the Gestapo." The teacher was a "kind of Hitler," directing everything that happened in the room. The teacher had conducted a Holocaust simulation, and for this student, the experience was emotionally powerful. She claimed that she would never forget it. I remember thinking at the time that in all probability, this student had indeed had a powerful learning experience, but that it must have come at the expense of trivializing the Holocaust. I thought then that no simulation, no matter how well done, could avoid that significant pitfall. How, after all, could a classroom encounter that didn't include *actual* barbarity—physical, emotional and spiritual—mimic Holocaust atrocity authentically? How could the finality of mass murder be conveyed to students in a meaningful way, without bastardizing its deepest and most personal consequences?

CONCERNS ABOUT CLASSROOM SIMULATIONS

What Thomas Laqueur (1994) lamented about the Holocaust Memorial Museum in Washington, DC, resonated with the reservations I held about classroom simulations of the Holocaust:

> Any simulacrum [of the Holocaust] would be unspeakably vulgar. The social history museum in Victoria uses odors of apple brown betty wafting from its model of a nineteenth-century kitchen to give us the feel of the times; but what might one do for Treblinka? It would be unthinkable to crowd visitors [to the Holocaust Memorial Museum], a hundred at a go, into the real cattle car which sits on a few feet of track on Floor Three in order to "experience" what "it felt like." ... [To mimic] smells, sounds,

> "experiences"—screams, hissing of gas, screeching of train brakes, barking of dogs, bursts of machine-gun fire, shouts—would be unbearable. (p. 31)

Laqueur here condemns such simulacra as not only aesthetically repugnant but also morally unbearable. To aestheticize the Holocaust was originally offensive to the theorist Theodore Adorno; to simulate it experientially might be to reduce it ad absurdum to kitsch, Disneyland, or blockbuster ("reality") television.

Similar concerns, I suspect, drove William Parsons and Samuel Totten (1994) to warn teachers against enacting Holocaust simulations. "Even when teachers take great care to prepare a class for such an activity," they write, "simulating experiences from the Holocaust remains pedagogically unsound" (p. 8). They continue:

> The problem with trying to simulate situations from the Holocaust is that complex events and actions are oversimplified, and students are left with a skewed view of history. Since there are numerous primary source accounts, both written and visual, as well as survivors and eyewitnesses who can describe actual choices faced and made by individuals, groups, and nations during this period, teachers should draw upon these resources and refrain from simulation games that lead to trivialization of the subject matter. (p. 8)

In an article devoted exclusively to dissuading teachers from enacting simulations, Totten (2000) goes so far as to suggest that teachers who use simulations are not only "minimizing, simplifiying, [and] distorting" the Holocaust, but "possibly even 'denying'" it (p. 170); that is, aiding those Holocaust deniers who dispute its very facticity.

Like Laqueur, Totten, Parsons, and others (Dawidowicz, 1992; Wiesel, 1990; Wieser, 2001), I used to share central assumptions about Holocaust simulations and about what it means to "trivialize" the Holocaust. The assumptions may be classified in two intricately related categories of curriculum, what might be called the representational (or symbolic) dimensions and the consequential ones. The representational set is primarily concerned with the image of the subject matter, specifically its (re-)presentation in classrooms. The consequential category centers on the domain of actual human impact, what students learn.

The representational assumptions tend to run this way: classroom simulations, as representations of the Holocaust, inevitably pervert Holocaust history, since the form of a simulation warps its historical referent. By treating tragic subject matter as a game, by making it fun for students to learn, by leavening the heavy history of this era, one compromises or diminishes the seriousness of the events themselves. As the Holocaust is inherently tragic, so tragedy demands reverence or at least a serious venue. By contrast, simulations are inherently irreverent, if not outright farcical, and thus an inappropriate medium.

Given these assumptions, it follows that students participating in a simulation run the risk of learning about the Holocaust *as* its trivialized form. This is the consequentialist claim. Students risk coming to think that what they have simulated is a close replica of the historical reality rather than a distant, distorted echo, only partially intelligible. As Totten (2000) writes, "For students to walk away [from a simulation experience] thinking that they have either experienced what a victim went through or have a greater understanding of what the victims suffered is shocking in its naiveté" (p. 170). As I see it, there is an important distinction between the two parts of Totten's argument. "For students to walk away thinking that they have . . . experienced what a victim went through" seems to me indeed to constitute "naiveté"; for students to gain "a greater understanding of what the victims suffered," by contrast, seems to me a laudable goal, a worthy exercise in historical imagination. Whereas the former leads to hubris, the latter leads, at least potentially, to humility in the face of this history, hopefully even to wisdom.

Totten's coupling, however misleading in its substance, is nonetheless illustrative of the tight linkage between representational and consequentialist assumptions. The fear is that a Holocaust simulation necessarily collapses the important distinctions between the experiences of Holocaust victims/survivors and present-day students, desensitizing students to those very real differences, and allowing a "shocking naiveté" to masquerade as "greater understanding" of Holocaust atrocity. The Holocaust historian Lucy Dawidowicz (1992) summarized the problem of trivialization succinctly and derisively, asking, "What kind of [understandings] can come from American children who think of the Gestapo as the name of a game?"

According to Sam Wineburg (2001), all endeavors in history education inevitably encounter the tension between the knowable and the unknowable as it is woven into the very fabric of the discipline. As Wineburg writes,

> Coming to know others, whether they live on the other side of the tracks or the other side of the millennium, requires the education of our sensibilities, [and] that is what history, when taught well, gives us practice in doing. Paradoxically, what allows us to come to know others is our distrust of our capacity to know them, a skepticism toward the extraordinary sense-making abilities that allow us to construct the world around us. (p. 24)

The consequentialist position, as articulated forcefully by Totten, claims that classroom simulations necessarily sabotage the precarious balance of understanding toward which all history education ought to aspire, according to Wineburg. In having students role-play the parts of historical actors, simulations encourage students to elide the tremendous disparities between themselves and others.

There are other dimensions to each of these categories as well as other kinds of arguments altogether that may be levied against the use of Holocaust simulations. Anxiety over the possibility of harming students psychologically, for example, is a consequentialist claim that deserves mention. In role-playing the part of victims, are students not in some way psychically victimized themselves, temporarily or not? Worse yet, what happens to students who play the part of victimizers? Are they not encouraged, again at least temporarily, to imagine themselves as perpetrators of brutal acts? And doesn't such an imaginative leap carry implications for their behavior outside school? How might such role-playing affect students' perceptions of Jews? Will they, whether Jews or non-Jews, think of Jews only as victims? Considering the impressive literature on the impact of role-taking on image-making, of action on thought (Jones, 1981; Peters, 1987; Zimbardo, 1999; Zimbardo, Maslach, & Haney, 2000), it is clear that the psychological dimensions of simulations are not trivial matters.

The concerns revolving around Holocaust simulations thus converge in the following constellation of symbolic and consequential questions:

- Might it be possible for a simulation to represent the Holocaust without trivializing it?
- What if a well-crafted simulation *could* end up giving students a strong knowledge base about the Holocaust, a heightened sensitivity to historical contingency, and a greater empathy for its actors?
- Under such circumstances, would the symbolic objections be worth disregarding for the consequentialist achievements?

I conducted research on Ms. Bess's Holocaust simulation in an attempt to answer these questions. I should restate that rather than entering her classroom with an open mind, I was mostly sure of my answers and was seeking empirical support for my claims. Since hearing about her from my former student, I had been referred to her numerous times by educators, researchers, and district administrators, many of whom gave me her name somewhat cautiously, saying she was an "excellent history teacher" but that her treatment of the Holocaust was "controversial." Given the objections outlined above, the hesitancy with which she was recommended was not unexpected. I was surprised, though, when my research on her class didn't unfold to support the prejudices I had held upon entering it.

GAUCHO HIGH SCHOOL AND MS. BESS

Gaucho High School, where Ms. Bess teaches, sits high on a hillside overlooking the ocean in Northern California. Surrounding it are tree-lined streets, well-manicured lawns, and the tidy houses of a mostly White, middle-class, suburban neighborhood. Although the view from the street is one of Stepford serenity, the view behind the school's main building is very different. Gaucho's student population outgrew its main facility by the late-1950s, and most classes now are held in nine portable buildings that sprouted seemingly haphazardly from concrete fields sprawling behind it. A few faded murals adorn the windowless walls of the portables; for the most part, the space between structures is punctuated only by teachers' cars. An occasional tree brightens the landscape, and a constant police presence quells any hints of unrest. As Ms. Bess describes it, Gaucho is a wonderful public school, despite the ugliness of its plant, "the best school in the district by far."

> It's a very liberal, progressive, PC [politically correct] kind of high school. There are no gangs; kids are polite to one another. But basically there's social segregation—kids hang out with kids that look like they do, but that's something, I think, that's part of high school.

Gaucho serves 1,400 students, with fewer than 10% being limited English proficient. Despite the school's mostly White, suburban surroundings, Gaucho's student population consists mostly of African American, inner-city youth, bused from the neighboring city. The school district in 1995–96 reported the following ethnic distribution at Gaucho: African American, 45.81%; Caucasian, 23.18%; Asian, 19.73%; Hispanic, 8.65%; and Filipino, 2.43%.

Ms. Bess is a tall woman whose attractive face and dancer's physique make her age unidentifiable. She has been teaching history at Gaucho for 24 years, and she has taught about the Holocaust since 1973, a time when few published Holocaust curricula existed and few teachers taught the subject in public schools. Over the years, her teaching of the subject has evolved dramatically, though her goals have remained mostly unchanged. As she explained to me,

> What initially years ago made me want to try something different was that I had kids say, "Well I would have hid," or "That wouldn't have happened to me." I was sort of outraged that they were so cold-hearted. . . . I realized that they don't understand evil, and they don't understand the circumstances, the play of the hand

> that history deals, not just in the Holocaust but it happens a lot, a lot. And, you don't have many choices. Initially that's what I wanted. I wanted them to be humbled, and I wanted them to—I didn't ever want to hear a kid say that to me again.

Implied in Ms. Bess's wording are a few of the goals she had for student learning, namely, that students would investigate the historical circumstances of the Holocaust, clarify their values, and gain humility in the face of that tragedy. In a sense, it was the very seriousness of the subject matter that encouraged her to experiment with its form. Personalizing this history through a simulation model, she felt, would help to humble her students.

Ms. Bess developed her simulation out of initial encounters with an experiential board game titled Gestapo: A Learning Experience About the Holocaust (Zwerlin, Friedman Marcus, & Kramish, 1976), and over the years its form had changed radically. Ms. Bess moved the simulation from her ninth-grade World History class to her full-semester, upper level history elective, and, unlike the simulation experienced by my ninth grader, the one I observed didn't involve previous years' students playing Gestapo agents. Although her simulation no longer resembled the board game and no one played the part, the name Gestapo had stuck.

COURSE DESCRIPTION

The simulation was part of a larger history elective course Ms. Bess taught on World War II, a very popular, honors-level class open to 10th, 11th, and 12th graders. In the course were five chronologically ordered units of study in addition to Gestapo, which Ms. Bess had titled The Road to War, The Happy Times of the Axis, America Fights the Good War, The Tide Turns for the Allies, and Final Reckoning. Each unit was fact filled, and each student was given a list of terms that he or she had to define throughout the unit.

Many of Ms. Bess's students had enrolled in this elective class because they had had her as a teacher the year before for World History and appreciated her innovative pedagogy. As one of the four target students, James, a talkative football player of Italian descent, explained, "She's cool," elaborating that "she takes different approaches to stuff than usual teachers will." By this, James meant that her classes were "real interactive . . . , [which] makes you understand more; you're not just lookin' in books, read about Adolf Hitler, write a sentence." As her course description promised, Ms. Bess did use a "wide variety of teaching methods . . . to make this history class challenging, informative, and fun." Because of Gaucho's block scheduling, the class met 5 days a week for 1½ hours each day, and, on average, Ms. Bess changed activity formats five times each class session. Additionally, over the 3-month course, she spent almost all her lunch hours showing extra-credit movies set during the World War II era.

Ms. Bess's windowless room was ideal for showing movies and videos, and when the lights were on, the wall-to-wall posters brightened its interior. Ms. Bess had literally covered her classroom's concrete walls from floor to ceiling with graphic images. Only the front wall contained some blank space, in the form of three blackboards, aligned side by side. Three tables spanned the space in front of the boards, and Ms. Bess's had materials splayed out all over them. I sat at the front of the class in the farthest right-hand corner, boxes of magazines stacked near my feet. Ms. Bess's teaching assistant, a senior at Gaucho, often sat behind the table farthest from me, quietly correcting students' work.

Ms. Bess had selected Studs Turkel's anthology, *The Good War* (1984), to serve as the students' main resource outside class. The assigned readings were short, usually less than five pages, and all illuminated some war experience from the point of view of an individual. As the course proceeded, I came to view this choice of text as emblematic of one of the strengths of Ms. Bess's simulation as a whole. As Terkel's book was read, the individual threads of each personal narrative wove together into the textured pattern of collective history, an interplay that characterized the entirety of Ms. Bess's course.

The students' homework, usually based on the readings, was composed of two parts. The front side of the worksheet involved amassing details from the reading and using them to construct what Ms. Bess called "truths" but what might be alternatively called historical generalizations. On the backside, students were asked to express themselves about the reading any way they chose—in poetry, artwork, music, prose, or other forms.

Each of the five units in her course ended with a cumulative test. Although Ms. Bess's teaching was highly content driven, she did not emphasize memorization. The students were allowed to bring to their exams one index card full of information, and certain other documents that might be useful to them during the test, such as maps of Europe they had coded. All tests, homework assignments, and in-class work were allotted a certain number of points, which were then tallied for each student at the end of the term. Assignments typically varied from 10 to 100 points, depending on their labor intensity, and "over 800 points of work" were assigned during the semester.

The simulation wove through the course, making surprise appearances. At almost any time during class, except during a quiz or test, Ms. Bess would cue the students, saying, "OK, put away your papers, clear your desks; we're now going back to [1933] . . . ."

SIMULATION SET-UP

Ms. Bess started the simulation during the second week of the course. On Monday, she handed out playing cards, one to each student. "Starting on Tuesday," she announced, "I'd like you to declare something." She continued:

> Some of you are going to take one or two cherished ones with you [on our simulation], but there's no fair way to do it [to decide who gets to take more than one person along]. Of course I'm not talking about really taking someone along, because we can't do that. What I'm describing is an imaginative journey. But you know what? I have kids who tell me, "Ms. Bess, I feel like I'm back there." . . . It's important for you to think about who you'd like to bring. And it's important for you to be traveling with someone you love.

At this point, James interjected, "Mushroom," referring to Ms. Bess's dog, whose photograph adorned the front wall. "Another *person*," Ms. Bess replied. Those students whose cards were marked with a black dot, it turned out, could take two "cherished ones" with them instead of just one; Ms. Bess wanted the total number of students and their Cherished Ones participating in the simulation to equal 60, an even 100,000th of 6 million. "You'll be living in Germany, and you'll make up only a very small minority of the population, . . . only 1% of the population," Ms. Bess explained, continuing, "Take a moment now and think about who you'd like to take with you on this journey."

Ms. Bess then asked random students whom they would take along. James reported that he'd take his "mom and dad." Another young man in the class was planning on bringing his "sweetheart." Other students cracked jokes, mentioning various (sexy) TV stars they would like to take along. "It's gotta be someone you know," Ms. Bess chastised, with some humor in her voice. She then handed out a form for homework; on it, the students had to write their names, their birthdays, and the names of one or two people, "family or close friends that [they] CHER-

ISH," along with their ages and the nature of their relationships to the students.

To prepare for the simulation, Ms. Bess handed each student a packet of information she had written. The rules of Gestapo were followed by a list of "common jobs held before WWII," a "Holocaust census" and a Gestapo terms list. On the last sheet, a list of 25 undefined terms stood waiting to be defined, terms such as *typhus, Krakow Ghetto, Dr. Joseph Mengele, Auschwitz,* and *Kapo.* For all their unit tests and the final exam, the students would need to know the information about the simulators they were to record in the columns of the Holocaust Census chart: the age, name, relation to class member, dead or alive, and exactly how this person died or survived. The Common Jobs list was included to help students in choosing professions for themselves and their Cherished Ones. The top sheet of rules was the most informative. Ms. Bess expected the students to have read it by class the following day. I quote the text of this sheet almost in full, as it conveys a sense of what was to come in the simulation as well as some of Ms. Bess's reasons for doing it:

> Very soon your class will begin participating in a simulation called Gestapo. I have written this simulation so you can connect more personally and emotionally to the infamous World War II event known as the Holocaust where over six million Jews were murdered between 1933 and 1945. You will learn how the philosophy and practice of racial hatred shattered the lives of millions of Jews living in Europe. Very simply, you and your cherished friends and family members will embrace the fate of Jews who tried to survive the planned extermination of their culture. In each of our 5 units, we will "return" to history as Jews and learn what happened to us in each year we are studying. . . . Sometimes, the simulation will last 5 minutes or 2 continuous days! You will never know in advance when we are "playing" Gestapo. Did Jews living before and during the war know what to expect? Below are a list of rules for how this simulation is conducted.
>
> Soon you will receive an envelope with the names, ages, and numbers of you and your cherished ones. Memorize your numbers! This envelope serves another purpose. Every day we "play" Gestapo, class will begin with what is called ROLL CALL. The purpose of this kinesthetic activity is to "test" the luck and health of you and your cherished ones. The rule is that the last person to complete roll call (find your envelope) will be punished appropriately according to the year we are "living" in. Never take your envelope out of class.

Since all Jews were required to carry ID, you must bring the ID of you and your cherished ones to class every day. This number must be easily seen by me. Failure to have your ID will mean that you or a cherished one will be punished. Once you and your cherished ones are dead, then you no longer need to present this ID.

Every day Gestapo is simulated and you are in class on time, you will earn from 2–10 points. This applies even if you are dead. . . . If you are absent, then you cannot earn any points that day. Sorry! . . . This activity is worth a total of 100 points.

You may find it advantageous to bring money to class. The most money you can bring is 50 cents. Jews were routinely assessed fines. Sometimes, the ability to bribe an official meant the difference between life and death. Failure to pay a fine could have serious consequences for you or a cherished one. The only units of currency that the "Germans" will accept are dimes.

IF YOU DIE, then 20 points will be subtracted from your total grade. So . . . you should complete a one hour homework assignment worth 20 points. It is due the following school day [after you've died]. Even if you die, you may still earn a grade of "A." Here's how: Have perfect attendance every day Gestapo happens, [and] complete your "dead" homework on time.

Assuming your attendance is perfect and you are never the last in roll call, then how can you or a cherished one die? A number of factors are involved. They include your age, the decisions you will be asked to make during the simulation, your failure to wear your ID or a Star of David arm band, your inability to pay money if so ordered, the dice number you roll, or an I.D. number chosen randomly from a jar.

If you "survive" the Holocaust, you may take 15 free questions on the final exam. Your envelope will join my wall of survivors. If a cherished one survives, then you may take 10 free questions on the final. . . .

. . . I hope you will find this different approach to learning more interesting and more powerful than other teaching strategies. This is not a game. We're simulating a nightmare that millions of people had to endure for years. Please don't lose your respect for humanity and suffering. There is never anything funny about racism and mass murder. It is my hope that you will practice empathy. Empathy is putting oneself in another person's shoes and practicing empathy means listening not only with the head but with the heart. I think learning empathy is the most effective weapon you can carry to combat personal prejudice.

Although Ms. Bess read some of these directions aloud to students as she handed them out, it became clear that some students never read the directions in full on their own as she had assigned. As James told me at the end of the course, he had stopped caring about coming to class regularly after his character "died" because he hadn't realized that attendance alone earned students points in the simulation. Other students, however, had clearly read the directions, as shown by the fact that they came to class prepared with pockets full of dimes.

The following day was an "ordinary" day. Ms. Bess reminded students of upcoming homework as she returned the papers they had handed in earlier. As she called out students' names so the students could retrieve their work, she pointed out good grades and showed off especially creative assignments to the other students. The new reading assigned was an oral history from a victim of Kristallnacht, the Night of the Broken Glass; Ms. Bess warned the students not to glue broken shards of glass on the "backsides" of their homework without covering it afterward with Saran Wrap. She had already cut her hand once on a student's assignment. After this class business was over, Ms. Bess explained that she would spend the rest of the class session lecturing on the levels of terrorization incurred through the Nazi hierarchy of power, from the Hitler Youth up through the Gestapo. Before starting, though, she passed around a single sheet for students to check that their birthdays and the jobs they had chosen had been recorded accurately. Ms. Bess had assigned fictitious ages to the class members based on their real ages, such that the oldest student in the class, a senior taking the course to graduate, became the oldest character in the simulation at 75. The youngest student in the class was assigned to be only 6.

Some of the students, by asking previous years' participants in the simulation, had researched which jobs might help their characters stay alive. Other students chose jobs for their characters based on their real-life counterparts' characteristics. Some students used both strategies. Pepe, an adventurous, athletic young man whose Peruvian grandparents lived with him, had flipped a coin between "mom, dad, friend, and sister," in order to decide whom to "take along" on the simulation. In the end, he took two characters: a female friend, 15, whom he thought would survive because he had chosen for her to be a translator even though she didn't speak another language in real life, and his sister, 18, whom he thought was "probably gonna die" because he had made her a musician, on the basis of her real-life passion for violin. Pepe's own character was a 20-year-old male doctor; he had chosen a medical career for his character because he himself wanted to become a doctor one day. Vanessa, a shy, hardworking student of Mexican descent, had decided to be a nurse and to take along her sister. She chose a medical career, not because it was reflective of her own goals, but because she thought it might aid her in surviving. "I thought that maybe, perhaps," she explained slowly, her sister would be useful "in a concentration camp to help the people that were sick," since, as she understood it, the SS "don't want to spread around disease or something like that." She had thought up this strategy herself. James, Pepe, and Vanessa were three of the four students whom I followed through the course. As the list continued on its journey from desk to desk, Ms. Bess explained, "You've also been assigned a number, and I intend it to be depersonalizing." "It's horrible, but you'll get used to it," she elaborated. "We all do."

Ms. Bess's tone was hard edged and tough as nails. She swore occasionally, and she rarely smiled, but she was not humorless. She ended this class session with the first part of a slide show on Dachau, the concentration camp, which she and her husband had visited on their honeymoon.

The following day, Ms. Bess finished the slide show, the lights went up, and she eased the students into their first experience of the simulation by distributing copies of the class census. The students read the list, looking for their own names and the names of their cherished ones as Ms. Bess explained roll call. Each student's identity number had been written in bold marker on the face of a small button envelope. At roll call, she would distribute the envelopes on the desks across the rooms, and each student would scramble to find the one with his or her number on it. "The purpose of roll call is to weed out the weak," Ms. Bess explained, hinting at the authoritarian character she would play in the simulation. "So we can do anything we want just to stay alive?" James asked, clearly taking the simulation seriously. "James is dirty," another student remarked, thinking he might not play fair. "James," Ms. Bess cautioned, "If you want to learn a lesson, 'loose lips sink ships.'"

"OK, Clear your desks," Ms. Bess told the students, and the noise of dropping books filled the room. In the first row sat Desmond, a talkative young African American man with a set of crutches leaning against his desk. Desmond had just had an operation to remove cancer from his left kneecap, and the scars showed beneath his shorts. "Desmond has a problem," Ms. Bess broadcast as the tension in the room built, "If anybody finds his number—what number are you, Desmond?—if anybody finds number 318, that's Desmond's." "I want you all to help each other," she entreated. "Now put your hands in your laps," she commanded. As she walked around the class, placing the envelopes, number down, on each desk, she told a story from a past year's roll call:

> Now, Rosa Michaels, she was lucky. Twice it turned out that her number was right on her own desk. That's luck. Other times, she

> survived because somebody called out her number and helped her out. You'll see.
>
> ["Oh, we can do that?" asks Pepe.] Absolutely. Stick together; help each other. I promise you that you will live longer. If you go cutthroat, I will cut you down.

Ms. Bess explained that this first practice run would happen in two phases, odds and evens. "Three hundred and two is even, right?" James double checked. "Everyone ready?" Ms. Bess asked. The odds went first. Wordlessly, Ms. Bess started flashing the lights on and off in the room, as half the students in the class ran from desk to desk looking for their numbers. The effect was eerie. The dark moments were pitch black, punctured by the impression of student statues, stilted and strobelike in their movements. A long 2 minutes passed this way as each of the students lurched to his or her seat, envelope in hand. The evens had their turn next. A young White woman, Adrienne, had grabbed Desmond's number and placed it on his desk while searching for her own. The last student sat down, and Ms. Bess kept the lights on. This had been a test run only, a preparation for the real simulation, so this last student's "life" was spared for the moment.

Inside the envelopes, the students found identity cards, small passport-size cards they were instructed to fill out and keep with them at all times. The students wrote in their names, ages, occupations, and nationalities. "You're all German," Ms. Bess informed them. In past years, Ms. Bess explained as she moved around the room, stamping their cards with the word *Gestapo* in tiny, red, Old English letters, students had duplicated these cards, such that now she stamped them to guarantee their authenticity. "You've had some mean-ass students," Calypso, a young African American woman muttered. Calypso was the fourth student whose experience of the simulation I monitored closely.

THE SIMULATION ENACTED

The following day, the second Thursday of the term, Ms. Bess began the simulation. Twenty-five minutes of class had passed in a discussion of the Great Depression when Calypso asked, "Are we gonna play today?"

> [Ms. Bess responds.] Oh, I wish there was another word besides *play*. Learning should be enjoyable, but I don't want to hear someone claim, "Oh, Ms. Bess, you're trivializing the Holocaust." It just makes me cringe.

With that, the class began their first real Gestapo activity. Ms. Bess, after explaining that the students would need money on occasion, "opened a bank" in which the students could store it. Pepe was suspicious of Ms. Bess, asking, "Is your bank honest?" Ms. Bess assured him that it was, and a number of students made deposits, dropping their dimes in the canister on her desk. Ms. Bess wrote down each name and, beside it, the amount deposited. This first day was worth 8 points, and Ms. Bess instructed her teaching assistant to grant the points to every student in attendance.

Ms. Bess sat at the "bank" in front of the class and eyed the students seriously as she talked and then read from her script of the simulation:

> OK, We're about to begin. As I look across all of your faces, sometimes I ask myself, "Do I have any feeling about what might happen to you?" [pause] and I truly don't. I truly don't. I had one girl last year, and I just had a feeling about her. I thought, "She's lucky." I had her as a ninth grader, and I just watched her use her charm and her luck and her looks, and I just had the feeling that she would make it. And sure enough, she did. And . . . that's exactly how this woman I think will go through her life. As I look at all of you, I really don't know; I don't get a strong hit about any of you. So, if you think I know what's gonna happen, I don't. I don't have a clue. . . . [The script begins here, with Ms. Bess's downward glance serving as a cue that she has begun reading from it. Almost immediately, though, Ms. Bess clearly ad libs; only the first few sentences are read verbatim.]
>
> This simulation begins in 1932. Now we know from class that the Great Depression has raged across Germany. Forty percent of the people in Germany are unemployed, cannot find work—want to, but cannot find work. Now everyone in this classroom is Jewish, except for one, and I'll explain that later.
>
> Now because we're Jewish, we're affected as well. The 40% applies to us, too. We are unemployed, many of us. Some of you have lost your businesses. The Great Depression has not spared us, but guess who the Nazis blame? They blame the Jews; the Jewish conspiracy, the Jewish bankers, the "international Jewish businessmen" have somehow caused this calamity to happen. And we must, I imagine we must stay home at night reading Nazi propaganda and thinking, "They're blaming us? And we're suffering just as much as everyone else is?"
>
> Who in here has a cherished one who may be 45 or 50 or older? [Four hands are raised.] . . . And are they male? [One hand

remains.] You might have had a relative, or maybe you [yourself] fought in World War I. Of all the soldiers in World War I, the Jewish soldiers actually received more medals than the non-Jewish soldiers. So, many of you may have lost parents in the war, patriotic Germans who were also Jewish who fought for their country and died for their country.

Now, Jews have lived in Germany for thousands of years. Most of us can trace our ancestry back hundreds of years we've lived in Germany. We're not newcomers; we're not immigrants. We have lived in this place for a long time. Chances are the home where we live is the home where your great-grandmother was born. The town where you live is the town where your family has lived for hundreds of years.

[A complete silence had enveloped the students by this point.]

We've heard stories from our parents and our grandparents about persecution.—One of my speakers, she said that she heard a story that when her great-grandmother was a child, somebody in her town gave birth to a baby with two heads. ["Really?" James can't help but ask.] . . . It happens. And who did they blame for this—they blamed the Jewish people in the town, OK? And someone's house was burnt. She said people were lynched—that's more of an American term, but Jews would routinely be victims of persecution. There would be a wave of violence that would strike, and I don't think any one of us in here probably lives in a place where we haven't heard stories of Jews being persecuted, but it seems that times always got better; we continued our lives, and we just are maybe used to suffering. We've gotten used to being a small minority. What percentage? [Ms. Bess quizzes the students.]

["One," some students reply.]

OK, that's on the test. Please have that little, tiny "one" ready. One percent.

In this last exchange, Ms. Bess's role as the teacher of the class, the reinforcer of historical facts, shows through the simulation script; rather than talking in the first person, she momentarily switches to the second person. What struck me from the moment Ms. Bess started to read from the script, though, was the uniqueness of speaking in the first person about Jews. In reality, I was the only Jewish person in the room, and yet, Ms. Bess was pretending that all the students and she herself were Jewish. This narrative gesture became increasingly important to me as the students themselves began to speak about this history in the first person, too, an indication that they were developing the sense of empathy Ms. Bess wanted to cultivate in them.

In the following few minutes, Ms. Bess described that Jews need not be religious, may not believe in God, and could still be culturally Jewish. She used the example of her Jewish husband, who did not believe in God, but who grew up in Brooklyn, New York, speaking Yiddish. (When one student asks for an example of a Yiddish term, Ms. Bess mentions "*shiksa*, like me." *Shiksa* is the Yiddish term for a non-Jewish woman. "A couple others I know, but they're real vulgar," she jokes.) When the giggles settle, Ms. Bess continues:

> Now I'm going to ask all of you to say something to the class. I'd like you to ask yourself, "Am I a religious person?" I don't care what your faith is, but, "Is religion important to me?" Is church important, or whatever—temple? Are you a devout believer?

As she did throughout the simulation, Ms. Bess here overlaid the present situations of the students onto the past realities of German Jews. She was asking each student to consider his or her own religious attitude in order to answer the question on behalf of the Jewish character to be played. Ms. Bess then asked the students each to declare to the class whether they were "Jewish first" or "German first." Were they "more Jewish" or "more German?" In fact, she was asking how they thought of themselves in their own American context; were they more religious or more American? One by one, the students answered, dividing the class roughly evenly. James answered, "German," without having to think about it. Pepe similarly identified as "German first." Vanessa, who in real life attended Catholic mass with her family every Sunday and was looking forward to becoming confirmed when I first interviewed her, answered, "Jewish." "You see, we're different," Ms. Bess concluded, "not all Jews were religious, and it's important to understand that."

Again Ms. Bess read from her script, occasionally embellishing it with her own stories. Ms. Bess described the 1932 elections and Hitler's subsequent seizing of power. The students asked factual questions, and Ms. Bess answered them. Essentially, she was lecturing exactly as she would do throughout the other, nonsimulated units in the course. Nonetheless, the seriousness in the class, the level of engagement of the students, had been unrivaled in the preceeding 2 weeks. The students were absolutely enthralled by the information. Ms. Bess continued to heighten their sense of relevancy by asking questions that called on them to give personal responses: "What do you say to yourselves when you see all this anti-Semitic propaganda? Do you believe it? What do you say to your daughter when she comes home with a black eye because somebody hit her [and] called her a 'dirty Jew'?" Through this kind of questioning, Ms. Bess carved space in the curriculum for her students to engage moral questions seriously and to become emotionally entangled with their [imagined] historical counterparts.

Later in the lesson, Ms. Bess defined the word *Mischling*, the Nazi term for people of "mixed-race" heritage. The students dutifully wrote down the definition. "Now." Ms. Bess gathered their attention to ask, "Is there anyone in here whose mother and father are of . . . different race[s]?" Two students in the class raised their hands. Ms. Bess saw Calypso's first.

> Calypso, I'm going to ask you to play the role of a *Mischling*, ok? Your mother is Aryan; you're father is Jewish. Now, Calyspo, this may work to your benefit, and you may survive because of this.
>
> . . . Half of her blood is regarded as superior, but half is inferior [Ms. Bess has turned to the rest of the class, and now turns back to Calypso], and they don't know what to do with people like you. Hitler is truly a racist. So the laws will be different for you. . . . When we roll call, Calypso, you roll call both times. You get to go twice.
>
> [Calypso interrupts.] But doesn't that increase my chances of dying?
>
> [Ms. Bess replies.] No, it increases your chances of living. You get to roll call twice; you have less chance of being the last person. . . . You should be fine. But, if we ever do Gestapo on a day that you're absent, we'll assume that your mother has died and that you are no longer protected by her blood, and then you'll be in the situation with the rest of us.

Ms. Bess implored the students to write down the identity number of their class's *Mischling*; "You'll need it for the test," she cautioned them.

By the close of the session, Ms. Bess had told the students about ways to identify Jews, the boycott of April 1, 1933, the Nuremberg Laws, and the disappearance of opponents of the Nazi regime. Only a few minutes were left of class time when Ms. Bess announced that someone from the class would be "arrested" and "sent to Dachau" as a political prisoner. She looked around the room, eyeing the students, her gaze settling on James. "James, I think I'm going to have you arrested because . . . you're very firm in your opinions and there's something about you that would scare me, . . . if I were the Gestapo," she said.

Ms. Bess's choice of James puzzled me. I found it hard to consider him "most likely to be sent to Dachau" given that during a classroom debate earlier in the semester, he had aligned himself strongly with livelihood over liberty, expressing avid support of even a fascistic government if it would guarantee his family sustenance. He was willing, at that time, to dismiss the importance of preserving individual liberties. What the choice highlights, though, is the speed and dynamism of the simulation setting; as with many who need to make pedagogical choices (Jackson, 1968; Shulman, 1987), Ms. Bess had very little time to reflect, because she was making split-second decisions. Although James didn't fit the precise category of political opinion she sought to fill, he was "outspoken" and willing to challenge authority. "But, James, thank your mother and father tonight when you go home," Ms. Bess added, "because, you know what? You're only 8 years old." Ms. Bess paused dramatically between each word as she stated James's fictitious age. "They're not sending an 8-year-old to Dachau [in 1933]; if you were 18, you'd be in Dachau," she continued.

Looking around the room for another candidate, Ms. Bess found none. "As I look across the room at the rest of you, I don't think there's anyone in here that would have been sent to Dachau," she said, definitive in her judgment. "I don't have a defiant, in-my-face kind of student," Ms. Bess said as James interrupted, "Except for me?" Some jockeying by Desmond followed, as he tried to claim that he was that kind of student, too, but Ms. Bess was not convinced. Instead, she noted who was absent that day, reminding students, "If you are absent, you are prey." Because the absent student's character was female, and all the political prisoners sent to Dachau in the early 1930s were male, Ms. Bess spared her, "arresting" in her place a cherished one. "I need a dime because that is the rent and board at Dachau," Ms. Bess explained, warning that if a dime didn't show up on her table within 10 seconds, the cherished one would "die." Ms. Bess began to count as conversation erupted among the students. "I'm not giving up my dime," remarked one young woman. The young man at the desk next to me, whom I happened to know had four dimes in his pocket, sat wordlessly and motionless. Ms. Bess counted to 7 at an even, fast pace. At "8," Adrienne rushed up to the desk in a panic, and some students applauded as she paid the dime.

In an unusual move, Ms. Bess took the final moment of class to reveal that the next day, they would have two roll calls, and the last person standing would have a cherished one arrested. "If we have a death, then we'll have a death," she remarked, her tone hard-boiled. "Tomorrow night we've got the prom," one student reminded her. Other students chimed in that they had competing commitments for Friday, too; Desmond had to go to the hospital, James was getting a manicure for the prom. . . . Ms. Bess replied coolly, "If you're looking for fairness in Nazi Germany, you're looking in the wrong place." One student, in an audible but subdued voice, uttered, "I don't wanna play anymore," just before the bell rang.

Early Reactions

I have quoted the students' first experience with Gestapo at some length because many of its themes recurred as the simulation played out, themes such as Ms. Bess's dual roles as simulator and teacher, the ensuing environments of competition and cooperation, the thrill of surprise, and the overlapping of histories. Before discussing how the simulation played out, I pause here to consider these important motifs.

Ms. Bess's role consistently trampled on the boundary between controller and comrade, the shifts being demarcated by her use of pronouns. At times, she used the first person to signify her allegiance with the class, her membership as one of the group; at other times, and increasingly often, she used the second person, singular or plural, as evidence of her godlike status in the simulation. Because of her dual role, a split morality emerged, one that already appears in nascent form above. As stager of events, Ms. Bess often dictated interactions, the effects and evidence of her hierarchical power, for example, "If you go cutthroat, I will cut you down." And yet, as comrade at arms, she would practically enlist the students to defy the authority of her other role, beseeching them to help one another and sharing tips with them on how to "survive." I remember a moment, not too long after this class, when I was shocked that Ms. Bess showed students how to "tag" their envelopes for easier recognition during roll call. The juxtaposition of her conducting roll calls and then showing students how to "win" at them was startling. Ms. Bess was thus both tormentor and savior, torturer and saint, dualities with problematic moral implications. Her role as simulator—controlling, cold, and calculating—necessarily compromised the students' trust that she could foster as their teacher.

In the classroom, these roles translated into two occasionally conflicting tendencies. When Ms. Bess was acting as the former, the simulation dictator, the students were almost always set against one another, forced to compete for precious few rewards: racing to find their identity cards, vying for exit visas, turning one another in, and so on. At these times, each student acted on his or her own behalf only; for the students, the individual became a means and an end in itself. By contrast, there were times when the students indeed helped one another as Ms. Bess in her latter role, as teacher, entreated; the students gave one another dimes, handed off identity envelopes, divulged crucial pieces of information and the like, sharing in a profound, if fleeting, sense of community. Adrienne's act of retrieving Desmond's envelope, for example, was repeated again and again by other students in the class. These two environments, of competition and cooperation, symbiotically thrived throughout the simulation, trading positions in the fore- and backgrounds, and occasionally colliding full force.

A sense of surprise wove through the simulation regardless of which role Ms. Bess was playing or which environment held center stage. For the most part, no one except Ms. Bess knew when the simulation would resurface. Moreover, when it did, none of its component parts reappeared in the same form. No two roll calls and no two "deaths" were alike; both became more brutal as the imagined years passed. Roll calls, for example, transformed in shape; from the cards being placed on desks, they were moved to all over the room, to a big pile on the floor; and the participants themselves moved outside the class to take a running start to get to the classroom door. The "deaths" became more gruesome as well; from a Dachau political opponent's death to a car striking a Jew forced to walk in the street under the Nuremberg Laws, to ghetto deaths, to a Babi Yar shooting, and of course, to the symbolic center of the Holocaust, the gas chambers.

Throughout the simulation Ms. Bess often used the students' present realities to shape the historical reality of the simulation, and vice versa. When seeking out the class *Mischling*, for example, Ms. Bess chose Calypso because of her biracial heritage, a loose, historical parallel. When deciding who ought to be arrested as a political prisoner, Ms. Bess singled out James (though his "in-your-face" attitude lacked political overtones). These moves collapsed the lived present onto the distant past. In these ways, Ms. Bess normalized Holocaust history for the students, bridging the potential gaps in students' historical imagination by allowing them to see Holocaust history as at least loosely related to their own lives.

As engaging as these moves made that history, Ms. Bess's kaleidoscopic maneuvers sometimes worked against students' gaining a historically accurate perception of the Holocaust; for many students, the simulation itself shaped some misguided notions of the historical reality. In this first session, students may have gotten the impression that Jews in Weimar Germany were as diverse in their senses of Jewishness as the students sitting in the room were in their religious affiliations, when, in fact, the majority of German Jews at the time were assimilated and probably thought of themselves as being German first. Furthermore, the comparison alone somewhat diminishes the special status of Jewishness as imbued with both religion and ethnicity at that time, not to mention that it was defined biologically as race by the Nazis. Ms. Bess's historical conflation in this activity may have misguided students both about the proportions of religious to assimilated German Jews and about the special statuses involved in being a European Jew in the early 1930s, and yet the point remains that it clearly heightened the students' potential to empathize across continents, situations, and time.

Vanessa, for example, thought the simulation was "really interesting" because it spurred her historical imagination of the plight of Jewish victims; in her words, "You just get to, not really feel like it, 'cause I could never feel how they did, but try to take a little part of how they were treated in those days." Even in its first week, the simulation was powerful enough for her that it reached into the life of her mind outside of school. When she heard of racist incidents, she thought about "how the Jewish people were treated during World War II." For Pepe, too, the simulation was something "different from other classes," as he explained because it "kinda gets you feeling like other people might have felt during World War II." When I asked him how he'd respond to critics who might object to the simulation for making a game out of truly tragic events, Pepe rejected the possibility almost indignantly. "It's not a game," he insisted. "She's teaching you something and taking you through the steps. She's just showing examples. She's just using you as an example of the statistics and the people."

Even Calypso, who had been bored by the course in its first weeks, had become engaged by the simulation, justifying its use as a teaching technique and thinking of class material beyond class time.

> It's like hard enough for me to deal with and think about . . . the civil rights movement, like [that] I couldn't go to school, or like be sitting here with you [a White person], you know? That's hard for me to realize, so *this* [the Holocaust] is like . . . it has *no* reality to me.

The simulation, she implied, was meant to bridge that gap by trying "to put the reality of the Holocaust into our lives." Judging from her other remarks during the interview, the simulation was accomplishing that goal. "Ms. Bess's class really has a big impact on my life now," she said to me during our second interview, illustrating that sense with an example of imaginatively applying the Nuremberg Laws to her own life: "Sometimes I'll be walking down the street and I'll be thinking, 'Damn,' you know? What if I had to like walk in the street? What if I wasn't just allowed to walk on the sidewalk? I was thinking about that, and thinking like that's so crazy." She even called the simulation "fun," embellishing her explanation with an anecdote:

> When [Ms. Bess] first told us, you know, like, "Yah, there's this one girl who came from the hospital" [rather than miss a class that might involve simulating], I was like, "Whatever, you're lying." I was like, no student cares that much. But then, like last Monday, I didn't go to school, and then I woke up at like 12, and I was like, "Damn, I need to get to Ms. Bess's class!" and I just threw on a T-shirt and jeans just for that class! [Calypso's laughter tumbles into her story.] And then I didn't even go to track practice; I just went home! And then, [when] I went home . . . I was like, "Oh God, I'm like one of those kids," and I was like, "Na ah."

It is impossible for me to gauge how representative these students' reactions were of the class as a whole; nonetheless, their enthusiasm certainly seemed to have been shared by their peers; the other students in the class seemed just as attentive to the simulation, and attendance rates remained high.

The Simulation Continued

Over the following few weeks, the simulation escalated. On Friday, the day of the junior prom, many students were absent, so rather than roll call to determine the victims of the day's events, Ms. Bess simply assigned fates to those who were absent or to their cherished ones. James' cherished one was "killed" that day for having being housed in a mental institution in 1936. In our interview months later, he was still furious at what he perceived as the injustice of this untimely "death." "She only lived like one day," he fumed to me about the character of his mother. James claimed it was unfair for his character to be "taken" that day, "because it was Senior Cut Day *and* junior prom," he explained, utterly serious. "Eight hundred and sixty seven students were gone that day; that's more than half the school." James knew these statistics because of his participation in student government.

After giving numerous examples of early Nazi anti-Jewish legislation, Ms. Bess described for the few students in that day the process of emigration from Germany, the forms, the lines, and the money involved. She then opened a "visa office" for a limited time, exactly 1 minute. For 50¢ per family member, all in dimes, Ms. Bess allowed the payer to roll a die and immigrate to the country assigned to the number rolled: number 1, Czechoslovakia; 2, Greece; 3, Denmark; 4, Poland; 5, France; 6, Palestine. The students ran to the front of the room, lining up to "get out." One young man paid for Adrienne to emigrate because she was absent. Desmond rolled Palestine (which in later weeks he would remember as "Pakistan"). Nine students were able to "emigrate" in the time allotted.

Other "deaths" occurred in the simulation that day, too. Ms. Bess drew randomly from the absentees to determine that someone would "die" because she couldn't get insulin from her Jewish pharmacist and naively turned instead to a "die-hard Nazi" pharmacist who killed her in cold blood. Near the end of the class session, Ms. Bess described the events of Kristallnacht, demanding payment for the cleanup of the streets and threatening a student with her character's arrest if she couldn't pay immediately. When the student whimpered that she didn't have any dimes with her, Desmond successfully solicited dimes for her from other class members.

At the beginning of the 3rd week, Ms. Bess brought the first unit, the Road to War, to a close, starting the second unit, which she nicknamed Happy Times for Hitler. In this unit, she taught students about the prowess of the Blitzkrieg, the invasion of Poland, and the occupation of Europe. The simulation reached the year 1939, when Jewish monies in German banks were seized. "That's shady; they take all *our* money?" asked a shocked Calypso, using the first person to describe her Jewish character.

In the fourth week, more "deaths" occurred when students forgot their ID's, did not complete their homework, or were absent. The remaining students had to choose between "hiding," "buying false papers," or doing nothing. Some students went into "hiding," and were assigned quotations to memorize and recite, acts that would serve as their protection; other students bought false identification. In the class session representing the year 1940, 11 students were "forced into the Lodz Ghetto" in Poland, including Pepe, Calypso, and Adrienne. Ms. Bess sold each of these students a bright yellow felt armband to wear.

At this point in the simulation, Pepe thought that his character was probably going to survive despite being sent to the ghetto, noting, "I'm the only doctor with a license" there. As a strategy for survival, Pepe had tried to keep his characters in the same place so that his attention wouldn't be divided. When I asked him during our second interview to tell me what had happened to his characters, he answered in the first person:

> First, we were in Germany, and then we emigrated to Czechoslovakia. And then the next day, Czechoslovakia had gotten like taken

> over by Germany, so we were at home, and I decided not to hide or to get fake ID. So, we got sent to the ghetto and been there since.

He had decided not to go into hiding both because memorization was difficult for him and because he had heard that "only 1 in 10 survived from hiding, so not a very good chance."

Because of his fictitious age as the oldest male in the ghetto, Isaiah was assigned to represent the leader of the Jewish Council, or Judenrat. As a result, Isaiah didn't have to participate in roll calls, but was guaranteed "life" as long as he attended class and did Ms. Bess's bidding. In his first day as Judenrat leader, for example, Ms. Bess had him borrow the canister marked "Ghetto" and copy down all the names and corresponding ages on the identity cards therein, making a list of those under his dominion. As Isaiah diligently copied the list, Ms. Bess presented a "window of opportunity" for survival to one student by sharing the experiences of a guest speaker who had visited her class years ago:

> One of my favorite speakers, a teacher, . . . [his] first name was Paul. And he doesn't talk anymore, I think he's just talked out. He was Belgian and Jewish. He was sitting with his mother at a train station, and they were waiting for this train that was going to come pick them up. They were waiting there with their armbands on. And a Catholic priest walked up to the mother and said, "Excuse me, madam, I see that both of you are Jewish. My name is Father So-and-So, and I run a school in France, a school for boys. I'm afraid that if you and your son remain here, you'll both die. I'd like to offer you help. I'd like to take your son. I'll take him back to my school in France. I'm going to give him a different identity, a new name, and I'm going to try to keep him alive."
>
> And this poor woman had a moment, because this train was leaving, to decide what to do with her son, who was about 9 or 10. Now Paul remembers this moment clearly. He heard everything; he looked at his mother; he thought his mother would say, "No way." And his mother didn't say anything. . . . And he grabbed at his mother, and he was crying. "I don't want to lose you. I don't—I'd rather die with you. Don't, don't, don't." And his mother, he said, never said a word. She looked at the priest, and with her hand, she shoved Paul away. She never said a word. She didn't say good-bye, . . . but apparently she had spoken to the priest and said, "Tell him that if the war is over to come back, because he knows where we live, and I'll be there."

> And he went kicking and screaming. I imagine the scene in this bustling railroad station and this little kid, you know, he's taken off by the arm, and he doesn't want to go with this priest. For all he knows, the priest is a serial killer, I mean, he doesn't know. In fact the priest was a very, very tenderhearted man who kept Paul alive the entire war.

After telling this story, Ms. Bess gave a free, false identity to the only 10-year-old character in the simulation. She also warned him to remind her that from then on, he would be "in hiding" in France. Like Isaiah, he would not participate in roll calls.

That same day, Ms. Bess interspersed segments from the movie *Schindler's List* (Spielberg, 1993), and from the documentary film *Lodz Ghetto* (Adelson & Taverna, 1989), to illustrate the horrible conditions of ghetto life, the continuation of culture and distribution of resources, the distinctions between so-called essential and nonessential workers, and various forms of ghetto death. The three students in the class who had chosen to be "doctors" or other medical personnel presented in-depth reports from research they had been assigned to do about typhus. Then the students who had chosen to go into hiding took turns reciting the first of four quotations they would have to memorize in order to remain safely hidden:

> One betrayed one's Jewishness by every anxious movement one made; by every uncertain step one took; by one's eyes that were those of a hunted animal; by one's general appearance on which persecution had left its stamp. (source unkown)

Desmond was the first student to recite, and was thus shown leniency despite making a mistake; rather than being "killed," his character was "arrested" and taken to the "ghetto," where he subsequently became chief of the Jewish police. Vanessa recited perfectly, her eyes glued to the ceiling the entire time. Desmond mouthed the words to a friend who struggled to remember the complicated quotation at her turn, after Vanessa's. By the time James's turn arrived, he was able to recite most of the quotation, even though he had not prepared before class; he stalled out at the last few words, though, and was "arrested." The class fell silent each time a fellow student stood before them to recite. In the last 5 minutes of the session, Ms. Bess "announced a death." Calypso, who was absent that day, would "die" a "common death," by starvation. "Number 301, Ghetto Lodz, 1940," Ms. Bess commanded the students to note in their censuses.

Calypso had made sure to attend class fastidiously until that day, when she was so sick she "just could not get out of bed." Oddly, when she thought that Ms. Bess was probably going to "kill" her cherished one for being absent that day, she was "ready to be hella mad." (Ms. Bess had announced early on in the simulation that she would try to save the classroom characters by forfeiting cherished ones first.) When Calypso did return to class and found out that her own character had been "killed" instead of her cherished one, she was relieved; "I was like, 'Thank God,'" she told me. Calypso had been slightly ambivalent about her own character; she was attached to "her" but also slightly removed. When I asked her to recount this character's story months after her "death," Calypso said the following:

> I never really got to know her that much 'cause Ms. Bess killed her hella quick, but I was 46, Jewish, of course, and I . . . lived in Germany, and right when Hitler started taking over, at the very beginning, like '32, . . . I moved to Czechoslovakia. That cost me hella money. After that, Hitler eventually took over Czechoslovakia, in '39 or something, and then, he put me in a ghetto. He took away all my money and put me in a ghetto. And then I starved to death in the ghetto.

The next day, both James's own character and Calypso's cherished one were "killed." James had become the youngest character in the ghetto and thus had "died of starvation" in 1941. Not surprisingly, he became less engaged in the simulation as a result, this being marked by a change in his grades and attitude. By our second interview, he was no longer the A-minus student he expected to be, earning a B for having missed the quiz and not attending the extra-credit movies. (James ended up with a C-minus for his final grade of the semester.) When asked about the class, he said, "It's fine," but with a sarcastic tone that implied he didn't mean it. "Once you die, it's like, 'I don't care,'" he told me. At that point, he started to make fun of other students in the room who still seemed to take the simulation to heart; as James explained later, "Half of us was already dead, . . . and we were just joking with people that were alive, you know?"

Calypso's cherished one had died during a roll call. Calypso, despite being a track star at Gaucho, had been the last one to find her envelope that day. Unlike her own character's "death," this one, Abdul's, affected her deeply. She explained to me why in a voice that was uncharacteristically serious:

> The person I took with me, Abdul, was my ex-boyfriend. And in real life, he really did get killed on March 18th. He went to Murphy High [near Gaucho], and he was shot in the head, and so now when I think back on it, I wish I didn't take him because when [Ms. Bess] really killed him in class, I was like hella devastated. You know, I was like, "Nooo," . . . I was hella mad.
>
> We did roll call, and I wasn't there the day before, and she had told everybody to turn in their envelopes, but I still had mine 'cause I wasn't there the day before, and I didn't know, so, my envelope wasn't in the roll call, so I couldn't find it. So I was the last one. And then I was like, "Wait, Ms. Bess, how am I supposed to find it [if it's not even there]?" And she was like, "Ohhh," and then so she killed him, and I was like hella mad.
>
> When I was telling one of my friends from another class who did it [Gestapo] last year, he was like, "You shouldn't have taken "Dule" [Abdul] 'cause—you know, . . . because it was gonna be such a big deal, he said, 'cause it's so realistic." He was like, "You shoulda just taken your mom or something." I know I should have.

Abdul had been Calypso's boyfriend when he died. "I didn't like really think about it," she explained about choosing Abdul as her cherished one. "[Ms. Bess] was just like, 'You can bring one person,' and I was like, 'I know who *I'd* bring'." The structure of the simulation, in overlaying her life onto Holocaust history, prompted Calypso to reexperience her real-life loss. By the end of that week, 14 students had "died," their cards ceremonially tacked to the side board of the classroom. I was relieved when Ms. Bess returned to the regular curriculum for a few days.

On the Monday of the fifth week, the students returned to the simulation after taking group quizzes on the range of activities in which partisans participated. "This [video] segment is particularly hard for me to see, being a woman," Ms. Bess confessed to the class, before showing it, "but this happened in the Lodz Ghetto." "This will affect one woman in the ghetto," she warned, "and, Isaiah, it's your job to quickly give me that person; I need her to be of childbearing age." The moment of anticipation gave way to flurries of discussion as Ms. Bess had to fiddle with the VCR to make it work. "Does it have to be someone in the class—I mean, can it be a loved one?" one student asked, as James quickly moved over to consult Isaiah on whom to choose. "Not me," Adrienne called out from across the room. The VCR stuttered to life suddenly, in the midst of the Lodz Ghetto hospital. In flat tones accompanied by stark photographs, the narrator described its destruction, focusing on newborn babies being thrown from its second-story windows and one new mother fleeing from her bed only to be shot. "Of course the Jewish police kept law and order" throughout the massacre, Ms. Bess explained. "This is a hard death to have anyone take on," Ms. Bess said almost apologetically, then hardening, "but Isaiah, I want you to give me the name of any female between the ages of 15 and 40." "Who is that?" she asked as Isaiah stared down at his list. "Quick," she added, not more than 2 seconds later. Isaiah quietly gave a number: 344. Ms. Bess and the students scanned their lists, and Ms. Bess pronounced, "That's Pepe's sister." Pepe, a little unbelieving, asked, "How'd she die again?" and Ms. Bess summarized, "She was killed in the massacre at the hospital, 1941." Pepe looked serious as the class members filled in their censuses. "This is a lovely lady, Pepe," Ms. Bess said to him consolingly, having taught his sister last year, "and I hate to ask her to take on this role; she was simply the right age."

No sooner had Pepe's sister "died" than Ms. Bess turned Isaiah's list over to Desmond. "Desmond is a sweet, charming young man," Ms. Bess said to the class, "but . . . he's part of the Jewish police, and I want you to understand what that means." "So, Desmond, I want you to kill somebody right now," she pronounced. Desmond seemed to smile a little, prompting Ms. Bess to probe him confrontationally, "You have a problem with that?" "No," he remarked, which she immediately challenged: "Why not? Not even a little problem?" After a shrug and a pause, Desmond shook his head, saying, "Naww." James piped in eagerly, "Make it somebody good." For the first time in the semester, I saw students besides James clearly treating the simulation lightly. "Who's somebody good, James?" Ms. Bess asked, her disapproval barely masked by toughness. "Well, like somebody you don't like or—" Ms. Bess interrupted him, not caring for his answer. "The people who are talking, I notice, are all dead," she proclaimed. "I don't know if you'd be talking if you were in the ghetto," she scolded, and the hum in the classroom subsided. "Is there like an age or anything you want?" Desmond asked, to which she replied, "I don't care. This is just a symbol, a gesture of your power."

Despite his protestations of not caring, Desmond interestingly chose to "take" not someone in the room, but rather a cherished one, moreover the cherished one of the only student in the class who got to play two characters in the simulation. (That student got to "travel" through the simulation twice because he himself was a member of the class, and a close friend of his in the class had chosen to take him along as a cherished one.) Ms. Bess dictated this death to the class: "Killed in the ghetto, by the Jewish police." Then she elaborated:

> These men were evil. I think they did things they didn't have to do. Imagine if . . . , at Gaucho High, 20 ninth graders were allowed to carry Mace, wear uniforms. . . . There are people at this high school that would love to play with you, mess with you. You know, maybe you beat them up in fourth grade; maybe you got a better test grade than they did in biology; maybe this, maybe that; maybe they're jealous because you've got a cute girlfriend. And they just want to make your life miserable because they're damaged. . . . The Jewish police are the victims, but they have been chosen to even victimize the victims.

I have to admit that this conversational moment made me uncomfortable. Although the Jewish police were clearly guilty and were much reviled postwar, were they less or more "damaged" than the Polish non-Jews living outside the ghetto walls within feet of rampant starvation while doing nothing or, worse yet, collaborating in and profiting from it? Ms. Bess was painting "evil" in broad strokes rather than encouraging her students to carefully consider the roles history casts people to play. It seemed to me that the momentum of the simulation itself didn't allow the class to stop and discuss the moral complexities of Ms. Bess's claims. I hoped she would return at some later point to the questions surrounding gradations of culpability.

Desmond raised his hand, and when called on, volunteered a justification for choosing the "death" he had; unwittingly, he adopted a kind of historically accurate instrumentalism when he remarked, "He was a butcher anyway, so he didn't have no use." Despite recognizing a note of guilt in Desmond's having supplied justification at all, Ms. Bess did not assuage him: "Now, I'm not trying to make you feel bad; I'm here to try to help you understand how these kinds of things happened, how the SS, which was very small in number, could dominate a huge ghetto of a half a million people, and they did it with collaborators, Jewish collaborators in the form of Isaiah and Desmond." (For a more nuanced and complex historical analysis of the roles of various Judenrate and Jewish police forces, see Bauer, 2001, pp. 143–166.)

Ms. Bess moved on to describe the slave labor camp Bergen-Belsen, demanding from Isaiah more characters to be interned there. Isaiah's first choice was a cherished one, and thus someone not in the room. The second name he uttered as he was thinking was Adrienne's. "Adrienne,"

Ms. Bess immediately announced. "I think that's a good choice." James let out a mocking "Ha!" but Adrienne's face was serious and her tone plaintive as she gently protested, "No." James started yelling, "Kill her! Kill her!" with some whimsy in his voice while Adrienne began to beg: "Isaiah, I let you borrow my pen." She moved across the room to stand over Isaiah, who was still seated at his desk. "You can't send me to a labor camp with my own pen!" she said, visibly upset. Isaiah looked up at her, clearly feeling awkward. "How 'bout Eva Black?" Ms. Bess asked, and for a moment it was unclear whether she was suggesting Eva Black instead of or in addition to Adrienne. When it turned out that Eva Black was Isaiah's mother, Ms. Bess moved on to the next name. "How 'bout Jill Johnson?" she asked, to which Pepe replied, "She's already dead." "Doesn't the person have to be from Ghetto B?" Pepe then asked, but Ms. Bess seemed slightly frustrated at not finding another name and said, "I don't care." "Ms. Bess, don't you ever get guilty conscience about playing this game?" Calypso cut in, uncomfortable with the bargaining in progress. "No," the matter-of-fact reply came.

> Because I know that the end product is better than what I have to do. Sometimes I feel bad that things happen to individual people, yes. But you know that I have to believe that what I'm doing is something larger than just the one on one, Adrienne's personal feelings. I know that Adrienne's a strong person. I know that Adrienne wants to live. But I know that Adrienne also wants to learn, and I assume that for all of you, although some of you mask it in funny ways. I know that you all want to learn.

Ms. Bess quickly turned her attention to the simulation, reading off the names of the eight characters "in Bergen-Belsen." The list included Adrienne. As Ms. Bess read her name, Hal uttered audibly, "Good." Adrienne shot back, more audibly, "Fuck you, Hal; shut up." Ms. Bess continued reading, undaunted. When the list ended, Desmond called out on Adrienne's behalf, "I thought [Isaiah] gave another name other than Adrienne's." Chatter swelled. "He didn't say me," Adrienne maintained. Four or five voices answered Adrienne in unison, clearly pointing out Ms. Bess as the enemy—"*She* did." "She's not the Judenrat," Adrienne proclaimed indignantly, if gently. "Does the Judenrat want to disagree with me?" Ms. Bess challenged Isaiah, staring at him hard eyed. Isaiah and Adrienne responded together, "Yea." Without missing a beat, Ms. Bess, said, "Then you're dead."

I don't know whose sharp inhale punctuated the end of her sentence, but Desmond's surprised "Oh" could be heard clear across the room. "Is that what you want to do?" Ms. Bess questioned Isaiah, offering him the chance to wriggle out of his previous ethical stance. "No," he said. "All right," Ms. Bess continued, "if you want to stand on principle, Isaiah, then I will accept your death." Ms. Bess had begun to move on, but Desmond yelled, "I have a question" twice to stop her. He asked, "Who are you acting, like Hitler or something, or are you just like a person?" Desmond's outcry indicated a discomfort that many students were most likely experiencing as a result of Ms. Bess's dual roles. Ms. Bess began to respond, when James interrupted with an answer: "She's like the SS." This gave Ms. Bess a split second to think. "I'm a teacher," she declared. "I'm the teacher of this activity." As the students left class that day a little while later, Ms. Bess commented to me, "Finally, a little emotion!"

While Ms. Bess was pleased that the students had expressed themselves emotionally in this class, it was clear to me that most students had been emotionally invested in the simulation throughout its duration. Ms. Bess had ingeniously cultivated the students' identification with their characters from the outset, such that they became emotionally invested in their characters' fictional "lives." Layered onto this personal attachment was the thrill of never knowing what would come next. The constant surprise of the simulation made James consider Ms. Bess's class to be different from other teachers' and caused Vanessa to think of simulating as "nerve-wracking." For Calypso, the simulation had the surprising power to drag her into class on a day when she had stayed home sick. Generating and sustaining the students' engagement in the scenario was thus both their emotional investment in their characters and the unpredictability of the characters' fates; the simulation held the excitement of danger, though of course without actual physical consequences.

The emotional consequences, however, carried their own hidden costs. This class session stood out in many of the students' minds. As Vanessa described the day, "Ms. Bess seemed kind of mean just like throwing [Adrienne] in there." In fact, Ms. Bess's unilateral decision to "arrest" Adrienne had been made in such a way as to give Vanessa the impression that Ms. Bess had "just changed character." "That's what I thought," Vanessa continued. "I didn't want to talk to her afterwards; she seemed scary." Ms. Bess's role-switching had become confusing at least to Vanessa and probably to many more students as well, jeopardizing the students' trust in their teacher, even when the simulation was not in play. I doubted if any of Ms. Bess's students would have felt comfortable turning to her at this point in the semester for advice, help, care, or any of the kinds of counseling teachers often provide.

The next day, Ms. Bess devoted 15 minutes to Gestapo before giving out the Happy Times Unit test. After showing another video clip from *Schindler's List*, the shooting of a Jewish woman engineer who had dared to speak directly to an SS man, Ms. Bess assigned the same fate to a character in the simulation. She then discussed *Kapos*, concentration camp inmates who were assigned to oversee barracks and who were often criminals (see Eichengreen, 1994; Levi, 1960). Ms. Bess wanted Adrienne to play the role of a *Kapo*. "What if I don't?" Adrienne asked. "I won't tolerate that," Ms. Bess replied, elaborating, "You're 34; you're a doctor, and you didn't do the typhus report." Ms. Bess implied a threat, but quickly turned the decision over to the class at large: "Class, should she do it?" Conversation erupted from all sides of the room, with various voices vying for the floor. "She should do it," Desmond yelled. "No, she shouldn't," another shouted. "If it's gonna keep her alive, she should," Desmond retorted. "She's got her dignity though, and that's all she's got left," Calypso chimed in. "But she's gonna die if she doesn't," someone else argued. Discussion erupted everywhere in the room for a moment before Adrienne herself yelled out, "No!" Ms. Bess, unflustered, announced that another student would be the *Kapo*. Thomas did not object, even when asked to choose the following murder victim, whose death would result from I. G. Farben's testing of Zyklon B gas. The 4 points for the day were recorded for the students who attended, and the unit tests were distributed.

The students had been studying the following unit, America Fights the Good War, for a few days straight, when that Tuesday, Ms. Bess told the students to clear their desks and get ready for a 12-point day. The students understood this to mean that Gestapo would take up most, if not all, of the class period. "We're going to be back in 1942 all day today," Ms. Bess announced by way of introduction. "Let's review, because it's been a long time since—" she began, then was interrupted. "Since we died," a student cut in, finishing her sentence. Although he was clearly making a joke, the remark revealed a kind of weariness among the students. The simulation was taking its toll on their spirits. Ms. Bess summarized where each of the "living" characters was situated by pulling out their identity cards from the canisters: 14 characters were "in hiding," 7 were "in the ghetto," some were "in slave labor camps," and the rest had "emigrated." One student was absent, and though he and his mother had "immigrated" to Palestine, Ms. Bess "killed" both by means of "of natural causes."

"By the way," she remarked, "Adrienne, I didn't have a chance to ask you last time why you didn't want to be a *Kapo*." Adrienne responded quietly, "Because I didn't want to have to kill people." "Even though it's just a gesture, some paper thing, a name on the wall?" Ms. Bess pressed her by pointing out the artificiality of the simulation itself, asking, "It bothered you that much?" Adrienne nodded. "You didn't seem to have a problem," Ms. Bess continued, asking Thomas, "What do you say to Adrienne's objection?" Thomas shrugged his shoulders. "I'm just thinking like pretty realistically, [and] I think if my life was on the line and I was gonna be killed if I didn't do that, I'd do anything to save my own life." Ms. Bess turned this answer on Adrienne, part challenge and part question: "You would not do anything to save your own life." Adrienne responded, "No." Ms. Bess reconciled their two positions in a rhetorical move I found both graceful and troubling:

> These are two parts of humans. There's not a right or wrong. I respect Adrienne's position; I understand Thomas's. I'm not sure I'd be any different than Thomas; I'd like to believe that I would be like Adrienne, but I don't know. In reality, I don't know if I was given a choice. I know many of you—James, I'm real clear on, you'd be with Thomas, right? [James nods.] One, I'd like to know that I live in a world where there are more Adriennes, but I don't. I know that each one of us has an Adrienne part, but we [don't always] listen to it. And circumstances definitely affect us.

Ms. Bess's answer was graceful in that she managed to weave these two positions into the fabric of each single human being; I also found her willingness to admit her own uncertainty admirable. I like to think that none of us who didn't live through the Holocaust knows what we would have done when faced with the harrowing moral dilemmas it presented, and I appreciated Ms. Bess's modeling that unknowingness. Problematically, though, Ms. Bess was speaking in the role of teacher here, not simulator, and while she was helping students understand the choices of historical actors and clarify their own value systems, she was also hurling at them appraisals of their moral fiber, casting them into restrictive models of behavior and claiming to know how they would react to a truly unknowable situation. Ironically, she was claiming to know better how the students would react than how she herself would, the result of her privileged position, in that she controlled the simulation rather than participated in it.

Ms. Bess then solicited random students' opinions about whether they would align with Adrienne's or Thomas's position. At one point, James commented that "the girls" seemed to choose Adrienne's and "the guys," Thomas's. "Isaiah, you didn't have a problem being the Judenrat, and some people have died because of your assistance. Has that bothered you?" Ms. Bess asked. "I didn't know what it was at first," Isaiah answered, and the room dissolved in laughter; by this point in the simulation, it was hard for the students to remember not being familiar with the Jewish Council. Ms. Bess tied this rejoinder in by saying, "I don't think the Judenrats knew exactly what they were gonna be asked to do, Isaiah." James added, "They probably thought they were gonna help people at first"; and Isaiah confirmed, "That's what I thought, too." "Well, you wanna quit?" Ms. Bess asked him, her tone slightly changed to indicate that she was now acting as simulator. Fearing the consequences of agreeing, Isaiah said, "No."

That same day, Ms. Bess held a roll call for all the "Jews in the ghetto" and for all the "Jews in hiding." The third and final roll call of the day was planned for the Jews "in the slave labor camp." To make these roll calls more competitive, Ms. Bess had them begin outside the classroom. The students participating had to run down a stretch of tarmac, up the stairs to the portable, and into the darkened classroom to find their envelopes from around the room. I recall distinctly that when Ms. Bess opened the door for the first of the three roll calls, the sunshine that poured in seemed incongruous.

The end of the simulation came quickly. In the seventh week, Ms. Bess showed a video clip from *War and Remembrance* (Wouk & Wallace, 1988), a graphic portrayal of Jewish victims being "processed" for assembly-line mass murder at Auschwitz/Birkenau. The clip took a grueling 20 minutes to watch. Just as it began, though, an announcement was read over the PA system about a statewide science exam, and four students, including Thomas, left the room. When the lights went up, Ms. Bess announced the "deaths" of three of the four test takers to the stunned students.

The last day of Gestapo started out like many other classes had. The students handed in oral history projects, from which Ms. Bess asked them to share highlights. Then she took care of class business and engaged students' questions. At 12:55, she announced that this would be the final day of Gestapo. She described the infamous death marches, illustrating the facts powerfully with another survivor's story. Ernie Hollander, an inmate originally from the Carpathian Mountains region of Hungary, had had to bury those who died on the death march from Auschwitz to Dachau, sometimes even those who were not yet dead. "He was a killer if he was gonna bury people alive," James blurted out. "No, he had no choice," Ms. Bess corrected. She told James that "Ernie had turned off his heart," after having watched his father and brothers murdered in the camp. "If you felt anything, you'd die," she told the class. Ernie and a few fellow inmates finally ran away from the column of marchers to hide in the cupboards of an abandoned kitchen. Days later, they heard English spoken, and though they were initially afraid of the Japanese faces they saw, they were eventually convinced that these were Japanese American soldiers liberating them, literally, from the cabinets. After telling Ernie's story, Ms. Bess announced the names of some "survivors" in the class: Ryan and Lee had survived in Denmark; Desmond and his mother had survived in Palestine; Isaiah, Adrienne, Pepe, and three cherished ones were on the death march; Vanessa and her cherished ones and all the other remaining characters were in hiding.

Ms. Bess took a moment out to double check her numbers before allowing four of the characters on the "death march" to "live." This left Isaiah and Thomas, the symbolic Judenrat, in limbo; both of them had cherished ones, only one of whom was allowed to "survive." Thomas had a cherished one on the "death march" and was thus participating in order to "save" her; Isaiah had himself and his mother to keep "alive." To simulate the march, Ms. Bess had each of the two students stand on one foot while watching the videotaped testimony of another survivor's death march experience and subsequent liberation. The film footage was powerful, and the students watched both the video and their two classmates standing to watch it. Ms. Bess encouraged Isaiah and Thomas, saying, "You're doing great," and "I'm very proud of you." As the clip ended, however, she required each to take three hops forward, and then each to take three hops backward, switching roles. "Where is it hurting you?" she asked both, and both indicated their held up feet. "Can I go to the bathroom?" asked James, disrupting the drama of his peers' bodily pain with his own ordinary needs. "No, nobody move out of respect for Isaiah and Thomas," Ms. Bess commanded. Isaiah and Thomas stood, immovable, as Ms. Bess had each of the characters in hiding recite the fourth passage they were to have memorized. All of them "survived" after reciting flawlessly, and their classmates noted in their censuses whether they had had false identification or were in hiding.

Twenty minutes had passed since the start of the video when Ms. Bess realized that Jonny, whose character was in hiding, was absent, and that therefore both Isaiah and Thomas could "survive." They released their feet with obvious relief. Ms. Bess continued to list the "survivors" by number and name, listing the circumstances of each. "Vanessa survived, which is not surprising," she read out, repeating the information for the students' censuses, "Number 309 survived with false identification in hiding." At the end of the count, however, Alyana pointed out to Ms. Bess that she had miscounted. There were actually 16 characters left "alive," not 15, the number Ms. Bess had wanted for its symbolic content;

15 would be an exact quarter, representing the quarter of European Jewry who lived to see the liberation of the concentration camps. "Nooo!" Ms. Bess cried out, audibly annoyed. Immediately, she regained her composure, saying, "OK, then, we'll have 16. I'm not going to do it again." The toll the simulation had taken on Ms. Bess was evident. "So we're done with Gestapo?" a student queried. "Almost," she replied.

DEBRIEFING

One by one, Ms. Bess encouraged the "survivors" of the simulation to speak, to take a moment to thank anyone or anything that helped them through. Ms. Bess interspersed questions. When it was Pepe's turn, he thanked Adrienne and two other students. "Did you cheat?" Ms. Bess asked, and Pepe answered, "Yes." He told me later that he was not immediately forthcoming with the particulars because he still felt slightly suspicious that Ms. Bess would change roles and "punish" him in some way. But when she asked how he had cheated, he did answer, proudly for having "pulled it off": "I never paid my fees to immigrate. You never asked me for the money; I just walked up, told you I had paid, and rolled." "Kill him," one student joked, and laughter erupted. There was finally no tension in the room. "I'm sure that happened," Ms. Bess noted. "I'm sure there's a historical parallel there."

Vanessa thanked Adrienne for her help at one point, but for the most part shyly refrained from saying much. Ms. Bess tried to draw her out, asking if the memorization was tough for her to master and which stanza was hardest, but Vanessa answered quietly that the stanzas "all seemed the same" and weren't hard to learn. Isaiah, usually reticent in class, thanked many, including Adrienne and Hatsue, who helped him, "when [he] didn't have no money like to emigrate." He hadn't cheated. Adrienne thanked Desmond and Ms. Bess's teaching aide, a senior student who had sat at the front of the room, wordlessly grading quizzes or arranging papers. "How did Tina [the aide] help you?" Ms. Bess asked her, and it was clear from the surprise in the room that the other students were eager to know, too. "She put my number on that desk a couple of times," Adrienne explained; sometimes Tina had managed to put Adrienne's number at the top of Ms. Bess's pile so that Adrienne had a better idea of where to look in the classroom for hers. It turned out that Adrienne and Tina had become friendly while playing on the volleyball team together. "Does it anger the rest of you that Tina helped Adrienne?" Ms. Bess asked, and both nods and frowns greeted the question. Adrienne didn't feel guilty about it. "All of you who helped," Ms.

Bess pronounced, "you may not be alive, but you let other people live." Desmond thanked many and had not cheated. Ms. Bess credited him for having "stuck it out" despite his numerous medical appointments. Isaiah had managed to keep himself and *two* cherished ones "alive," and Ms. Bess started to say, "You're the best—" but corrected herself, adding, "the luckiest one." The student victims, those who didn't "survive" the simulation, didn't share their reactions.

I found this last discussion about the simulation disappointing. I wished that the class had tackled what Ms. Bess had called the "historical parallels" explicitly, such questions as, Was there a moral victory in having "survived" the simulation? Does one's integrity have anything to do with one's fate—in both the spiritual and earthy senses of the word—in the simulation? Was cheating or lying acceptable in order to "survive"? "All of you who helped," Ms. Bess had pronounced, "you may not be alive, but you let other people live"; the question left hanging was what this statement meant morally. Was Ms. Bess saying students should have helped one another even though their characters may not have benefited? At issue is the question of transferability; the extent to which the lessons of the simulation were transferable, or applicable to the students' real lives, was never addressed. Instead, Ms. Bess left the implicit, tough, moral, and existential issues hanging, leaving her students to draw their own conclusions, if they considered the questions at all. When is cheating or lying warranted? What does "survival," or possibly its modern American counterpart, "success," mean at the expense of someone else's? Is "survival" worth any price? How ought people respond in the face of inhumanity, injustice, brutality, or suffering? And, why didn't Ms. Bess ask the "victims" to share their experiences? Was she equating winning/surviving with the power to speak?

These questions, hovering at the edges of the conversation, constitute what I consider a missed opportunity, but a minor one, because they were left hanging in what was otherwise a unit rich in discussions of morality—for the most part, allowing students the opportunity to engage in moral deliberation with some sense of consequence was part and parcel of Ms. Bess's typical teaching practice, a significant accomplishment in and of itself. In a fascinating study, Katherine Simon (2001) shows that most teachers in disciplines across the curriculum rarely, if ever, allow students such opportunities. Moreover, the discussions in Ms. Bess's class had real consequences. The thorny moral dilemmas Ms. Bess pushed her students to confront were not hypothetical ones, but determined the characters' fates in the simulation. Because it was so much a part of Ms. Bess's teaching practice, it was surprising to see her not connect what was revealed in the debriefing session to the students' modern contexts in the same way. Given her facility with conducting discussions of morally complex issues, it is easy to imagine Ms. Bess skillfully pushing the students to reflect on the transferability of the simulation's moral lessons. Although the debriefing had not engaged students in sophisticated moral deliberation, other key moments in the simulation certainly had. Ms. Bess had frequently confronted the students with morally intricate stories, anecdotes, and events, lacing Holocaust history with dimensions of moral complexity that rarely appear in history classrooms. Ms. Bess's students had learned about this history by investigating much of its moral richness.

In closing, Ms. Bess showed a 2-minute video of survivor Gerda Weissman Klein's acceptance speech at the 1995 Academy Awards. Klein had written a powerful memoir, *All But My Life* (Weissman Klein, 1957), which was subsequently made into a documentary film (Weissman Klein, 1995). Despite the music swelling to cue Klein to stop speaking, she refused to forgo her remarks, dedicating her award "to all my friends who have died who will never know the magic of a boring night at home." The Hollywood glitterati in attendance gave her a standing ovation, and Ms. Bess stopped the video, reiterating Klein's message for her students. "No one's trying to kill you; lice aren't trying to bite you; you're not on a transport; you're not in Mengele's lab," she said, trying to encourage them to recognize the quality of their own lives by contrast. She didn't want them to take the gifts of their circumstances lightly. James interrupted:

> Everyone's like that, though. You always take for granted what you have; it's just human nature. . . . I don't think, like, that my life's better off than people in the Holocaust. I mean, I can think like that in school, but not outside of it. You can't think like that all the time.

In this brief response, I saw that one of Ms. Bess's goals, at least for this student, had been met. Although Ms. Bess may not have recognized a victory in James's remarks, his implication was that he had been provoked to consider his life in these terms at least while in her class.

The rest of that week, the students learned about the end of the war in Japan, debating the options Truman confronted and voting against dropping the bomb without warning the Japanese. On Monday of the ninth week, the "survivors" of the simulation handed in their decorated envelopes for Ms. Bess to post on the wall. Then small groups of students "buddied up" to quiz one another for the upcoming final exam. Ms. Bess handed out the free answers to "survivors" of the simulation; the students who had "survived" themselves or "saved" a cherished one needed only to circle the questions they did not want to answer for up to the number of points they had won in the simulation. Students received 15 free points for "surviving" themselves and an additional 10 points for each "surviving" cherished one.

Because she had many students, little time, and minimal assistance in grading students' work, Ms. Bess relied wholly on short-answer quizzes and exams throughout the semester, and the final exam was no different. I was surprised, though, when the exam reduced even the experiential dimensions of the simulation to testable information. In one section of the final, for example, Ms. Bess asked a series of questions that required students to regurgitate simulation information, such as "Exactly how many people in class died on a death march?" "Who died as a result of medical experiments performed by Dr. Mengele?" and "How old was the oldest survivor of the Holocaust?" In a sense, questions like these implied that what happened in the simulation was at least as important to know, if not more so, as what had happened during the Holocaust itself. I had expected to see Ms. Bess test students on the Holocaust as learned about via the simulation, and I was disappointed that the final examination didn't betray the larger purpose behind the simulation, that is, to teach students about the Holocaust.

In the 2 days of school after the final exam, attendance predictably dwindled. Ms. Bess showed *Schindler's List* in its entirety to the few students who showed up for class, and they signed each other's yearbooks, munching on doughnuts while the videotape played. Ms. Bess was relieved that the year had ended.

STUDENT REFLECTIONS

When I had finished observing Ms. Bess's class, I was mostly awed by what I considered her tremendous accomplishments and only somewhat concerned about what I saw as missed opportunities. Both the achievements and shortfalls were representational and consequential. Among the significant accomplishments of her unit, I count the high level of engagement Ms. Bess fostered in students, the impressive volume of information she was able to cover and instill in them, the opportunities she structured for them to discuss moral questions, as well as certain aspects of her Holocaust representation. The missed opportunities—among them a short-shrifted debriefing and other aspects of the Holocaust representation—pale in importance by comparison.

The students' responses on the second and final survey I administered revealed their overall engagement in the simulation. All 23 students who took the survey reported liking Ms. Bess's course. In addition, almost all the students, 91.3% of them, agreed that "Ms. Bess is a great teacher." The students also unanimously agreed on three other items that point toward their approval of the experience: they would recommend this course to friends of theirs, they would recommend studying the Holocaust to friends of theirs, and there was nothing they had expected or wanted to learn about the Holocaust in this course that they hadn't. The students also almost unanimously agreed on the way to learn about the Holocaust. Almost all the students, 22 of the 23 who took the final survey, or 95.7%, responded affirmatively when asked whether they had liked studying about the Holocaust by simulating. In short, the students had enjoyed the course, felt they had learned much, and, I would argue, had gained a sense of the importance of the topic itself.

The students had also learned basic information about the Holocaust. Given the same list of eight Holocaust-related terms to define on both surveys, the students' scores improved greatly. The average score on this identification task in the first survey is 2.73 out of a possible 8, whereas it is 5.9 on the second. Likewise, the median score on the first survey is 3 out of a possible 8, whereas it moves up to 6 on the second. Moreover, many students were able to identify more of the sophisticated terms on the second survey than they had been able to on the first, and the quality of the definitions supplied improved on the second survey; more details were included, such as names and dates. The four students whom I interviewed repeatedly over the course of the semester—Calypso, James, Pepe, and Vanessa—could also easily explain by the end of the course how Hitler rose to power and what countries fought in World War II. As Calypso explained, before taking Ms. Bess's class, she knew "that there was a Holocaust, and there was a guy named Adolf Hitler, and he didn't like Jews, and he tried to kill 'em all," but "that was basically all." This was a far cry from what she could discuss at the end of the course.

More impressive to me than the amount of information students learned, however, was the way in which they had learned it. The students in Ms. Bess's class had learned about this history by becoming emotionally engaged in it. Serving as at least a partial indicator of the rest of their peers, all four focus students had been emotionally struck by the tragic dimensions of the Holocaust while learning new information. For Vanessa and Calypso, the emotional experience of the simulation overshadowed the impact of their informational learning. While both young women had increased their knowledge as indicated by the increase in their number of identifiable terminology, the core of what they felt they had learned was experiential and emotional, something uneasily put into words or captured in interviews. Vanessa had been struck by the cruelty of the experience of the Holocaust despite the fact that her characters had survived the simulation; Calypso had been affected by the tragedy of the Holocaust in overlaying on it her own tragic personal circumstances.

Although Pepe and James didn't easily admit so, it seemed clear to me that both had been emotionally involved in the simulation. Both young men spoke in the first person to describe their characters' fates (as had their classmates); neither made fun of the activity in talking about it to me; and Pepe was quietly proud of his character's survival, while James was resentful of and disappointed in his characters' early demise. For these two young men, the emotional impact of the simulation may not have been foremost in their minds, as it had been for Vanessa and Calypso, but neither was it absent from their assessments.

While these students' reactions only hint at those of their peers in the class, I would argue that all the students in the class had been engaged by the simulation, even if not all had "liked" it. Only one student of the 23 who took the survey at the end of class replied in the negative to the question "Did you like learning about the Holocaust by simulating?" When asked "Why or why not?" this student wrote that he or she hadn't liked simulating because it involved "too much pressure, and I don't think we will ever know how the Jews really felt."

Embedded within that emotional impact and intense engagement is a necessarily changed attitude toward Jewish victimization and survival during the Holocaust. In the empathy expressed by the four students in their interviews, by the rest of the students in their answers on the surveys, and in their new understandings of the impossibilities inherent in the situations of European Jewry during the Holocaust, Ms. Bess's goal that her students become humbled by this history was fulfilled, genuinely and deeply. All four interviewed students had come to recognize the arbitrariness of who survived and who didn't, and all had gained a sense of the magnitude of that tragedy in the fabric of individual lives. Even James, who hadn't consistently taken the simulation seriously, had gained the sense that the events of the Holocaust were unpredictable from the standpoint of the victims:

> If that happened to us right now, we wouldn't even know it until it was too late, because you don't know—you wouldn't know at first. People didn't know at first till it finally got real bad; I don't

> even think they knew what was happening at Auschwitz till the last minute.

Whether or not James's assessment is historically accurate, it's clearly a valuable orientation to hold toward innocent victims of atrocity; in his eyes, they were not blameworthy. The simulation had also taught James the lessons to "value what you have now; [and] live every day, you know, like it's the last one," lessons he had been able to take to heart at least "a little bit" from learning about the victims. When pushed to consider what she thought she had learned from the simulation, Vanessa explained:

> I think I feel more sad because I kind of experienced it, and it felt kind of like nerve-wracking; you didn't know what would happen and stuff. Before, I was learning from the notes, so I'm just not really feeling anything, but then when I experienced it, I did. ["Even though you survived?" I asked her.] Yah. . . . I feel lucky.

In an earlier interview, Vanessa had expressed similar reactions. She felt she had been learning about a Jewish experience of the Holocaust, the experience of "fear and terror, not knowing what'll happen; not knowing if you'll see the next day." For her, the moral lesson of the Holocaust was simple: "Everybody should treat everybody as an equal, an equal person, and like, that's it."

REFLECTIONS

Ms. Bess had achieved her goals for the course in part by skillfully balancing individual stories with collective experience such that these students, and I suspect many other students as well, understood both the larger historical context and its impact on real people's lives. In order to represent this history fairly, some notion of the large numbers of victims, Jewish and otherwise, needs to be conveyed; in order to bring it to life, however, a sense of the individuality of each victim needs to be conveyed. These two forces work at cross-purposes. Ms. Bess, in structuring the simulation as the entanglement of 60 individual lives, kept these two tendencies in a kind of perfect tension, such that students determined to some extent what happened to individuals, but understood it in the context of millions. Furthermore, the students had learned these lessons by psychologically identifying with both imagined Jewish lives and actual (if fictionalized) Jewish fates during the Holocaust, as Ms. Bess used both in constructing the simulation. The four students, in describing their "own" Jewish life stories in the first person, and the other students in the class, who used first-person language throughout the simulation, exhibited that they had learned to think of themselves as Jews living under persecution, if only for the space and time of the simulation. Why is this so remarkable?

Getting the students to metaphorically step into the shoes of other people's experience was an accomplishment in itself, a rare move for teenagers, and not one that is easily manipulated or artificially manufactured. Rather than reifying stereotypically negative or Nazi-propagated images of Jews, Ms. Bess's simulation structure implicitly battled against them. Ms. Bess very easily could have done the opposite. Ms. Bess could have easily taught Holocaust history from the perspective of the perpetrators, in other words, a phenomenon that probably inadvertently occurs more frequently than not at the high school level.

After my first few years of teaching this subject, I realized that in my own courses, the students finished my Holocaust unit having viewed only negative images of Jews, either stereotyped, propagandistic, and Nazi-generated ones or ones in which Jews were degraded, humiliated, and dehumanized, standing at the edges of mass graves or already in them. I assumed that by viewing such images, my students would automatically empathize with such victims. I still believe that in order to understand Holocaust history thoroughly, students need to confront these images; they need to understand how Nazi ideology, legislation, and activity vilified Jews, and such images are thus illustrative. However, by not showing positive, realistic images of living, "normal" Jews (materials that, by the way, are much harder to come by) to balance these other images, I believe that inadvertently, I may have perpetuated or helped entrench negative stereotypes of Jews. Two of the four students I interviewed from Ms. Bess's class, after all, had held negative associations with the word *Jew* before learning about the Holocaust. Unlike my past students, however, Ms. Bess's students understood that the stories of Jewish lives are as individual as the students in the class and that Jews are as "normal" as they themselves are, by no means a small or usual accomplishment.

This normalized representation of Jews, however, bore hidden, consequential costs. What this normalized representation necessarily obviated was the history of pre-Holocaust (religious) anti-Semitism, arguably foundational for a deep understanding of Holocaust history. In the process of historical Jewish lives during the Holocaust being shaped to fit in with students' own self-representations, the history of anti-Semitism was necessarily neglected. In order to make Jews seem "normal" to the students, in order to make Jewish people from history seem like these students in the present, the history of anti-Semitism was overlooked or bypassed. It would be very difficult to represent Jews as similar to non-Jewish students if more of their differences—embodied in Jewish rituals, traditions, beliefs, and history, including the history of anti-Semitism—were emphasized. As a result, none of the four focus students, and probably none of the other students in the class, understood the larger historical context playing into why Jews were the main group targeted by Nazi policy and action.

When pushed to explain why Jews were targeted, Calypso responded that anti-Semitism had probably started with the Nazi Party and that the scapegoating of Jews was more of a power play than a particular hatred. "I don't know why," James had responded when asked the same question. When pressured, he ventured an answer that involved the Jews as a convenient scapegoat in the immediate situation: "I guess that they needed a scapegoat; and then, I guess they were only 1% but they had a lot of business and money and stuff, I guess they took it out on them, I don't know why," he repeated. Long pauses in Vanessa's response indicated to me that she was struggling to find an answer she didn't have: "I didn't really understand that; I thought that . . . , I think they targeted them because they thought they were inferior because, . . . I'm not sure why though. . . . Maybe it was because they were such a small group?" Like Calypso and James, Vanessa had not learned to view this instance of scapegoating in the context of historical anti-Semitism.

Ms. Bess may have neglected this thread of Holocaust history because it was not part of her original curriculum. Alternatives in Religious Education (ARE), the publishing house of Gestapo: A Learning Experience About the Holocaust (Zwerin et al., 1976), is a Jewish organization that designs and markets educational materials specifically geared to Jewish contexts. In fact, Gestapo is the only educational material that ARE markets in a non-Jewish arena, Social Studies School Service, a national distributor of educational materials from which Ms. Bess first ordered the simulation. It is quite likely that the original game, though it doesn't say so in its introduction, was designed with a Jewish audience in mind. The writers may have assumed that by the time Jewish teens simulated this game, they would already have been familiarized with historical anti-Semitism. This may be one of the liabilities of Ms. Bess's considerable creativity; in having based her entire curriculum on a game originally designed as an educational supplement only, a crucial piece of history was left out.

In our final interview, Calypso exhibited another knowledge gap that troubled her. She recognized that she had no idea whether "the

Jewish community had tried to do anything in their defense," and if so, what and how. "That's like a question I started really having towards the end," Calypso added, continuing:

> I don't believe that this is a group of like completely weak people that just let somebody come in and dominate their lives. Granted, it probably happened 'cause they didn't have any power, political, but I don't think they just let it happen. They must have done something!
>
> . . . If we have Americans now that go out and put their lives on the line in war, I'm sure there were some Jewish people that put their lives on the line for their people too. People do that all the time. I don't know if I'm strong enough to do that, but it's part of human nature.

While she may not have had the historical information about Jewish partisans and resisters, interestingly, Calypso's moral learning here dwarfed her informational gap. Calypso's pondering reveals an internalized, normalized image of Jews and a faith in the commonalities across human groups. To Calypso, European Jews living then were as brave and as cowardly, in sum, as various, as Americans living now, an equivalence I consider to be positive, whether or not historically precise. Calypso had learned about Jewish victimization, if not in all its historical complexity, at least in meaningful, moral depth.

While I have argued above that part of the genius of Ms. Bess's simulation was the framework of students' learning this history from the perspective of its main victims (Jews), this structure posed other problematic implications. Perhaps rightly so, given the historical centrality of Jewish victimization in the Holocaust, Ms. Bess's simulation nonetheless didn't prompt students to consider the plight of non-Jewish victims of Nazism, such as the Sinti and Roma (commonly called Gypsies), male homosexuals, the Polish intelligentsia, the so-called hereditarily ill and "asocial," and other groups. More important, perhaps, the students weren't encouraged to connect the fates of their Jewish characters to the role of bystanders and non-Jewish collaborators in this history, but only directly to the role of perpetrators and Jewish cooperators as represented by Ms. Bess and her instruments. The role of the bystander, therefore, a naturally more hidden role than that of the perpetrator or victim, remained invisible to students.

As previously mentioned, the discussion devoted to debriefing the simulation and the final exam marked other missed opportunities for deepening students' learning. Rather than mining the simulation's moral complexities and discussing the transferability of its moral lessons, the debriefing session was overly brief. And rather than assessing students' knowledge of the Holocaust, the section devoted to the subject in Ms. Bess's final exam focused instead on what students had learned about the simulation. The experiential richness of the simulation didn't lend itself to a fact-based, multiple-choice test.

Indeed, one reason Calypso stopped liking Ms. Bess's course as much as she had at its beginning was because of this emphasis on the factual. When Calypso's grades plummeted, she explained the slump by saying that she had become bored by the class, feeling that her "other classes were just so much more interesting." In Ms. Bess's class, the assignments were all the same to Calypso; they all emphasized factual knowledge over expressing opinions, and as such, "they never made you think." Referring to the recitations that "hiding Jews" had to perform, Calypso made the sophisticated analogy "That's like, after a while, how the whole class seemed to me," a rote performance of regurgitated information. "That was like a perfect example of how she taught everything; either you know it or you don't know it." Despite this sharp criticism, however, Calypso had felt that the simulation was worthwhile. She felt that she had learned deeply, though it was not reflected in her grade; and she was thankful for the experience, though she felt estranged from Ms. Bess.

This last point highlights the most distressing aspect of the simulation, its greatest consequential problem: Ms. Bess's role as authoritative dictator in the simulation compromised her role as caring teacher in the classroom. Ms. Bess did not know about Calypso's boyfriend, for example, until reading the first draft of this case study (well after the end of the school year). Had I not been researching her simulation, in other words, she would likely never have known about the emotional upheaval the simulation caused Calypso to relive.

Researchers and educational theorists have long bemoaned the lack of intimacy that characterizes public schools. And though the structure of schooling is largely to blame for the isolation students often feel—because of features such as the large numbers of students per teacher, the compartmentalization of the school day, the focus on subject matter rather than students at the secondary level—certainly the simulation itself exacerbated such tendencies. Whether or not Ms. Bess would have been able to serve as a comfort to Calypso had the simulation not occurred is of course unknowable; what is clear is that the simulation prevented Calypso and probably her peers from considering Ms. Bess as even a potential school ally, one of the most important functions teachers can fulfill (Noddings, 1992; Palmer, 1993; Pope, 2001). That Calypso could feel unknown, however much that feeling was predicated on the structure of schooling more generally, was certainly intensified by the role Ms. Bess played as persecutor.

The moral trade-offs of Ms. Bess's simulation are thus quite complex. When I first entered Ms. Bess's classroom with elaborate biases against simulations, I was unaware of just how morally complicated simulations necessarily are. Although I did not leave Ms. Bess's simulation unwary of their potential pitfalls, my admiration for the successes of this simulation in particular overwhelmed my prejudices.

Before studying Ms. Bess's class, I had thought that a simulation format would be fun for students and thus trivialize the seriousness of the Holocaust, that the consequences of its gamelike features would compromise its representation to students. What I came to realize after observing the class is that student enjoyment should not be mistaken for student engagement; while Ms. Bess's students were deeply engaged, they were in no way making fun of or having fun in their reconstruction of the Holocaust. The fact that they used the word *fun* to describe their experience did not mean that they weren't taking the subject matter seriously; they simply lacked a language to express respectful, wholehearted engagement. I had also believed that students of a simulation would mistake what they experienced for the real thing. I thought they would consider their experience in the simulation to be an exact replica rather than a remote representation of actual events. After experiencing Ms. Bess's simulation and interviewing the students, however, my opinions changed. These students were clearly able to draw differentiations. As Vanessa explained to me, even during the simulation, she was aware of the differences between the students' experience of the simulation and Jews' experiences of the Holocaust; to her, the simulation served as a glimpse rather than a totality. "I don't really know what happened back then," she explained, "but I have a little idea about what did happen; . . . [the simulation is] not as big as what really happened, but it's kind of a short introduction to what *could* have happened." Not only did she understand the historical and psychological distance between the simulation and its historical anchor, she understood the fiction that the simulation generated. Even in our first interview, when the simulation had just started, she saw the differences, explaining that in the simulation, "you just get to—not really feel like it, 'cause I could never feel how they did, but try to take a little part of how they were treated in those days." Although Ms. Bess's evaluations of students' learning didn't reflect it, the simulation was an imaginative venue rather than an end in itself.

Finally, I had come into Ms. Bess's class with the presumption that a simulation's emotional intensity would necessarily eclipse the intellectual dimensions of the learning. I came to understand, however, that at least in Ms. Bess's class, the experiential and intellectual components of the simulation were mutually reinforcing. The obvious informational learning that went on in Ms. Bess's class was, for the most part, enhanced by its simulation format and vice versa. One clear element of power of the simulation may be that it challenged students' minds by engaging their hearts and challenged their hearts by engaging their minds; the moral and informational dimensions of this simulation were inextricably fused (Ball & Wilson, 1996; Simon, 2001).

Ms. Bess's simulation format spelled out the possibility for students to deliberate very powerful moral dilemmas with a sense of real consequences. In its emotional intensity, the simulation also provided students with a deep learning opportunity, to be personally engaged in studying history, to be passionate about its results. To set up such a simulation and play it out, acting as an enemy, alternately authoritarian, arbitrary, and helpful, is no mean feat for a teacher, and neither psychically untaxing nor morally uncompromising. It is for these reasons that I am so very impressed with Ms. Bess still, though my enthusiasm for atrocity simulations in particular remains tempered.

I hasten to add, however, that this tempering of my biases does not lead me to advocate the use of simulations to teach Holocaust history. While simulations do not *necessarily* trivialize Holocaust history, nor *necessarily* lead students to learn about the Holocaust as a trivialized event, this does not mean that simulations cannot or do not often do so. What I hope is clear from the analysis above is that the crucial distinctions between what might be called constructive and destructive simulations inhere in the particularities of their presentations rather than the generalities of their form, a point that raises other questions: Are there critical attributes that separate educative simulations from miseducative ones? If so, what are they? Although it lies outside the realm of this research to state an answer with certainty, I find it tempting to speculate.

In a sense, the power of the simulation described above lies in the magnitude of the fiction it generated. It was ultimately a series of paradoxes in play: a fictional cast of characters that allowed real people to come to imaginative life, a partially scripted drama that enlivened a nonscripted historical reality; a simplified narrative that illuminated a multifaceted and barbarously complex history; a series of playacted events, gamelike in quality, which nonetheless lent an emotional seriousness to truly dramatic, tragic, and murderous circumstances. Ironically, perhaps, it was the grandeur of Ms. Bess's fiction that allowed for the authenticity of her results. It may be that a simulation that is full enough to generate its own emotional "reality" is less conducive to trivializing history by virtue of encouraging students to recognize the historical distance between the simulacrum and its historical referent.

According to this argument, metaphorically, a thin screen overlaid on this history could be more illusory than the plush curtain Ms. Bess's simulation threw before it. The density of her historical coverage, the fabric she wove, substantiated her simulation's "reality," enough for students to see what was both hidden and revealed by the curtain, to understand the fictiveness of their classroom creation, and ultimately, to recognize its inability to represent more than a fiction of the past.

Ms. Bess's simulation worked, in other words, as do good theater, fine literature, even powerful qualitative research, which bring into being, at least temporarily, an imaginative world in its entirety. In the words of Lee Shulman (1983), "The well-crafted case instantiates the possible" (p. 495). Ms. Bess's simulation, by functioning as provocative theater, created a powerful fiction that never attempted to represent history authentically, but rather, strove to "instantiate . . . [a] possible" history of the Holocaust in her students' minds. In short, it is mistaken to judge the simulation by the sole criterion of historical authenticity; simulations, by their very nature, cannot duplicate historical realities nor even represent them authentically, but rather form their own parallel versions of those histories.

According to one staff member at the U.S. Holocaust Memorial museum, people frequently call the museum's education department seeking the dimensions of the rail cars used to transport Holocaust victims to the concentration and "extermination" camps. "We don't give them out," I was told. Why? Because presumably such callers are teachers, and

> because I know they're going to take masking tape and go in the gym and mark off the size of a rail car and jam all of [the students] in there, explain what the death trains were like . . . [of course] with the best of intentions. But what does that teach [those students really]? It doesn't teach them about a death train. It teaches them about being crowded for 5 minutes together.

I don't dispute the wisdom of this decision; indeed, I support it. The mental image of giggling teenagers aping tragedy is patently offensive. And yet isn't it possible that learning about "being crowded for 5 minutes together," *if done seriously* as part of a richly based historical unit, could help students understand victims' experiences on those trains? And, in turn, couldn't that albeit limited understanding pave the way for students to gain fuller knowledge, even wisdom, about the Holocaust?

Ms. Bess's simulation, though hardly generalizeable, nonetheless "instantiated the possible" for her students, allowing us to recognize that simulations, even simulations of atrocity, like all pedagogical arrangements, pose moral trade-offs (Cuban, 2001; Hansen, 1995). Done well, they allow students emotional and intellectual access to past events; done poorly, they pose miseducative, indeed harmful, opportunities galore. While Ms. Bess's Holocaust simulation was not morally uncomplicated, it was nonetheless impressive enough to change this researcher's biases against the possibilities of the genre.

Chapter 4

The Drama of the Holocaust

When I entered Jim Dennis's classroom for the first time in May, near the end of the school year, I was surprised by its starkness. I had expected to see at least some indication that this was the site of his yearlong ninth-grade World History course. Instead, the three long bulletin boards lining the back wall stood empty, and no posters or student work adorned the walls. Even the blackboards defining the front of the room had nothing on them. A tall cabinet, maybe 8 feet high, anchored the front right corner of the room, a television monitor perched on top of it, and a line of paint stains ran along the far wall from the door. The desks were lined up in short rows of four to five seats, all facing the blackboards. As the students trickled in for their second-period class, though, their chattering brightened the room.

After a brief introduction, I stood in front of the students, explaining what my research involved and why I needed their parents' approval. As I had in every classroom I had visited, I said something about researching teachers whose reputations preceded them. As if on cue, a sea of arms pointed to my right, where Mr. Dennis was leaning against the wall, and a spring of confirming remarks bubbled up: "You came to the right place," "Mr. Dennis is the best," and "Spectacular," they told me, unsolicited. Mr. Dennis waved at the air, fanning away the compliments in mock embarrassment.

As this show of hands attested, Mr. Dennis was a beloved figure at Palmer High School. It wasn't unusual, for example, for the students I observed to express sincere gratitude and interest during class time. At the conclusion of a rapid-fire lecture the first day I observed, Mr. Dennis checked to make sure that everyone had understood the information he had whizzed through: "Did you guys all get that?" he asked. "Yes," one student replied: "It was amazing," another volunteered, without a trace of cynicism. Another morning, while I was waiting for Mr. Dennis to open his classroom door, I happened to yawn as a former student of his walked by. "You're going to Mr. Dennis's class?" he asked me, possibly mistaking me for a student. "You can't be tired going to *his* class," he continued. "He's the best thing at this school."

Mr. Dennis's prematurely gray hair was cut close to his head. When he smiled, which was often, his boyish face took on a somewhat mischievous look, as if he had a present hidden behind his back. He majored in history at an elite private college, and went on to receive a joint master's degree and certificate in teaching. Lanky, clean-shaven, and somewhere in his 40s, Mr. Dennis was married, had two young children, and was a devoted member of a fundamentalist Christian community. He had been teaching high school for 14 years, 11 of them at Palmer.

PALMER HIGH SCHOOL

Palmer High School is a suburban public high school serving 1,320 students. Scenic and sun-soaked, its campus stretches over more than 49 acres of well-groomed lawns in Northern California. Paved pathways twist between its buildings, connecting them only indirectly as if implying that no one should rush across these grounds. The status of the school, though, sends a different message. Palmer High has a national reputation for academic excellence; it is not a place where, metaphorically, students stroll at leisure. In fact, a publication of the College Board named Palmer one of "the five high schools in California perceived to provide outstanding preparation for highly selective college admission." As such, Palmer offers more than 12 Advanced Placement courses in a wide range of subjects, and almost 80% of its students head directly to 4-year colleges after graduating with "over 90% . . . go[ing] to 2–4 year colleges."

Nestled between a major university and a booming industrial center, Palmer enrolls students who are mostly children of white-collar professionals, most of whom are doing well. As one student whose family had immigrated recently from Hungary told me with obvious disdain, "There are people [*kids*] here who have cell phones and Mercedes, and they're only 18." According to Palmer's Unified School District, the ethnic/racial constitution of Palmer's student body breaks down as follows; 78% are White, 11% Asian, 5% Black, 4% Hispanic, and 2% other.

Well funded and well paying, Palmer pays its teachers salaries ranging from $35,072 to $64,008. Above and beyond its fiscal health, the school boasts a tremendously active parent population, which logged "more than 17,000 hours of volunteer time" in a single year. Mr. Dennis talked about the parents of students in his classes as "eager and anxious to jump in and help; these are not passive, apathetic or indifferent people." As he described it, all these factors, but especially the students' motivation to learn, make Palmer High School "an awesome place to be."

Part of a team of five teachers, Mr. Dennis teaches the first 2 semesters of a 3-semester sequence of World History. The year that I observed, he taught five sections of the course, with a total of about 140 students, or 28 students per class, which was the same teacher-student ratio of all of Palmer's classes and one of the lowest ratios in California at that time. Four of Mr. Dennis's sections were part of a "house" system, wherein its students shared the same teachers, all of whom integrated the contents of their core courses: math, science, English, and social studies. The section of Mr. Dennis's class I observed contained the only students he taught who were not selected for participation in the house; these students felt lucky to have Mr. Dennis at all. Mr. Dennis described the group as "definitely Honors level." Though it allows brief forays into China, Africa, and India, Mr. Dennis's course mainly conforms to the traditional boundaries delineating the Western historical canon; beginning with ancient Greece and Rome, the course surveys the Middle Ages and the Renaissance and eventually deposits students in modern Europe.

One student, Geku, described Mr. Dennis's course as "an adrenaline rush." Describing himself as a "person who listens" and "usually doesn't talk a lot," Geku is athletic and serious. He is interested in the "CIA, FBI, and espionage," and he enjoys learning about "war stuff," even though he recognizes that "it's not that great of a thing because people die." Mr. Dennis's course was a thrill for him because he never knew what to expect. He recounted one class session on the French Revolution in which the class held a mock trial and Geku was pulled into the drama as a suspect. It was "easy to pay attention" in the course, he summarized, because Mr. Dennis was so entertaining and the activities so varied. As the young Hungarian student, Gordy, put it, in Mr. Dennis's class, "you dance, sing, you reenact, you fight, you watch videos, draw; you really get to be friendly with your classmates 'cause like you're acting with them." All four students I interviewed used the word *different* at some point to describe Mr. Dennis's pedagogy. Cindy, a Mexican American student who had been dropped out of the house system when two of its courses proved too difficult for her, explained:

> I've always hated social studies until this year. Mr. Dennis is like my favorite teacher; he's like the best history teacher I've ever had. He teaches things so easy to understand, the way he teaches them. He does a lot of neat things, like reenactments and stuff, so you understand it more than just like writing it down. He hardly ever has us take notes, but occasionally he [does]. He's different. . . . A lot of teachers just like read materials out of books, but Mr. Dennis, he'll like research the whole thing, and then he'll make it up into like either a song or a dance or a reenactment or something to

> make it different, interesting, so people understand it. I personally don't understand it if I read it out of a book. I have to have someone tell me or show me what it is.

While the students adored Mr. Dennis and what they described as his nutty teaching antics, those with whom I spoke agreed that Mr. Dennis toned down his typically exuberant playfulness while teaching his unit on the Holocaust, matching his pedagogy to the seriousness of the subject matter. To Gordy, the shift was "like a big cloud came over the classroom; [and Mr. Dennis] wasn't like cheery, singing."

MR. DENNIS'S CURRICULUM GOALS

Despite seeming to have less fun while teaching about the Holocaust, one of the last units of the year, Mr. Dennis told me that it was his favorite unit to teach, as he explained, "because of . . . the moral and ethical issues, because it is so full of that." Mr. Dennis had first heard of the Holocaust while working toward his master's degree in education, in 1977. The National Council on the Social Studies had published a special issue devoted to teaching the Holocaust as an accompaniment to the NBC movie *Holocaust* (Green, 1978), which aired earlier that year. Mr. Dennis became very interested in the topic, especially in what he saw as the connections between that past and then-present devaluations of human life, among which he included American perceptions of the severely disabled and the My Lai Massacre.

When I asked whether his goals for student learning in his Holocaust unit were different from his goals in other units, he responded with a resounding "Definitely." He qualified the statement quickly, though, pointing out some common goals across his units; "My goal is always to teach them for life—I want them to remember for the rest of their lives." He stressed the role of knowledge in all his units: "I try to give them notes, an outline of what happened," he told me, as "they need to know what happened." As he expanded on his answer, he implied that the goals for student learning particular to his unit on the Holocaust were moral in nature:

> Maybe the whole point of this is to turn kids into rescuers, to instill in them the mentality that will say, "When I see something happen on campus to somebody, do I turn my head and walk the other way or do I try to help?" And, yes, I know there are lots of consequences of trying to help, but if the mentality is, "I'm not re-

> sponsible; this is somebody else's responsibility," then that's exactly what allowed the trains to roll; that's exactly what allowed the people to be arrested; it's what kept them quiet. And I really, really want my two girls to be rescuers; I want them to go to Auschwitz. . . . They need to be willing to risk their lives for somebody else. I need to be willing to risk my life for somebody else. . . . That's what we need the kids to think about, . . . to let the pictures of the victims of the Holocaust be a backdrop on the front of which would be, "Will you have the courage to care?"

Mr. Dennis here quoted the title of a video he shows as part of his unit: *Courage to Care* (Gardner, 1985). "I wish I could say that about my other units," he concluded, regretting that the other units he taught did not include such crucial, applicable moral lessons as does this one.

Mr. Dennis's official curriculum was self-constructed, a collage of plans and materials from a variety of sources. His lectures included condensations of books he had read, copies of which he sometimes brought to class or mentioned in passing. As a modified textbook for the unit, Mr. Dennis handed out a pamphlet of 15 pages copied from a trade book, a cartoon-based primer on the Holocaust titled *Introducing the Holocaust* (Bresheeth, Hood, & Jansz, 2002). In addition, Mr. Dennis had written the script of one play and adapted the script of another, both of which students performed under his direction. Mr. Dennis's 2-week unit was filled with information and images and anchored by these two dramatic performances, which he called "reenactments."

MR. DENNIS'S SHOW

The first day that I observed Mr. Dennis teaching, he started the lesson by guiding students through a fast-paced, joke-studded review. He asked students strings of questions such as, How is it possible that Jews are a race? Are Christians a race? Are Muslims? What should Germany do, according to Adolf Hitler? Why do people follow him? Many of the students in the room raised their hands to offer succinct answers or make related comments, and Mr. Dennis assigned to the whole class points for many of the individual student's contributions. "There's no such thing as a pure anything," one Persian student commented. "I'm part Mongol way, way back, because the Persians were taken over by the Mongols." Another student, Gordy, added, "I've heard that the furthest person in the world from you is still like your 34th cousin." In response to the question, What should Germany do? one student volunteered, "Expand," and another responded, "Raise arms." In what I soon learned was typical humor for Mr. Dennis, he punned with the students by raising both his arms above his head as if being held up at gunpoint, "Raise arms like this?" he asked rhetorically, answering himself by lowering one arm and straightening the other in a Heil Hitler salute and saying ominously, "No, like this." Later, in describing the nature of totalitarian dictatorship, Mr. Dennis had all the students say, "Whoof" while tightening their fists in a gesture of strength. "Germany needed 'whoof' government," he had them chant in unison. The review covered the impact of the depression, the elections in Germany, and the appeal of communism before seamlessly presenting new information on Adolf Hitler's biography, the machinery of terror, the invasion of the Sudetenland, and the bombing of Pearl Harbor.

It became obvious to me very quickly that Mr. Dennis's punning, spontaneous dramatizations and his singing of information he wanted to get across mesmerized his students. Using a combination of humor, performance, gags, audience participation, and general goofiness, he was practically a vaudeville act unto himself, enlivening the historical information with imaginary voices and dramatic gestures. In discussing the Nazi state's "octopus arms" of fear, for example, Mr. Dennis drew an octopus on the board. He then acted out a short scene of a woman being arrested by the Gestapo, playing both the role of the terrified woman and that of the policeman doffing an imaginary hat before telling her, "Ms. Kiley, you don't have time to say good-bye to your kids, you come now." Mr. Dennis sang a march and goose-stepped to illustrate the takeover of the Rhineland. When France and Britain "complain" to Hitler after the Evian Conference, saying, "You lied to us," Mr. Dennis joked, "And Hitler thought, 'They can be taught!'" Mr. Dennis also repeatedly joked with the students about the very speed of his lecturing, remarking as asides, "How fast can I talk?" and "I cannot teach this in 2 minutes." With these pseudo-self-deprecations, Mr. Dennis drew his students into the game; the lecture became almost a test to see if he could do what he claimed he couldn't, but was in fact doing. Throughout the lecture, students interrupted to ask questions or express their opinions, and Mr. Dennis would occasionally ask them whether they had "gotten it" despite the breakneck speed of the information. As he did much of the time, too, Mr. Dennis ended this class by showing a video, this one a 20-minute segment about Hitler's early life, during which the students also asked questions. Mr. Dennis was a master lecturer; his lectures were entertaining and interactive, and his classroom was clearly a place where student talk had been valued and encouraged all year.

The First Reenactment

The 2nd day of the unit, I was surprised to learn that the class would be meeting in the auditorium to view the rest of the videotape on Hitler's biography. The students understood this to mean that there would be a surprise reenactment that day, and they had trouble focusing on the film. "Settle down," Mr. Dennis had to tell them a few times as they joked while watching. When the video had concluded, Mr. Dennis told the students that they would be seeing a "Degenerate Art Exhibit," and he invited them to follow him. Excitedly, the students chattered as they walked hurriedly. Mr. Dennis stopped them outside a doorway:

> Now, guys, I just want to remind you that they've put a lot of hours into this, so please be on your best behavior. They practiced until 10 P.M. last night. Don't get fidgety in there. They did this for you, and for the 6 million who can't be here.

Mr. Dennis then drew back a heavy black curtain draping the door and the students passed through it, quieted. The transition from the brilliant sun outdoors to the darkened classroom was temporarily blinding. Solo violin music, poignant and haunting (the soundtrack from the movie *Schindler's List* [Williams & Perlman, 1993]) encircled the room as each student found a place to sit on the floor. As my eyes adjusted, the walls of the room materialized, covered in Nazi symbols painted in red and black. The word *Judenfrei* dripped from one wall, and the words *Juden Raus!* emblazoned another. The back wall, wrapped in white butcher paper, served as a screen; the words *Arbeit Macht Frei* had been painted in an arch over it and were entangled with barbed wire. A young man in a historically accurate Nazi uniform stood stone faced and motionless in the center of the room, holding what looked like a real rifle. The students seated themselves carefully around him, and when they seemed settled, he spoke, using no script:

> Welcome to our very special art exhibit. Here, for you to view, the Nazi Party has hung the paintings of Jews and other rats. This degenerate art, if it is not stopped, is the horror that German culture may become. The purity of our supreme culture is threatened by this new, deviant style which has affected not only art but films, music, and literature as well. We in the Nazi Party have destroyed the degenerate films, banned the records, and burned the books. Today, with this exhibit which makes plain everything which must be hated in the artwork of the rats, we will cripple the artists of

this so called Impressionistic style. . . . We have gathered it here for you to behold, to see how degraded your culture is becoming. Together we can fight this plague. . . . Behold the triumph of the Nazis and the funeral of the degenerates!

The spotlight on the soldier dimmed while another rose on two more "German soldiers" ushering in an artist. The soldiers pretend to view the art, then laugh and move on, leaving the desperate artist behind.

Artist: What have they done? . . . These paintings are mine. . . . What have they done to them? [She tears one painting from the wall.] I know what is going on here, what will happen, what the Nazis will do. And so I paint, I must express the hatred and fear that is everywhere now. You wonder what will happen with the Nazis in power? Look around you! [Gestures to the paintings] Pain. And death. The agony of genocide, the killing of a race. My paintings are tools of resistance against the Nazis because they show what is really happening and so they are here, not where they can warn, but where they will be laughed at and thrown away. My paintings are more than canvas and paint, they are lives and deaths of a persecuted people. Look, this is someone's life, this picture, it is a young woman and a child. . . .

Voice 1: The Nazis made me wear a sign. That was the first time I felt true humiliation. It said that all Jews were swine. I knew I could do nothing. There was nothing I could do.

What followed was a highly stylized and sophisticated play that combined pathos, drama, and technology. Each "painting" came to life in the voices of different students posed around the room. A single spotlight would encapsulate the speaker, leaving the rest of the room swathed in darkness while hearing a vignette from the life of a Holocaust victim or survivor. One voice was meant to represent the Jewish assassin Herschel Grynszpan, explaining why he had shot the third secretary of the German embassy in Paris, Ernst von Rath. As the actor spoke about the shooting, she pulled out a revolver, which fired an alarmingly authentic noise. Another voice was Elie Wiesel's, reading excerpts from his acceptance speech upon receiving the Presidential Humanitarian Medal. Other voices described the process of ghettoization, the cattle cars, the concentration camps, and the after-effects of survival. One poignant vignette related the story of a young man who planned to jump off a truck with his father and on the count of 3 jumped, only to look back and see his father waving to him from the vehicle. "Since Auschwitz, I have never taken a shower, only baths," another voice recounted. Throughout, illustrative photographs were projected in slide form on the far wall so that the students saw, in addition to hearing about, the atrocities; with rapt attention, the students shifted their gaze from the slides to the speakers and back again. Near the end of the presentation, the Nazi guard returned, beating up the artist and leaving her body in a heap on the floor. A modern folksong filled the room as the slides continued.

When the lights went up in the room to signal the end of the 45-minute presentation, the student actors maintained their poses and the clapping, which tentatively arose, seemed incongruous. The students and I filed out of the room wordlessly, they to their next classes, I to my car. It was only then, as we left the room, that I realized we had been sitting on the linoleum floor of Mr. Dennis's classroom the entire time; it had been so transformed by the performance set that I hadn't realized it was his room.

The Next Surprise

The following class meeting was important to Mr. Dennis. He mentioned to me before class began that he was nervous; he had "a lot to cover," and he wanted to "do it just right." "Guys, good morning, nice to see you," he said as the students entered. "Mr. Dennis?" said one student who stood with a large box in her arms, "our class has a birthday present for you." At that, the whole class broke into a somewhat off-pitch but loudly sung rendition of "Happy Birthday." "Open it!" cried a few students while the singing continued. Mr. Dennis beamed while tearing into the wrapping, uncovering a brand-new portable CD player with a radio, tape player, and microphone. Mr. Dennis thanked the students, joking with them affectionately, "I don't know what to say. No final. All tests are off."

After a few more minutes of teasing, laughter, and thanks, Mr. Dennis turned the students' attention to the actors in the previous class session's reenactment. The students spontaneously clapped for the performers and the two "techies" in their class. Mr. Dennis selects the actors and technical support staff (or techies, who do the lighting, sound, and stage work) for each of his reenactments from his entire population of students. Thus, in any given reenactment, there may be only a few student participants from each section he teaches. Unfortunately, there are not enough parts for every student in his classes to have one. Geku, for example, was disappointed that he was never chosen to play a part in a reenactment.

Mr. Dennis asked one student actor, Talia, to share with the class why she had written the truck-jumping episode into the script. "That happened to my grandfather; he went through it," Talia responded quietly. Mr. Dennis reiterated slowly, "It was a true story." Nina, the fourth student I followed and one of the few African Americans in the class, told me later that Talia's revelation had impressed her. The reenactment "was good; it was real good," she said. "They all did a good job explaining those personal stories." But Talia's story especially, in its authenticity, had struck her:

> Once I found out that that was true, that was her grandfather—that really hit me. . . . Kids today, they're lucky; they have a pager or they have a cellular phone, but back in those days, you didn't have that, and it's because somebody took your father. That's just that, "whoah, where did he go?" That hit me; it really, really did. That was powerful.

The rest of the day's lecture and the following day's covered the phases of the Holocaust, which Mr. Dennis labeled "Identification," "Persecution," "Isolation," "Concentration," and "Violence." On the center board in colored chalk was an outline, along with a list of events corresponding to each header, which he narrated more fully. On the side board, the word *Shoah* was emblazoned in bulbous red chalk letters, both in Hebrew script and in English print. The students took notes and, as before, peppered his lectures with questions. In closing both days, Mr. Dennis showed short video clips to illustrate Kristallnacht and to portray the "liquidation" of the ghettos.

The Second Reenactment

On the 5th day of the unit, Mr. Dennis reached the section of his outline titled "Violence." The original outline from which he worked marked the fifth stage as "Extermination," for which he substituted the term *violence* perhaps in recognition of the fact that *extermination* is a term reflective of Nazi ideology, implying that Jews were vermin. Although this is understandable as a rhetorical move, I would argue that the term *violence* isn't strong enough, considering that all previous phases of the Holocaust included substantial violence as well; perhaps, a more appropriate term that does not employ Nazi language might be *systematic murder*.

In serious tones and dramatic style, Mr. Dennis narrated the activities of the Einsatzgruppen and the functioning of the gas chambers at Auschwitz. To help the students visualize the machinery of murder, Mr.

Dennis drew a gas chamber on the board, complete with valves and a Zyklon B canister slot.

> Just one of those cans, about the size of a Quaker Oats can, would kill 1,000 to 2,000 people. It would travel down here through these water pipes and escape through these holes in the ceiling, emitting a hissing sound as it vaporized immediately upon contact with the air. The gas was a bluish greenish color— and it's a gas used today, the same kind of chemical used today to kill rats or clear out a house of termites. Zyklon B was meant to kill you quickly. The people in the chamber would see it, smell it, and run to the door, trying to get out, leaving fingernail indentations on the cement ceiling. How desperate do you have to be to leave fingernail indentations on a ceiling? I don't know about you, but the last time I checked, my flesh gave way long before the cement would have. [Intoned slowly in an even pace] How desperate do you have to be before you leave fingernail indentations on cement?

The students and I sat silently as the emotionally riveting lecture continued. Mr. Dennis went on to describe the Sonderkommandos, their extraction of teeth and burning of bodies. "Today, at Auschwitz, at the edge of the Szola River, you can bend down and scoop up a handful of ash, and in it will be shards of bone, bits of teeth, and scraps of what was once human life," he said. He then listed the numbers of Jews killed at Auschwitz, Treblinka, and the other so-called extermination camps, concluding, "Fortunately, the war ended before the rest of Europe's Jews were killed." Mr. Dennis seemed to take a deep breath at that point, pausing dramatically for the full effect of his words to sink in. He then changed tack:

> Last year, I had the pleasure of seeing the movie *Anne Frank Remembered* [Blair & Frank, 1995], which tells the poignant story of Anne Frank, her brutal murder after years in hiding. With her death and the deaths of millions of others, Hitler thought that he had forever silenced voices like Anne Frank's and her family's. Well, he was wrong. They're not silent at all. She still speaks to us today; in fact, . . . I'd like to take you someplace to hear some of those voices.

With a few words about the hard work of the student actors about to perform ("They've worked on this for 4 months, with late nights of exhausting work"), and a few words of instruction ("No pagers, no talking, no walkmen, come with me, and walk lively"), Mr. Dennis had the students follow him out of the classroom and across Palmer's open quadrangle for another surprise dramatic reenactment, the one that for Mr. Dennis marked the culmination of his unit.

The students and I walked quietly as upper class Palmer students who had this period off looked on, bemused. Mr. Dennis led the way, looking increasingly worried. We rounded a corner behind the cafeteria and Student Center building and were suddenly confronted with two young men in full Nazi regalia. Standing in tall black boots, guns loosely propped at their sides, they stood, as if guarding the custodian's complex. One young man threw down a partially smoked cigarette as he addressed Mr. Dennis in immaculate German. "Anybody speak German?" Mr. Dennis asked the students, acting anxious. When none of the students volunteered, Mr. Dennis replied in halting German. The guards yelled at him; he seemed to jump and then passed a $20 bill to one of them. "Form a line, quickly," Mr. Dennis urged us. "They're letting us in, single file." "Schnell!" yelled one of the guards. A few student giggles escaped in trepidation and excitement, but the Nazi guards remained completely in character, joking together in German. We filed into a large storage area, where blackboards, lawn mowers, desks, chairs, and random equipment was housed in seeming disarray. A young woman descended a set of stairs against the back wall, greeting Mr. Dennis warmly.

"How long have they been out there?" Mr. Dennis asked her, as if muffling his voice but speaking loudly enough for all of us to hear. "Not very long," she replied. "I don't think we should do this, not now; I had to bribe them to let us in," Mr. Dennis told her. "I think we should," the woman answered. "It's the only time they'll get the chance, and visitors mean so much to them." Mr. Dennis nodded, eyes downcast. He had clearly become a part in the play that was unfolding. "By the way, this is Mrs. Kraler," he told the students, then abruptly he instructed them to look to the left and point at something, as the guards were looking in at that moment; Mr. Dennis wanted the audience to play along with the play. He counted each head as we walked up the cramped stairway, following Mrs. Kraler. At the top of the stairs a small landing stood encased by bookcases filled with books. Mr. Dennis asked that the students leave their belongings on this landing, and they dutifully complied, strewing the tight space with nylon knapsacks and leather satchels. Mr. Dennis then helped Mrs. Kraler swivel one of the bookcases sideways on its axis, revealing a narrow entrance to an attic. The students entered, pressing against one another for spaces on the floor of an elaborate set surrounding them.

To the left was a bunk bed, with a young actress clearly meant to be Anne Frank sitting on the lower bunk, looking through a photo album. Tacked to the wall behind her were photos of Vivian Leigh, Veronica Lake, and Clark Gable. Directly in front of where the students sat, a tiny living room was set up with a couch and two chairs on a flowered rug. Laundry hung on a line suspended across the room. To the right, next to the bookcase we had entered, a 1930s radio sat on a shelf next to a glass-paned hutch. Everything in the room, in fact, down to the dishes in the hutch and the few books on the bookshelves, seemed to be historically accurate period pieces. The student playing Peter Van Daan, perched on the upper bunk of the bed, was reading an oversized cartoon book while Mrs. Frank sewed quietly on a living-room chair. The other characters were similarly engaged in solitary activities, ignoring the students gathering at their feet.

When everyone had found a place to sit, with some help from Mr. Dennis, Mrs. Kraler introduced the characters and provided background on their situation, presumably for those who might not have read Anne Frank's diary. An air raid siren suddenly blared as she finished, and the lights in the room flickered. Peter jumped down from his perch, nearly squashing Cindy, the slight-framed Mexican American student seated beside the bed. Although some of the audience members whispered to one another briefly, excited by recognizing cast members from their class, the murmuring soon died down, and the play began.

Over the following 45 minutes, the student audience was completely engaged as the characters lamented their situation, dreamed of the outside world, talked about movie stars and schoolwork, reminisced, argued, struggled through Mr. Van Daan's stealing bread, suffered through Mrs. Van Daan's flirtatiousness, waltzed to sung music, and witnessed Anne and Peter's growing infatuation. The play had uncomfortable, touching, funny, sweet, and painful moments, and the acting was convincing. Finally, the air raid sirens sounded again, as the announcement of D-Day was heard over the radio. The thrilled attic inhabitants discussed the prospect of the war ending as the annex was discovered; Margot, Anne, and their parents were teasing one another when loud voices uttering German were heard below. The actors froze, and the students in the audience became very serious; only one girl's nervous laughter sputtered up, but then quieted in dismay. Heavy boots could be heard climbing the stairs with ominous certainty. In the annex, the tension was visible, not only on the actors' faces but on the audiences' as well. I saw some students with their mouths hanging open in anticipation. After pounding on the wall, two Nazi guards forced open the bookcase-door, ushering in Mr. Dennis, almost unrecognizable in the costume of a Gestapo agent.

In the original play, the arrest of the attic members is a brief affair. The Franks and Van Daans pack silently as the Nazis pound down the door and yell for them to leave. The audience doesn't view the arrest or, importantly, its consequences. Mr. Dennis, however, screamed at the attic inhabitants, calling them "Jewish rats!" and demanding that Peter sing "Mary Had a Little Lamb" while the two guards held him down, knocked over furniture, and knocked the hanging light off its moorings. Mr. Dennis sustained his verbal attack, forcing Peter to "point out the whore who bore you and the pimp who raped her." Anne screamed; Mrs. Frank looked on, horrified, clutching her husband; Margot hid her face. Mr. Dennis had told me earlier that this part of the production, the discovery of the hidden Jews, was unrehearsed and unscripted; the actors hadn't known exactly how the play would end and were improvising their characters' reactions. They cringed and sobbed and desperately held on to one another. Cindy, sitting near me in the audience, I noticed was crying.

The attic inhabitants finally exited as commanded by the guards, huddled together in family groups. The guards went with them, smashing the glass in the hutch as they left in a barrage of sound. Only Mr. Dennis was left on stage. He paced, soliloquizing directly to the students in the audience in a thick German accent: "Look at the way they live. Filthy, like little rats in a hole." He poked around the room, and happened upon Anne's diary. Loudly and contemptuously, he read Anne's famous line "In spite of everything, I still believe that people are good at heart." "You think I'm good at heart? Are *you* good at heart?" he questioned the students rhetorically. He left, and none of the students knew quite what to do. A moment passed where no one moved. Mrs. Kraler returned, visibly upset, saying simply, "Please leave." There was no clapping. The students walked down the stairs and out into the brazen sunlight to confront their next classes.

Reflections on the Reenactment

Because I was somewhat familiar with the original play, *The Diary of Anne Frank*, by Frances Goodrich and Albert Hackett (1958), I couldn't help comparing Mr. Dennis's version to its forebear as I watched. Although many of the scenes and dialogue sequences were the same, Mr. Dennis's adaptation differed from the original in significant ways. In a minor change, Mr. Dennis had the student performers update some of the language the characters used to suit their 1990s audience, as when Peter remarked, "And all my friends from school? Who wants to be around a *guy* with a star on his sleeve?" A more pronounced change from the original play involved the explicitness of the characters' Jewishness. Whereas the original play stripped Anne and the other attic dwellers of most references to their Jewish identities, the same characters in Mr. Dennis's production were presented as far less assimilated. In his rendition, the attic group in unison recites the Hebrew prayer thanking God for bread before eating, with Mrs. Frank prodding an eager Mr. Van Daan to stop him from biting before the prayer is complete.

In the original rendition of the play, the Jewishness of the attic's inhabitants is referenced minimally by their singing of a Chanukah song in English. In reality, the Frank family was an assimilated Jewish family. That is, they participated fully—socially, economically, and politically—in the non-Jewish worlds they inhabited in Germany and Holland, feeling themselves not to be outsiders in those realms until being named as such. They were also committed to Jewish causes, Jewish agencies, and Jewish learning, practicing religious observance liberally. So, for example, before the invasion of Holland, and indeed in the early stages of occupation, Anne had both Jewish and non-Jewish friends, although she was accepted into the Jewish school (by choice) before going into hiding. It is unlikely, then, that the Franks would have said a Hebrew blessing together before eating a regular meal, as they do in Mr. Dennis's adaptation of the play. Interestingly, though, the Franks probably had a more complicated relationship to their own Jewish identities than either Goodrich and Hackett or Dennis's renditions suggest. In the unedited version of Anne Frank's diary, *The Critical Edition* (Barnouw & van der Stroom, 1989), for example, Anne describes the Frank family celebrating Christmas more fully than Chanukah during their first year in hiding (p. 321). While Goodrich and Hackett (1958) universalized the Franks, downplaying their Jewish observance, Mr. Dennis's production, by contrast, may have exaggerated their Jewishness as an educative device. This shift reflects not only the different purposes of the productions, but among other things, their radically different sociopolitical contexts in 1954 versus 1997. Neither the embracing of multiculturalism, nor indeed the era of identity politics, had yet arrived in 1954. Mr. Dennis's production sought both to modernize the language used and to particularize the victims represented. Strikingly different in this rendition, too, was the role of Anne's now famous optimism as expressed in the line "In spite of everything, I still believe that people are good at heart." This quotation from Anne's diary, taken out of context, closes Goodrich and Hackett's play, a rhetorical move that, in later years, incited criticism for its uplifting message in the midst of tragedy (Ozick, 1996). Bruno Bettelheim (1960) wrote extensively on this tendency to mitigate the tragic dimensions of the Holocaust, emblematized by the icon Anne Frank has become.

> Her seeming survival through her moving statement about the goodness of men releases us effectively of the need to cope with the problems Auschwitz presents. . . . [Her comment] explains why millions loved play and movie [and, I would add, diary and girl], because while it confronts us with the fact that Auschwitz existed, it encourages us at the same time to ignore any of its implications. (p. 251)

Because Anne's diary ends before her life does, because her narrative does not describe the concentration camps, because her ideas are very much ideals, Anne Frank has come to represent hope despite tragic circumstances, faith amid inhumanity, life despite murder. While Goodrich and Hackett's play avoided the horror of the Holocaust, Mr. Dennis's plainly pointed toward the concentration camps, showing the arrest of the attic inhabitants and concretizing the abstractness of their murders in the form of Mr. Dennis's confrontational Gestapo agent.

As a result of including the Nazi character, though, a problematic tension arises in Mr. Dennis's production: His play represents Nazis solely as driven anti-Semites, rather than as ordinary men (Browning, 1992), who, through a variety of social pressures and historical circumstances developed the capacity for brutality. This distinction, in part, lies at the nexus of the debate between Christopher Browning and Daniel Jonah Goldhagen (1996) on the explanation of perpetrators' behavior. Mr. Dennis, having mentioned in class Goldhagen's book, *Hitler's Willing Executioners,* sided with Goldhagen, painting persecutors as deranged and cruel.

Nina's comments in her closing interview indicated that Goldhagen's representation of Germans had been conveyed to her. When I asked what she thought about the Nazis and their collaborators, she replied:

> I think they're very crazy, nutcase people. And what Mr. Dennis said is that these people chose to do it. They had a decision. Sometimes people just go the wrong way; when you kill somebody, you would have to know that this is wrong. They chose to do that, and for that, I just really think they're crazy.

Regardless of the changes Mr. Dennis made to the play, the students loved the version they saw. A substantial majority, 86% of those who handed in their final surveys, wrote that the best part of the Holocaust unit had been the Anne Frank reenactment. All four of the students I interviewed mentioned the power of the reenactment in their assessments of the unit as well. I spoke with Geku just minutes after the reenactment had ended; he was very enthusiastic about it, though he had trouble putting his response into words. "The Nazis seemed violent enough," he said first, warming to the task. "It seemed like they [the attic inhabitants] might have gotten claustrophobic from like all being stuck in one room together like that, two families."

Cindy had felt more involved throughout the reenactment. As she put it: "I was kinda like there. I guess that's what Mr. Dennis wants us to feel like we were there and we know what's going on. It was sad." Cindy had expected the reenactment to be "kinda boring," but when it had concluded, she "was like 'Wow, that really happened?' It seemed like that could never happen." The play had struck her as so realistic, in fact, that it prompted her to consider her own reactions to such a situation. "I can't even stay at my house for more than 2 hours," she remarked in all seriousness.

Nina thought that the reenactment was "fantastic." She elaborated:

> The Nazis, when they came in, they just tore up everything, and, with that, I was like, people always say, "Well, I would have done, I wouldn't back up" and everything like that, "I woulda come up and punched 'em or something like that," you know. If you try to do that, you're dead in one second. So, you see that that's what it really was like.

Only Gordy was somewhat critical of the production, feeling that it paled in comparison to the video the class watched about Anne Frank a few days later. He explained to me that the video was much more moving than the reenactment because, in the reenactment, "You know it's your friends, and you know they're just acting, but when you see the video, you know that that happened, like the people you're seeing were actually there."

The actors in the Anne Frank reenactment spent the rest of their school day performing for Mr. Dennis's other classes and that evening performing for their parents; they spent the following day, a Friday, performing for other classes in the school. Mr. Dennis was thus absent from his own class that Friday. The substitute handed out copies of the assignment Mr. Dennis had left for them in which he asked students to evaluate the reenactment using mock diary entries. The students wrote earnestly, and the talking and showmanship for the substitute died down.

The substitute then played a videotape selected by Mr. Dennis, a half-hour-long, hard-hitting excerpt from the movie *War and Remem-*

brance (Wouk & Wallace, 1988). (This was the same video excerpt that Ms. Bess had shown in her class.) In it, a group of victims arrive at Auschwitz and are subsequently murdered in the gas chambers. The excerpt is a popular one to show because of the starkness of its images as well as the exactness of its detail. As Mr. Dennis described the scene, "All the gloves are off, . . . and you know exactly what happened." As the VCR played, a few of Mr. Dennis's students completed their homework for other classes; Talia walked out; another young woman had her head down on her desk. When the video ended, the class was dismissed, and the students and I walked out, again wordlessly. I passed Cindy. "That was so gross," she said to me quietly. Nina mentioned in class later that it had been "very intense." I think all of us were thankful that a long weekend awaited.

When school resumed the following Tuesday, the classroom had been transformed again. Although pieces of the first reenactment's *mise-en-scène* remained, Mr. Dennis had plastered the back and side bulletin boards with Holocaust-related articles, posters, pamphlets, and announcements. The day's session was divided into two activities. For 10 minutes, the students read silently to themselves from compilations of articles about the Holocaust printed in American newspapers between 1933 and 1945. "Every one of these articles appeared on a date at the bottom of the article," Mr. Dennis remarked, "so there's no saying we didn't know."

The second part of the class session was dedicated to learning about rescuers. "If there's one ray of hope in the Holocaust it was that individuals took it upon themselves to care for those who were being persecuted," Mr. Dennis said to the class. By way of further introduction, he spoke about a teachers' conference he had attended some years earlier. Pacing back and forth at the front of the room, he made eye contact slowly with each student in the class as he acted out the voices he described, speaking in a lower register to represent his own voice:

> [At the conference,] they brought people up who had risked their lives to save Jews during the Holocaust, and they were called the Righteous Gentiles. And they recognized them, and it was so *so* powerful; if I think about it now, I get goose bumps to remember what they said.
>
> [In contrast to when bystanders were asked]—I think I told you this before, but if I did, just tell me, "You told us this before"—when asked, "Why didn't you save the Jews, the ones you had grown up with, the children who your children had included in bar mitzvahs they'd gone to, whose synagogues you'd gone to,

who had come to your house to Christmas and vice versa on Chanukah, why didn't you save them? Why didn't you do anything about them?" And, the response was, . . . "What else could I do? The Nazis were in power. There was a totalitarian regime, you know, the octopus, I mean, what could I do? I couldn't risk my own family. I mean, I'm sorry about what happened to them, but I can't risk my family because to help the Jews was to suffer the same fate as they if you got caught."

And what was so powerful was to hear the same response from those we call rescuers. When asked, "Why did you do what you did? Why did you risk your life, your family's life, your children's life? Why did you risk everything you had to save these people?" And the answer was, "What else could I do?" The same five words! I mean it was chilling.

"They're my friends," like Miep [the rescuer of Anne Frank] says. "They're my family. It's not us-them, they're us. We're together. They're people; they're human beings, who because of a particular religion they happen to practice are being terribly persecuted. What else could I do? I had no choice; I had to save them." "I had no choice"; the same four words . . . justified doing nothing and justified risking one's life. The same four words.

Mr. Dennis then played *The Courage to Care* (Gardner, 1985), a video profiling four women from different countries; of these women, one was rescued and three were rescuers. Each protagonist tells her story, and each story complicates stereotypical notions of rescue. One woman from Denmark, for example, tells of having shot her local policeman rather than let him arrest the Jews hiding on her farm. Another woman, from Poland, discreetly implies having slept with the Nazi official in whose villa she hid a group of Jews in order to secure his affections and safeguard her charges. While Mr. Dennis's introduction and the film text itself were thought provoking and morally inspiring, no time in class was as yet spent in discussion of the issues. The video showing was perfectly timed to finish at the end of the class period. Two sessions remained in Mr. Dennis's Holocaust unit.

DISCUSSING THE HOLOCAUST'S MEANINGS

Mr. Dennis started the first of these sessions on a light note. He had prepared Academy Award ballots for the students to fill out. (Just after the final examination in the course, Mr. Dennis supplied the winners in the various categories with miniature plastic Academy Award trophy replicas, which many of the participants from the two Holocaust reenactments won.) He then showed the second half of the video *Anne Frank Remembered* (Blair & Frank, 1995), which documents the last 7 months of Anne Frank's life with moving testimonies from those who knew her in the Bergen-Belsen concentration camp. The film showed gruesome footage of bodies bulldozed into mass graves at liberation and shared the postliberation letters of Otto Frank, seeking to find his family. Although it ended on a hopeful note, recounting the widespread influence and popularity of Anne Frank's diary, the mood in the room was unsurprisingly somber when Mr. Dennis turned off the VCR. He left the overhead lights off in the room as he spoke quietly:

> You know, guys, I always move right on, "OK, guys, take out your notes," or "Keep the quiz face down until I ask you to turn it over." [His intonation imitated his own voice in a bouncier mood.] . . . I want to stop for a minute, and let you ask questions, or reflect or give voice to what you've experienced in the last 2 weeks if you'd like.

A heavy pause hung in the air before the young woman who had played Mrs. Van Daan in the play, Melinda, raised her hand. With a nod from Mr. Dennis, she spoke, opening the floodgates of expression in the class. Below, I quote the conversation almost in its entirety because it is remarkable for the students' eloquence and openness, for the teacher's willingness to let student discourse dominate in place of a planned quiz, and for the sophistication of the issues raised. The students spoke softly.

Melinda: Before we started doing the play, doing the rehearsals and learning about it, I never put the truth to it; I took it as a fiction kind of. I knew it was true, but I didn't understand it. It was just the past.

Mr. Dennis: Was there anything that brought it home to you the most?

Melinda: One night my mom was yelling at me [to do my homework], and I was stressed out, and I told her, I'm like "No! You don't know what it's like to remember the deaths of 6 million Jews!" And like I had never thought about it before; I didn't really feel like that before. . . .

After a 3-second pause, Mr. Dennis gently encourages others to speak, saying, "This is your time to give voice to whatever you'd like to say." He calls on Nina.

Nina: I think the reenactment didn't hit me as much. . . . I was upset, but I never knew what started the whole thing [the Holocaust]. I never knew anything. . . . Then, as I started to know about it, it affected me a *lot*. . . . It made me very upset. [It seems as though Nina might cry; her voice cracks, and she pauses before continuing.] But, uhh, still I think it's better to understand it, all what started it and all. We can start from there.

Not unlike the students in Ms. Bess's class, these two young women expressed the emotional nature of the reenactment's impact on them. Implicit in their remarks, too, was a dawning recognition of the enormity of the Holocaust and its tragic dimensions. Other students' remarks echoed these sentiments later in the conversation. What happened next, though, was that Kate, in a somewhat confrontational tone, interjected what might be considered a criticism of the unit:

Kate: I think the whole Holocaust was extremely sad, but it wasn't all about the Jews. It was about these people that were different, and that's not only 6 million Jews, but a lot of other people died, too. And, I don't know, it might sound kind of like bad, but I think that there's a lot more focused on the Jews than there are on the other people who died in the Holocaust. And, umm, I wish people would recognize the fact that it wasn't just the Jews; it was anyone that was different in Germany and wherever Germany occupied. It was everywhere. It was anybody who wasn't considered useful.

India: I think Kate is extremely right. I mean the reason why they're the main ones is because it was extremely terrible, and maybe that's who people know about. But there were other groups who really got persecuted, too, and the main ones were like gays and Gypsies and physically and mentally handicapped, and ummm, others.

Mr. Dennis: I have a response to that, but I'm gonna wait until you've all had, given voice, if you want to, but I've thought about that. Somebody else mentioned that last week. OK, Talia.

I was impressed that Mr. Dennis was able to restrain himself from commenting. Talia, who had written the sequence in the first reenactment about her father and grandfather, tacked the discussion's course back to the emotional impact the reenactment had levied on her personally. Kate's point, however, proved too powerful a current from which to be steered away, and from this point on, the discussion teetered precariously between the two topics raised. With few exceptions, the students either discussed their personal reactions to the reenactment and to the resonance of the Holocaust, or considered the dominance of the representation of Jews in its coverage; some students addressed both.

Talia: This is about Anne Frank. It's like I always knew about the story and stuff; I always knew how toward the end, they were taken, but until the reenactment, it's just like you were in there and you knew who they were, and you kind of felt like you were part of the family almost? So, when all of a sudden you hear the voices outside, you felt the fright that they felt. I actually sensed that it was different for me because I feel like, I just feel like it coulda happened to me or my father, and that scares me.

Mr. Dennis: So, the reenactment helped bring the reality of what happened to them home to you.

Talia: Yah, like I mean, at first, it was just like, you know, "Oh yah, they got taken," and I knew it must have been a very scary moment, but until I was in there actually feeling what they were feeling, I didn't know how scary, you know?

Gordy: I agree with Kate 'cause she said that it was only different people, too, but they probably don't show that many [different groups were persecuted] 'cause the funding was mainly from Jews, the money for all these films, and the Holocaust Museum and all that. I mean, I've been in there [the museum], and, it's kinda like, you focus on one person, but that's pretty good, 'cause it's not only Jews. You get a passport and you walk around, and you see what's happened to you, and you could be from other countries, you don't have to be Jewish. It's like I think it's mostly good, but like, most of the videos and most of these things are funded by Jewish people and that's why they don't have that much information on [other groups].

Mr. Dennis: Thanks, Gordy.

[Mr. Dennis calls on Jimmy, who played the part of Peter in the reenactment.]

Jimmy: I'm not really sure what to say, but umm, the Holocaust to me isn't about, umm, isn't about the Nazis picking on minorities, it's about hatred. And, I don't think we should think about who he mainly picked on, it's not about that. It's about people just forgetting about, forgetting about what we're really supposed to do here. We're not supposed to, I mean, [loud exhale]. This experience [loud sigh again]—it's so hard for me to talk about. It's like I was Peter, and when the Nazis came in, like, I don't know. I can't even talk right now. I don't know. I've grown so much in these past 2 weeks because of this. I just want to get out to people that this is a big deal; this is something that happened to real people and we can't forget about it. We just need, we always need to remember it and not let it happen again, 'cause you just have to really look at who was hurt by this, and we were all hurt by it.

[Jimmy sighs, feeling at a loss for words. He seems to finish off his remarks prematurely, giving up. Mr. Dennis waits a full 4 seconds before calling on the following student, a recent émigré from the former Soviet Union who speaks in heavily accented English.]

Tatiana: My great-grandma? She was in a concentration camp. They were like, they were standing in front of like a big hole—[her voice rises, and it is hard for her to continue] a big hole in the ground. And, they were about to be shot, and my [grand]mother? My great-grandma, she like pushed her [my grandma] down before the bullet came, and she was still alive. And, then her mom got shot, and everybody else did, and they all fell on top of her, like in the ground. And, like at night, or something, umm, I guess the guards were like, I don't know, sleeping or something. She like crawled out from under the bodies, and she escaped in the dark into like the forest to a ghetto in like a small, little Ukrainian town? And, umm, she lived with like my other grandma—she umm, they were also like hiding, and then the Germans came and they were like trying to find them, and she like threw some furniture and everything she could out the window, 'cause she was trying to like hit them before they came. And she was 18. And, like, umm, then one day, her whole head turned gray, and she was like taken away.

Mr. Dennis: Do you know where?

Tatiana: We don't know. They never really told us, and no one really talks about it much. . . . Also, I wanted to say about it that there's a difference between 6 million and several hundred thousands, and there's also a difference between people who die fighting in a war as soldiers, and children, like innocent people who don't choose to be in a war and who don't have anyone, who are just like taken away, and treated like animals. It's not the same thing as people who died like that. It's not the same thing, and it's not fair.

In response to Tatiana's claim of unfairness, Mr. Dennis talked briefly about the Nuremberg trials. He then turned the floor over to Debby, who had played Mrs. Frank in the reenactment. As a cast member, Debby, like Melinda and Jimmy, was perhaps more emotionally invested in the reenactment than her classmates who had been audience members. Debby was already crying as she began, and Mr. Dennis reassured her as she spoke, saying, "Take your time," to encourage her.

Debby: It's gonna be hard for me to talk. . . . Our homework assignment, for the people that were in the cast, was to read the diary over winter break. And, I remember reading it up at the lake, and I read it as a homework assignment, and I thought about it, but I couldn't, even though I saw Anne's picture on the front of it, and I saw pictures of where they lived, and I saw pictures of Otto that were included in the book I happened to pick up, . . . I didn't read it with these people having faces and these people being people. And, I guess it's been a week now since we've done it, and since then, I've reread parts of the diary, and it's so different to read it now because every time I read the words *Daddy* or *Mummy*, it's not just another person; it's not just someone in a book, even though I know that I'm not Edith Frank, and I don't have Anne as my daughter or anything like that, there's something in it that hits me so much deeper. And, I think that—in responding to what some people have said about not, umm, pinpointing the Jews and not showing anyone else—I don't think it's because of funding; I don't think that has anything to do with it. It might have some small thing to do with it, but I don't really think that's what it is. It has to do with the numbers and it has to do with the stories. I don't think it mattered that Anne Frank was Jewish. I don't think that had anything to do with it. I think all that mattered was that she was someone who had so much potential who can't be alive right now because of something that someone else did. And I don't think that her religion—it's not what made the book or it's not the reason her story is being told over and over again today.

. . . I think that people everywhere need to understand what's happened so that it doesn't happen again, but I think that in small ways, and in smaller numbers, it has happened again, and it keeps happening over and over again, and there's no way to show the whole world our Anne Frank reenactment, and there's no way to make some movie that you know everyone's gonna see. There's no way to do that, and there's no way to make the rest of the world feel like they were a part of that family for 40 minutes of their life, but it's so important. If it just made a difference to one person that saw that reenactment, if it just made a difference to one person, then it was worth the 4 months of work that I put into it. In a heartbeat I'd do it again. If they just thought about it for 15 minutes, then I'd do it again.

Mr. Dennis: As one who had the privilege of . . . reading the evaluations, it didn't change just one person. It touched deeply . . . many, *many* people, very, very deeply.

Talia: The reenactment affected me very much. For the next few days, I went around very depressed. I thought about it a lot after that day. All day, I couldn't concentrate—I couldn't think about just going to math. It stayed on my mind for the rest of the day, the rest of the week.

Kate: I think of the amount of hatred we have to have to ground people up, put them in gas chambers, like bulldoze bodies into big ditches [Kate's comment reveals a minor misunderstanding. Having seen the postliberation films of bulldozers burying corpses in mass graves, she assumes that these are atrocities in the act of being committed.] and mow people down with machine guns—I think it says a lot about human kindness that's like a whole, like all of us, not just the people who were living. I mean, because they were all willing; they were all willing to kill people. And I think it takes a lot of hatred in the world to be able to do this kind of thing, and to kill that many people. I mean this happened 50 years ago, but it's got repercussions today; it happens today. I don't know, I think it says a lot about people in general, . . . how people were willing to do that to others.

Melinda: When we first started, we had the previous cast come, and they were crying like every time they heard an air raid, . . . and we were like, why does this touch you so? . . . What's wrong with you guys? Why are you still caught up in this? And, like I read the diary, and Anne Frank getting taken away was just an ending to a story. It didn't really affect me. Then it finally hit me—they're gonna die. They're not going to live happily ever after. . . . It's amazing the change in me. I've become a lot more humble. My problems are petty compared to the things they went through . . . .

Clara: One thing I've thought about the last few weeks is umm, what I would do if I were in that situation. And, it scares me a lot to think that I might not have the courage to stand up for Jewish people or house them in my house. . . . Like the other day, I was talking to someone and they were like making fun of one of my friends, and I hardly even stood up for them, and so, it scared me, 'cause I thought, if I can't even stand up for one of my friends on a lower scale like that, what would I do if I was going to stand up to a bunch of Nazis and stuff?

Petal: I already thought about [how] could they do this to the Jews, and the only answer that makes sense to me is that maybe they just slowly degraded them until they didn't think of them as human anymore. But I still feel like how can people keep doing that?

Mr. Dennis: I'm going to leave that question open. Umm, let's hear from Gordy, Jimmy, then Edith—I mean Debby. [Mr. Dennis jokes with Debby, who had played Edith Frank in the reenactment.] You guys realize that you've talked yourselves out of a quiz.

The students continued to speak. Jimmy, frustrated and stuttering that he couldn't really say what he wanted to express, made a profound remark about Otto Frank: "Think how he felt, when he came back and found out that his wife was dead and his two daughters were dead." Debby, speaking in reference to her fellow actors, movingly related, "I still can't see the 6 million; I can only see 8." Kate mentioned that she used to believe that all people were really good. It was "something I really fiercely believed in," she said, until studying this unit, when the notion "that I could be wrong about something that means so much is just upsetting; that really struck a chord." Other students spoke, too, piping in comments about whether a Holocaust could happen in America or whether it already had.

A few minutes before the end of the period, Mr. Dennis closed the discussion, relaxing the intensity in the room first, by complimenting the students and commenting that he was glad I had my tape recorder running. He then addressed the difficult topic that had arisen, the uniqueness of Jewish victimhood in the Holocaust. In no uncertain terms, he spoke to the students, portentous in his tone and repeating himself to drive home his message:

> A couple of you asked, "Why so much emphasis on the Jews?" because, yes, almost 7 million were killed, but 5 million non-Jews were killed; [slowly, for emphasis, he repeats] 5 million non-Jews were killed, to make the total 11 to 12 million. And I was asked this question last week, and I've been asked this question almost every year. It's a very, *very* important question and it's a very good question.
>
> And my answer to this takes into account every other act of genocide, which means to kill a race, which in a sense doesn't apply here because the Jews were not a race, but were treated as such. When I think about the Native Americans, because on my mother's side, we have Native American ancestry, and the Armenians in Turkey in the 1900s, when I think about the Hutus and the Tutsis now in Zaire and Rwanda, to my knowledge, the only people in history who have been singled out for total annihilation

> were the Jews. The homosexuals in Nazi Germany were killed, sort of, in an orgy of violence. The Communists were killed in the same way; as many as they could get their hands on were killed. Social Democrats, social deviants, people who had birth defects or other kinds of physical or mental handicaps, yes, they were killed, too. But to my knowledge, no other group in the history of mankind has had it said of them by another group, "Our goal is the total, complete elimination of this group from the face of the earth." There was no Final Solution for the retarded in Germany; there was no Final Solution for the Gypsies and Slavs, or for the homosexuals. There was no Final Solution for the Communists; there was no Final Solution for the Social Democrats; there was no Final Solution for the criminals. These people were taken and, as compared with what happened to the Jews, in an almost haphazard way. There was no Final Solution for the Armenians; there was no Final Solution for the Native Americans. I am here because my ancestors were not completely wiped out; they were put on reservations. . . . Only once in history has anybody said, "We need a Final Solution for this problem, and the problem is represented by this group," and that was the Nazis to the Jews. Had the Americans and the British and the Russians not counterattacked when they did, where they did, the Nazis intended to wipe out all the other millions of Jews. They did not intend to fail. [Talia interrupted here, to say that the Nazis had failed. Her remark was murmured, almost as if she was saying it to reassure herself of that fact.] And Auschwitz would have been just the first of many, many camps they would have built. And remember Auschwitz, Treblinka, Sobibor, Belzec were not built for anybody else, specifically, except for the Jews. And then others were brought there and gassed as well, yes, Ukrainians, Lithuanians, Slavs, by the hundreds of thousands, that the Nazis also had little use for because as Kate said so well, they were different. But remember that, when someone says, "Yah, but many groups have been persecuted," that's right. "Many people have been picked on." That's right. "Hundreds of thousands of people have been murdered, *en masse*." That's right. But only one group in history, only one group, can say of them that there was a Final Solution to their problem. See you tomorrow.

Perfectly timed to the bell, Mr. Dennis dismissed the students. As they left, some students were still sniffling; others crept out in silence, and a few hung back to ask questions.

The range of reactions to this discussion among the four students I interviewed was fascinating. To the female students I interviewed, the experience of this conversation was momentous. For both Nina and Cindy, the sharing that went on between students was unusual, intimate, and powerful in cementing bonds. As Nina explained a few weeks later:

> With that conversation, we really got to share how we felt about it [the Holocaust], and we all felt that it was awful, and what Jimmy [who had played Peter] said really blew me off, and I just had to cry. He said that it's not only that it was Jews that died, that it was people. Just think of how America would die like that, just think of how awful it would feel. You just can't let that happen.

I have often wondered whether, in the wake of September 11, Nina recalled these reactions to the reenactment. While there are of course huge distinctions to be drawn between assembly-line mass murder under a totalitarian state and the terrorist acts levied against the United States, Nina had reckoned with the tragedies of human loss through this discussion. I can't help but imagine that this early learning resurfaced years later when the United States was attacked. Similarly affected by the discussion, Cindy reported:

> I liked that day. It was an important day, 'cause like, everybody just started crying, and like, *guys* were crying. . . . To hear what else people think about it, not just you—you know what you think about it and what your feelings are—but to hear other people's feelings and what they feel about it, . . . brought our class more together, 'cause like everybody let out their feelings.

For Geku and Gordy, however, the experience was less impressive. Geku had been surprised that the conversation went on for quite as long as it did; he felt it should have been curtailed earlier. Gordy, who had been deeply involved in it, felt that he had been misunderstood by his classmates. He hadn't meant his comments about the overrepresentation of Jews to be taken as something "negative." In an effort to absolve his sense that others thought of his remarks as "racist," Gordy explained to me weeks later what he had meant:

> More of them [Jews] were killed, and they probably just had enough of all the years of persecution. . . . Judaism is like a religion, and other people were just out of a country, and other coun-

> tries didn't have that much money and didn't care that much about the people. If you're like, I mean—there were Jews in America, there were Jews everywhere, so that's why probably there's more focus on them. My dad, he said this, and also my grandparents said that that's how it was. I was born in Hungary, and I know it was like a poor country and I don't think they have extra money to spend on research and museums and all that. They're trying hard to keep up the museums they have right now. But Jewish people are everywhere, rich countries, poor countries, so they have like funding.

When I asked Gordy how he had formulated these ideas, he reiterated that his Hungarian parents and grandparents held similar views. When I asked what he had thought about Mr. Dennis's strong statements made at the end of class, the ones historically justifying the special status of Jews, Gordy didn't remember to what I referred. Bearing out much research that suggests that students' home environments shape their understandings of the history they learn in school (Pesick, 1996; Seixas, 1993b), Mr. Dennis's closing remarks had not penetrated Gordy's thinking on these matters.

For the last session of the unit, Mr. Dennis showed the class the made-for-TV movie *The Wave* (Dawkins & Jones, 1981). Based on the experiences of a high school teacher (Jones, 1981), the movie portrays, as Mr. Dennis put it in his introduction, Jones's "2-week answer" to a student's single question about Nazism and the Holocaust, "How could so many go along with it?" In response, Jones had launched a simulation experience to teach his students the attractiveness of following a dictatorial leader even at the expense of sacrificing individual freedoms. In real life, Jones had been awed by the drive of the students to join and fortify the student organization he began in imitation of the Nazi Party. In the denouement of the movie, the teacher holds a student rally, unveiling the leader of the organization to have been, metaphorically, Adolf Hitler. The students are aghast and bereft. In the text of Jones's account, he had taught the students that "we would all have made good Germans," that, in other words, "fascism is not just something those other people did, . . . it's right here, in our own personal habits and way of life. Scratch the surface and it appears" (Jones 1981, pp. 21–22).

Watching the beginning of the film, Mr. Dennis's students made fun of the characters because of their outmoded dress and style of speech. Seeing the history teacher character studying textbooks late into the night, Gordy yelled out, "Mr. D, is that what you do?" Mimicking a student character in the movie, another student asked if he could be

Mr. Dennis's bodyguard. By the middle of the film, though, the students' teasing had stopped, and by the end, many of the students had understood the movie's message. Cindy told me that *The Wave* had affected her strongly:

> That was weird. I didn't understand it at the beginning, but then like at the end, when he said, "This is your leader," I understood like everything that was goin' on now, 'cause like this man turned all these people against each other, and it was just scary because it could happen again.

The moral messages she drew from the Holocaust unit were connected to having viewed *The Wave*. As she put it, "Don't be a follower," adding after a slight pause, "If you think you're higher than somebody, they're gonna prove you wrong one day, and you're gonna regret it."

As Geku told me, he had learned that the message of the Holocaust is, "Make sure you understand what you're following, who you're listening to, what you're reading 'cause there's propaganda out to trick you and take control of your life." As he had done consistently, Mr. Dennis fit the movie perfectly into two class periods, and no time was left for discussion. When the film ended, so had Mr. Dennis's unit on the Holocaust.

REFLECTIONS

Both Mr. Dennis's unit on the Holocaust and his teaching in general were highly dramatic. His reenactments were clearly built around drama, heightening his students' engagement with the material by involving them, literally, in its presentation. These plays, typically banished to the realm of the extracurricular in high schools, marked Mr. Dennis's course as the antithesis of "school as usual." Instead, they showed students how engaging historical material can be. In the Anne Frank reenactment, not only were there student actors and technicians creating the experience for other students (under Mr. Dennis's direction), but previous years' actors served as directors and assistant directors, role modeling for their younger peers an enthusiasm that historical engagement can generate even 2 and 3 years later.

And the plays themselves were highly impressive. Students, some of whom had never acted before, fell deeply into their roles, pouring their hearts, their bodies, and their considerable time into perfecting their performances. The technicians, set designers, and parent volunteers likewise functioned professionally, supporting the actors with elaborate costumes, sophisticated lighting, and intricate soundtracks.

As captivating as these performances was Mr. Dennis's lecturing style. Even at his most serious, dramatics dominated his lectures. His pacing, style, and movements effected a choreographed presentation, capturing and holding students' attention. The videos Mr. Dennis showed, whether excerpted or in full, were similarly selected for their powers to enchant through drama. Not unlike a well-crafted Hollywood movie or a July Fourth fireworks display, the representation of the Holocaust that resulted from Mr. Dennis's unit was thus, not surprisingly, a series of dramatic moments, acted by students, lectured by Mr. Dennis, or captured on film. His enacted curriculum, therefore, emplotted the Holocaust as a series of crystallized, climactic events. Rather than conveying the quotidian experience of living through the Holocaust, Mr. Dennis's dramatics etched powerful moments in high relief.

Like a fireworks show, too, Mr. Dennis's unit rarely paused for student reflection; only once in the midst of this emotionally riveting material did he carve out time for students to share their thoughts aloud. Furthermore, that this discussion was planned to occupy the space between a powerful video and a fill-in-the-blanks quiz in a single class period is indicative of how little reflection time Mr. Dennis had allotted. The unit Mr. Dennis constructed was emotionally rich and experientially thick, then, but it was nonetheless somehow intellectually thinner than it might have been. By allotting few venues in which students could reflect on the very intense experiences he constructed, Mr. Dennis didn't fully exploit the drama of his Holocaust unit. What it all could mean to students got lost in the excitement of the experience itself; the fireworks of Mr. Dennis's unit masked the ordinariness of its delivery model. For the most part, Mr. Dennis left it up to his audience to make sense of the experience, however breathtaking that experience was.

In this context, the one prolonged discussion the students commandeered was illuminating. As I mentioned above, the discussion was impressive for many reasons, among them the students' eloquence, self-confidence, and theatricality, and the teacher's willingness to allow the students the opportunity to voice their thoughts unmediated by him. As much educational research shows, having students talk in and of itself remains unusual in classrooms (Hess, 2002; Kahne, Rodriguez, Smith, & Thiede, 2000; Nystrand, Gamoran, & Carbonara, 1998). The complex interplay of factors that allowed for such a rich discussion must not be overlooked. While Mr. Dennis's mostly White and mostly upper middle-class students may indeed have been unusually articulate, they had also been trained to feel comfortable speaking in class. Mr. Dennis's classroom was clearly a place where student input had been encouraged and rewarded since the beginning of the year. His point system for student input and his consistent solicitation and praise for interesting contributions encouraged students to volunteer their thoughts, ultimately establishing a pattern whereby students participated without being asked. Moreover, Mr. Dennis's classroom was a place where students were taught to perform; thus the students had become used to their peers' holding spotlights. Added to this groundwork was the students' incentive that day of "talking [themselves] out of the quiz." Thus it was not surprising that in May, the time of their Holocaust unit, they were comfortable enough with one another to share deeply personal information during that discussion. I explicate these factors not in any way to diminish the masterful accomplishment on Mr. Dennis's part of evoking risky and authentic student comments, only to explain its context.

Especially revealing about the content of that discussion was the way in which, through this largely uninterrupted outpouring of feeling and thought, the students appropriated the enacted curriculum, breaking open some of the boundaries Mr. Dennis had intentionally set. In particular, Mr. Dennis's intended curriculum represented the Holocaust as a uniquely Jewish tragedy. Although there was some mention in his photocopied text of non-Jewish victims of the Holocaust, Mr. Dennis's in-class remarks focused almost exclusively on Jews. Unlike the other public school teachers I observed, in fact, Mr. Dennis explained to his students the term *Shoah*, expressing his own preference for that term over the more popular *Holocaust*. It was the students' discussion, and Kate's comments in particular, that exploded this aspect of Mr. Dennis's emplotment. By calling attention to non-Jewish, Nazi-targeted groups, Kate pushed the enacted curriculum toward a more universalized notion of Holocaust victimhood, which some of her fellow students embraced. Despite Mr. Dennis's closing remarks, the enacted curricula ended up holding in uneasy tension both Mr. Dennis's particularist and Kate's more universalistic approaches.

It was surprising to me that in the wake of this provocative discussion, Mr. Dennis's students were not assessed on their learning; the students had so successfully talked their way out of the quiz as to never be tested on the unit. This choice on Mr. Dennis's part conveyed contradictory messages, indicating that the Holocaust unit was either most valued or least valued by virtue of being the only one not tested that year. Aside from the brief Anne Frank "diary entries," Mr. Dennis used no formal mechanisms to assess whether his goals for student learning were being achieved.

Despite this lack of assessment, my surveys and interviews revealed that the students had indeed become acquainted with basic Holocaust information from his unit. Although most of the students, approximately two thirds of those I surveyed, reported having learned about the Holocaust before taking Mr. Dennis's class, they had clearly learned information from him as well. The average score on the informational section, where students were asked to define to the best of their abilities Holocaust-related terms, rose from 3.8 to 5.3 out of a possible 8 from the first to the second surveys. In addition, most of the students who turned in their second surveys felt that they had learned "a lot about the Holocaust" from Mr. Dennis's unit.

It was clear from their surveys, too, that they had appreciated their experience in Mr. Dennis's Holocaust unit, just as they had loved being in the rest of his course, an echo of the adulation his students expressed when I first walked into their classroom. All the students who submitted surveys responded in the affirmative when asked if they liked the course, and all reported that they would recommend the course to friends. And all said they would recommend that their friends study the Holocaust. As Nina told me in our closing interview, expressing what I suspect was a common feeling among Mr. Dennis's students, "I'm gonna miss him; I wish I could have him for the next 3 years." Geku remarked in his closing interview, "It kinda sucks that it's the end of the year [because it's been] a great class."

A more nuanced picture of what kind of information students gained and lacked at the conclusion of the unit emerged from my interviews with the four focus students, Geku, Gordy, Cindy, and Nina. Three of the four students felt that they had learned detailed historical information such as, according to Geku, the "number of deaths, how powerful it was, who the main leaders were, the sequence of things, [and] what happened first and last." Nina explained to me that before Mr. Dennis's unit she hadn't known "that there was a lot of ghettos . . . or how the concentration camps were involved"; she had known that the Nazis "had the Jews do a lot of crazy, ridiculous work," but not what, how, or under what circumstances, which she learned from Mr. Dennis. Cindy, though she "didn't really like the unit 'cause it was so sad," and though she reported being baffled by the packet of cartoon readings, nonetheless recognized that she "learned a lot . . . [about] how mean people can be to other people just because they think they're better than them, and [that] no one deserves to die in such cruel ways."

Of the four students, Gordy was the most critical of the unit, explaining that he didn't learn new information because he felt that the unit had treated the Holocaust too superficially. "It was maybe too much fun," Gordy told me, clarifying, "we did all this fun stuff, but I don't think we covered much information and we didn't go deeply. We didn't learn as much as we could [have]." Gordy had thought that maybe if he had been required to complete a research paper or had had the opportunity to hear a survivor speak, he would have been more challenged and learned more from the unit. Paradoxically perhaps, Gordy also thought that the Holocaust unit was too long. He felt that Mr. Dennis had "spent too much time" on the Holocaust at the expense of covering World War II more extensively. "We did one day for starting World War II, and we never finished the ending, and like, we didn't do the war in the Pacific, all that stuff," he complained. When I asked why Gordy thought Mr. Dennis might have dedicated so much time to the Holocaust, Gordy replied, "It's just a touchy subject—it's like a subject that you have to spend time on it."

Despite (or perhaps because of) this vision of Mr. Dennis's class, Gordy was one of the most adept at answering my factual questions. When asked, for example, which countries fought in World War II, Gordy could supply a comprehensive list of 12 countries, as could Geku, who supplied 6, whereas Nina and Cindy faltered uncomfortably. Nina could list 3 countries, Germany, France, and the United States, but then admitted that "the rest I'm not sure," volunteering "Russia," and "Denmark" with a puzzled look and a question mark in her voice. Cindy could only muster the country Germany, qualifying her meager answer by rolling her eyes, shrugging her shoulders, and apologetically telling me, "I don't remember any others; I just remember Germany for some reason." When asked how Hitler came to power, the four students provided answers that ranged from the detailed to the pedestrian, but all were correct.

The question that tripped up all four, though, was why Jews had been victimized during the Holocaust. In answer to that question, Cindy and Nina both guessed, Cindy looking to me for answers and Nina admitting her lack of knowledge. Geku provided a tautological answer, perhaps in order to avoid showing the gap in his knowledge, while Gordy's stereotyped preconceptions governed his factually incorrect account. The students' answers follow:

Cindy: 'Cause they were different maybe? Is it religion? Or, what they believe, their beliefs are different? Needed somebody to pick on?

Nina: I think that the Germans were jealous . . . I don't know. They probably just didn't have a reason to. They just felt like they had to have somebody to pick on so they picked on Jews.

Geku: Because they were part of Hitler's Final Solution to the so-called Jewish problem.

Gordy: Because they were an easy target; because there was such a big number and because they were easily identified. I mean like Blacks, they stick out of a crowd—like those rabbis with the long things and all that. They stick out of a crowd, and they're easy to spot. And also they were peace-loving people. I have a lot of Jewish friends, and they don't fight and all that. So they knew that if they would be mean to them, they wouldn't fight back.

None of these four students, in other words, felt confident answering the question of why Jews were persecuted. Although Mr. Dennis had talked about the history of anti-Semitism and it was mentioned in his packet of readings, the students had left his unit without an understanding of why Jews were persecuted. They also knew little about what distinguished Jews from Christians or of what the destroyed Jewish communities and cultures consisted. Mr. Dennis had inadvertently fallen into the trap of representing Jews in his unit solely through stereotyped, Nazi-propagated images or through images of emaciated Jewish victims. However, I think that at least some of the Nazi images were rejected because of the living, "normal" students in the class who identified themselves as Jews during the short time I observed.

The moral impact of the unit on the students is hard to gauge; especially difficult is assessing whether Mr. Dennis's goal of fostering rescuers in his class was met and in what ways. The surveys in this regard are rather unremarkable and somewhat unreliable. The student interviews revealed that all four students, when prompted, could provide moral lessons they considered the Holocaust to teach; whether those lessons will affect their attitudes or behavior in making decisions in their own lifetimes is impossible to ascertain. At least one student, Gordy, had traveled through the unit and its experiences with his opinions relatively unchallenged, despite what Mr. Dennis had specifically lectured. Gordy's stereotyped notions that world Jewry is both wealthy and passive remained unchanged.

And yet it does seem as though, for many other students in the class, the emotional impact of the Anne Frank reenactment would stay with them in some form for a long time, regardless of how it was articulated. And the tragedy of the Holocaust does seem to have been conveyed. Even Cindy, who readily told me that "black-and-white movies don't do anything for [her]" planned on watching *Schindler's List* in its entirety at home on the first day of her summer vacation. Watching the excerpts in class had been a powerful experience for her, and she wanted to understand "a little bit better." Despite the difficulty in assessing its moral impact, it is clear that Mr. Dennis's Holocaust unit moved some students and motivated at least one to learn more.

In the end, Mr. Dennis had used drama to provide his students with lots of emotionally gripping experiences in a short time-span, on top of which he used multiple modalities to embody them. Mr. Dennis's extensive range of activity formats, from play to lecture to film to newspaper to discussion, even to simulation (in the lead-up to the Anne Frank reenactment), allowed students access to this history through multiple venues, ultimately increasing their chances of "getting it." Most of the students had learned some information, even those who were well informed before taking his course, and many of the students were emotionally affected by what they experienced. Mr. Dennis's unit had left a powerful impression that most of the students thoroughly enjoyed regardless of the gaps in their knowledge it left. Like good theater, the unit had engaged them; the question that remains is whether good theater works, or doesn't, as education.

Chapter 5

The Inevitability of Lessons

It should come as no surprise, given the cases that comprise this book, that the teaching of the Holocaust looks very different in different teachers' hands. Historical information and moral messages change from teacher to teacher. In Mr. Zee's classroom, the Holocaust was a vehicle with which to teach students about interracial tolerance, respect for diversity, and personal empowerment, so much so that he didn't need historical information about the Holocaust, arguably even the Holocaust itself, to achieve his goals for student learning. Ms. Bess, however, wanted her students to gain humility in the face of atrocity, and to that end, she conveyed an enormous amount of information about the Holocaust through a simulation that assaulted her students' complacencies. Her simulation made students appreciate the humanity of Holocaust victims and the complexities of choices they faced. In short, all the cases presented here point to the tremendous disparities in the moral dimensions embedded in teachers' goals, materials, methods, personality styles, and ultimately, that elusive wholeness called their teaching.

Moreover, this research showed that students studying about the Holocaust come away with very different lessons depending on their teachers' enactments of this history. There is variation not only from class to class in terms of the lessons students learn, but also from student to student, since they come to class with already embedded ideas and assumptions about history in general and this history in particular. In Mr. Dennis's class alone, Cindy learned the lesson "Don't be a follower," having never learned about the Holocaust previously. Gordy, by contrast, understood Holocaust memory as perpetuated by the supposed wealth of world Jewry, an idea he had inherited from his family before entering Mr. Dennis's class.

No one familiar with the educational enterprise will be startled by this state of affairs. We know that students, like teachers, bring to class with them personal predilections, ideological convictions, and historical conceptions forged by their experiences of race, class, gender, family, education, circumstance, and religion. That they learn from the same material different lessons is not surprising. Human variability, in the fullness of its possibilities, comes with the territory of teaching and learning generally, not only with teaching and learning about the Holocaust.

The situation does raise important questions, though. If teachers are teaching different lessons about the Holocaust, and students are learning different (even occasionally objectionable) lessons from or despite their teachers, are then the lessons of the Holocaust so malleable as to be meaningless? Should the Holocaust be called so readily into service as moral education, given the variability of its messages? Should Holocaust education be mandated at all? Currently, many states across the country officially authorize that Holocaust education be taught in public schools, and those mandates usually position Holocaust education as an opportunity for moral education, chances for teachers to teach clear-cut moral values that, at least on the surface, would seem to garner agreement across diverse American groups (Novick, 1999). A close examination of the situation in California, the state wherein the previous cases were set, reveals the flexibility inherent in Holocaust messages at the level of policy, that is, even before policy hits the turbulent waters of classroom realities (Cuban, 1988, 1990).

MANDATING MORALITY

The History–Social Science Framework for California Public Schools (Department of Education California, 1988) was the first curricular framework to recommend study of the Holocaust in California schools. Although the framework was not tied to formal state tests, it nonetheless had an impact. According to its drafters, students were meant to study this genocide "in-depth" (p. 88), covering specific historical information:

> Students should learn about *Kristallnacht*; about the death camps; and about the Nazi persecution of Gypsies, homosexuals, and others who failed to meet the Aryan ideal. They should analyze the failure of Western governments to offer refuge to those fleeing Nazism. They should discuss abortive revolts such as that which occurred in the Warsaw Ghetto, and they should discuss the moral courage of Christians such as Dietrich Bonhoeffer and Raoul Wallenberg who risked their lives to save Jews. (p. 87)

Embedded in the historical information are moral goals, specifically those related to "the role of the individual in mass society" (p. 87). The framework drafters wrote that students should consider, "What is the ethical responsibility of the individual when confronted with governmental actions such as the 'Final Solution' and other violations of human rights?" (p. 88). The inclusion of righteous "Christians" in the list of suggested topics provides one implicit (if partial) answer. Clearly, students are meant to see rescuers as models to emulate, just as they are meant to see Nazis as those to excoriate. Two general goals of the state framework help orient careful readers of the document toward this answer as well. In a section analyzing aspects of historical literacy, the framework developers declare that students, through study of history, should both "develop a keen sense of historical empathy" (p. 12) and come to "recognize the sanctity of life and the dignity of the individual," (p. 14) which presumably means empathizing with and recognizing the sanctity of victims' lives.

The Katz Bill, passed by the California state legislature in 1992, further affirmed the importance of teaching about the Holocaust in California public schools by mandating the provision of reimbursement funds to local school districts for costs incurred in complying with the measure. The bill, in other words, provided the financial incentive the initial framework had lacked. The wording of the bill echoes the moral goals specified in the state framework's general goals for history education, elaborating only slightly in tying them directly to study of the Holocaust. Section 3(a) of the measure begins,

> The Legislature recognizes and affirms the importance to pupils of learning to appreciate the sanctity of life and the dignity of the individual. . . . Pupils must develop a respect for each person as a unique individual and understand the importance of a universal concern for ethics and human rights. (chap. 763, p. 94-160)

The text continues, arguing for "the importance of teaching our youth ethical and moral behavior specifically relating to human rights violations, genocide issues, and slavery as well as the Holocaust" (sec. 3[b]). The Holocaust is here positioned as a human rights issue, roughly equivalent to slavery and other instances of genocide rather than as a unique historical event. Both the Katz Bill and the History–Social Science State Framework thus mandate the teaching of the Holocaust with an eye toward the same moral goals. Explicitly, the "sanctity of [human] life" and the "dignity of the individual" are espoused; implicitly, the Holocaust is to be taught as an event with universal moral implications, profound historical resonance, and multiple groups of victims.

According to the historian Peter Novick (1999), "the problem with such lessons," or at least one problem with them, "is not that they're wrong but that they're empty, and not very useful" (p. 240). How we interpret what it means to act to preserve the "dignity of the individual" or maintain the "sanctity of human life" varies widely according to the value sets of our chosen communities. Indeed, their generality or, for Novick, their vapidity, allows them to garner agreement across the political spectrum and enables them to be propelled into the wording of mandates. Novick elucidates the seeming incompatibility between a generalized lesson and its specific prescriptive or behavioral implications. As he puts it, "What . . . does one do with [such a] lesson?" (p. 240). Does "maintaining the sanctity of human life," for example, imply that we ought to support the bombing of abortion clinics, the expansion of gay and lesbian rights, or legislation proposed to increase gun control? The usefulness of such lessons, for Novick, is limited in part by the breadth of their applicability to incompatible political agendas.

The assumption behind both the Katz Bill and the History–Social Science State Framework, by contrast, is that these lessons and therefore their teaching are somehow easy or at least straightforward. The moral lessons themselves, after all, are mandated in the same way that historical coverage of the period is. According to the Katz Bill, teachers are encouraged to draw on a multiplicity of official curricula in designing their units, as if not only all teachers, but all Holocaust curriculum writers would naturally agree on these particular moral tenets or ideological positions. Specifically, the text of the bill recommends use of materials "developed by publishers of nonfiction, trade books, and primary sources, or other public or private organizations, that are age-appropriate" (Chap. 763, p. 94-160). A public relations letter sent out by then governor Pete Wilson's office 2 days after the signing of the bill—cynics would say to attract Jewish votes in an election year—summarized that "schools [should] use available materials from private Holocaust education organizations such as the Anti-Defamation League, the Simon Wiesenthal Center, the Martyrs Museum of the Jewish Federation and the Holocaust Center of Northern California." The drafters and supporters of the bill seemed to assume that the lessons of the Holocaust were so inextricably bound to the historical material that the various curricula available in these organizations would all convey the same lessons as those advocated in the state framework and legislative bill.

Of course these Holocaust education organizations are not all alike, nor do their published curricula share the same moral messages about the Holocaust. The curriculum that Mr. Zee used, Facing History and Ourselves (Stern-Strom, 1982), was universalistically oriented, focusing much attention on non-Jewish victims of the Holocaust and dedicating a little more than one fifth of the text to another instance of genocide altogether, the massacre of Armenians by the Turks. By contrast, the published curriculum from which Mr. Jefferson drew his sources was

The Holocaust and Genocide: A Search for Conscience (Furman, 1983), which emphasizes the Holocaust as being primarily about Jewish victims, integral to an understanding of Jewish history, and unique in its implications. Accordingly, the historical information provided by these two texts also carries different moral implications. This level of nuance, if understood by the state legislators, was at least not formally recognized in either the framework or the bill mandating Holocaust education.

The curriculum developers, in turn, seem to make the same kind of assumptions as those revealed in the state mandate. In listing their moral goals for student learning, they similarly assume that the moral lessons themselves are clear and that teachers will implement them relatively intact. In the introduction to *The Holocaust and Genocide* (Furman, 1983), former New Jersey governor Thomas Kean proclaims, "The most important lesson of the Holocaust is that each individual is responsible not only for his or her own actions, but for the consequences which these actions hold for others" (p. xix). In the same introduction, Furman, the curriculum's editor, lists different moral questions he thinks central to study of the Holocaust:

1. How do we reconcile the belief in God with the Holocaust?
2. Why did the nations of the world and our major institutions respond so passively to the Holocaust?
3. What keeps a people from descending into the practice of genocide?
4. Why is it so difficult to act out of conscience? (p. xxii)

Furman's question format suggests the complexity of any answers, which, nonetheless, he assumes will be discussed in classrooms using his curriculum. Other moral questions follow every short reading selection in this voluminous compilation of sources, such that taken as a whole, it covers a huge moral terrain, far more elaborate than those suggested by the mandate. This text, then, illuminates what is clearly the case across all published curricula about the Holocaust: their moral messages, explicit and implicit, are far more numerous, nuanced, and complex than the mandate recognized or than the curriculum developers indicated.

Although some of the explicit moral messages of the state framework, Katz Bill, and various official curricula could be linked thematically under the umbrella concepts of "the sanctity of life," or "right action under difficult circumstances," there are inevitably areas of divergence between their moral messages and in some cases, wide gaps between them. By virtue of having recommended a variety of published curricula, the state mandate ensured that teachers could not be faithful to the mandate's stated moral goals alone. Even had the four teachers I observed used the same published curriculum, their intended curricula (or what they planned to do with that published curriculum) would no doubt have taken radically different forms, not only because of the multiplicity of moral messages embedded in any single, official curriculum, but also because of the nature of teacher adaptation itself (Ben-Peretz, 1990). The distance between the official curricula they did choose and their individual enactments supplies evidence enough for the power of teacher adaptation. Although curriculum developers, like state legislators, may assume a clarity of moral messages and a tight linkage between the stages of curricular implementation, in fact the structural autonomy built into our system of schooling ensures variation in the process of curricular transformation.

Thus it is not surprising that the teachers' enacted curricula—what happened in their classrooms as Holocaust education—varied tremendously, conveying far more complex moral messages than either their official curricula or they themselves anticipated. These teachers' expectations of their students, their conceptions of learning, their visions of the subject matter, and their understanding of their particular contexts encouraged them to adapt their official curricula in very different ways, such that their enacted curricula conveyed very different messages about the nature of the Holocaust, the concept of Judaism, and the representation of history—this despite the fact that some of the teachers' explicitly articulated moral goals for student learning were similar. Mr. Zee and Mr. Dennis both wanted their students to become more willing to intercede on behalf of the unjustly oppressed or victimized, more likely to become "rescuers" given the opportunities posed by modern American society. In other words, it might be generalized that even when a high degree of uniformity exists across teachers' stated moral goals for their intended curricula, there may be little to no resemblance in the moral lessons related across their enacted curricula. The complexity of moral messages inherent in any history unit make the connections necessarily loose within a single teacher's transformation of the intended into the enacted curriculum, all the more so across multiple teachers' adaptations.

In sum, at many levels of the curricular transformation—from framework and bill to official curricula, from planned lessons to classroom enactments, from classroom encounters to what students learned—are a set of faulty assumptions about the nature of Holocaust history and its moral dimensions. At the level of the state mandate for Holocaust education and at the levels of the official, intended, and enacted curricula, the assumption prevails that the moral dimensions of Holocaust study are, if not self-evident, then at least easily implemented. Although each curricular transformation of moral information is presumed to be straightforward by framework drafters, state legislators, official curriculum developers, possibly administrators, and in some cases, even teachers, the multiplicity of options at every level complicates the picture significantly. Therefore, a single mandate to teach about the Holocaust in California public high schools produced radically different curricular enactments, accompanied by widely divergent moral messages that are learned by students. Although these four highly regarded teachers were all teaching about the Holocaust before the mandate appeared, the point remains: Teaching about the same subject matter takes radically different forms in different teachers' hands and in different school and classroom contexts, and learning about the Holocaust is likewise various and complex, bound to be different from student to student.

In terms of Holocaust education, then, these cases call into question what it means to have a mandate in the first place. While the mandate may be significant, its import is mostly symbolic rather than directive; it catalyzes but cannot control. The moral goals of the state framework and Katz Bill, no matter how narrowly defined, are not simple to enact. The seemingly straightforward objectives of imbuing students with a sense of the sanctity of life or the dignity of the individual, indeed of moral goals in general, are not easily accomplished by any means and certainly not within the extreme flexibility of the process of curricular implementation. Morality, or at least generalized moral claims, cannot be educationally mandated. The mistake underpinning the mandate was to regard the moral lessons of the Holocaust as simple. This study, over and over again, reveals that, in practice, they are not.

THE ILLUSION OF SIMPLICITY

The idea that Holocaust lessons are anything but simple, that instead they are politically volatile, historically flexible, and various across groups, finds resonance in Peter Novick's (1999) book, *The Holocaust in American Life* (as mentioned above). Having carefully dissected the rhetoric of moral messages swirling around the Holocaust in American popular and political discourse, Novick concludes that there might not be anything "useful" to be drawn from the Holocaust (p. 263). One could imagine him criticizing those who draw simplistic lessons from the Holocaust on the same grounds that I have critiqued Mr. Zee's curriculum: In seeking out lessons from the Holocaust, we are looking for happy endings where there were painfully few, redeeming what was ultimately tragic. In so doing, we "Americanize" the Holocaust, molding it to conform to dominant tropes in our culture, sugarcoating its horrors and making digestible that which *should* stick in our throats.

Novick (1999) classifies the types of lessons typically drawn from the Holocaust into two categories. First are those that tend to be general in nature, such as the ones identified above in the California mandate. In this context, the Holocaust serves as a "salutary reminder of the presence of evil in the world" (p. 239). Other examples of generalizeable lessons include those "fundamental American values" that the Holocaust Memorial Museum in Washington, D.C., promotes, "the inalienable rights of individuals, the inability of government to enter into freedom of the press, freedom of assembly, freedom of religion and so forth" (p. 240). In Novick's second category are those lessons that are more "pointed," by which he means more politically targeted. In this second category are lessons that might plausibly draw on the Holocaust to promote particular political agendas, such as gun control or the right to bear arms, pro-life or pro-choice movements, opposing the fur industry and stem cell research. Put differently, people exploit the emotional power of the Holocaust to promote their own goals, and the Holocaust becomes a metaphorical bullhorn, amplifying their positions. Novick's proposition is borne out in this study: What Elizabeth Miranda and Gordy understood from their classroom enactments of Holocaust education was certainly driven at least in part by their familial and religious heritages. If we're shaped like hammers, we will tend to see nails, as the old saying goes.

Putting aside for the moment the considerable difficulties in teaching about the Holocaust and indeed any morally laden history, the question remains of what ought educators do with its so-called lessons. How ought teachers adjudicate between competing lessons? For Novick, what distinguishes "some lessons as proper or legitimate" from "others as improper or illegitimate" finally comes down to personal resonance, the question of whether an analogy between the Holocaust and another event or cause "click[s] . . . or doesn't" (1999, p. 243), making decisions about suitable lessons even more arbitrary. For Novick, the Holocaust, like all historical events, bears no lessons in and of itself and thus suggests no objective criteria for assessing what people might draw from it.

Novick's conclusions must be startling, if not dispiriting, to educators who believe that history, or education itself, is fundamentally about providing lessons. After all, if the Holocaust bears no lessons, why teach about it in our schools? Does the claim that the lessons of the Holocaust are so broad as to be ineffectual really vitiate their being taught? Does the fact that some of the lessons of the Holocaust are so general as to require personal judgment about their implementation necessarily imply that they ought not be taught? Does the notion that there is no national consensus over the particular lessons mean that those lessons also should not be taught?

Even granting Novick's claims about the malleability of the Holocaust's uses, however, does not release educators from the moral consequences of their teaching. In other words, whether moral lessons are intrinsic or extrinsic to Holocaust history per se, they are inextricable from Holocaust education. Here, the concerns of historians engaged at the level of theory depart radically from those of educators facing students in the classroom. Whether a teacher asks him- or herself "which moral lessons *of* the Holocaust will I be striving to teach?" or "which moral lessons will I be striving to teach *through* the Holocaust?" may be theoretically important, but it is practically of little consequence. The distinction between whether the Holocaust bears moral lessons intrinsically or has moral lessons imposed on it extrinsically matters little. In schools, teachers must choose what to teach about the Holocaust, ideally considering the reasons behind those decisions and, thus, what representations of the Holocaust will be constructed in their classroom. These choices are accompanied by a host of intended and unintended moral meanings. Unlike Holocaust history in the abstract, then, Holocaust education—the portrait of the Holocaust conveyed through narrative—necessarily evokes moral lessons, explicated or not.

THE INEVITABILITY OF LESSONS

The abundance and inevitability of moral meanings embedded in Holocaust education may not be equivalent to drawing lessons, however. The distinction lies perhaps in the fragmentary and implicit nature of the former and the summative and explicit nature of the latter. Indeed, as I mentioned in chapter 1, the historian Deborah Lipstadt upholds this distinction in her writings on Holocaust education. Lipstadt (1995) explains that in teaching about the Holocaust, she teaches "the particulars" and "let[s] the students apply them to their own universe" and that "they never fail to do so" (p. 26). In advocating that teachers teach only historical information about the Holocaust and thus allow students to draw from that information their own lessons, she is subscribing to the notion that the two are separable, that the moral meanings embedded in her information on the one hand are distinct from explicit lessons she (or her students) draw from it on the other.

The dissimilarity is important. It is the difference between Mr. Zee's course casting the Holocaust in highly individualistic terms—what might be called a moral orientation that patterned the content—and the list of "big ideas" he and his students drew up at the end of their course, what might be called his list of lessons. Lipstadt, I suspect, would disparage the paucity of Mr. Zee's informational coverage, arguing that without historical information, students can't be expected to draw their own lessons. I suspect, too, that Lipstadt would disapprove of Mr. Zee's emphasis on individualism, and therein lies the flaw in her approach to Holocaust teaching.

Although the distinction between implied moral meanings and explicated moral lessons is important, as I see it, its importance can be easily overemphasized. As Mr. Zee's course highlights, informational coverage itself communicates moral meanings, meanings that can function as lessons regardless of whether they're defined as such and that ultimately may bear more weight in students' perceptions than explicated lessons. In this study, both implicit meanings and explicit lessons bore consequences for what morals students learned from studying the Holocaust, the major pedagogical difference between them being solely their level of explicitness. Whereas Lipstadt argues that historical information should be covered explicitly while moral lessons should be communicated only implicitly, I am claiming that the gulf between the two is not as wide as it appears. The teaching of the facts themselves carries important moral lessons; the shape of the information matters.

THE MORAL GEOGRAPHY OF HOLOCAUST EDUCATION

In this study, three significant continua emerged on which that information can be mapped, thereby providing further insight into how the teachers represented the Holocaust in their classrooms. The first continuum may be thought of as the *emplotment* (White, 1992) of the Holocaust; I borrow this term from narrative theory to convey the importance of the "story line" or "plot" constructed about the Holocaust in the enacted unit. The second and third continua that emerged are the image of the historical actors within that story and the representations of history communicated by it. All three continua conveyed moral messages. While these messages were implied rather than explicated, they were nonetheless powerful. Rather than conveying random or fragmented messages, these constructions of the subject matter marked consistent and meaningful patterns that influenced students' understandings.

Emplotment

How a teacher storied the Holocaust, as tragic or redemptive, unique or universal, insular or expanded, conveyed moral lessons. Mr. Zee, for example, ended his full-semester course by showing videotaped testimony of Holocaust rescuers and contemporary Americans who sought social justice actively and (at least seemingly) individually. In that way, the narrative of the course constructed the Holocaust as having a happy ending; at the very least, it implied that the Holocaust had a substantial silver lining. In addition, throughout the semester, Mr. Zee tended to universalize the subject matter, representing the Holocaust not as a uniquely Jewish event but as one having both numerous groups of victims and universal implications for humanity. His orientation was similarly expansive in that he taught about the Holocaust as having parallels, echoes, and reverberations throughout history, rather than being insular, barring comparison with other events across time. Rarely, in other words, did he discuss the Holocaust in historical isolation.

Given this confluence of patterns, Mr. Zee's emplotment of the Holocaust might be called "Americanized" (Alter, 1981; Flanzbaum, 1999; Rosenfeld, 1995), insofar as his representation emphasized individual achievement over combative circumstances—the American mythos of the rugged individual overcoming adversity. It concluded with a triumphant message rather than a tragic one, and it stressed inclusiveness rather than exclusivity, multiculturalism rather than Jewishness, racism rather than anti-Semitism.

Image of Historical Actors

The second continuum concerned the representation of historical actors in this history, for example, whether Jews were individualized or collectively represented, normalized or exoticized, personalized or abstracted. A unit's placement along these lines affected the perception of Jews by the mostly non-Jewish students in the classes I observed. Here a brief juxtaposition of Mr. Jefferson (described in chapter 1) and Ms. Bess illustrates these polarities.

Mr. Jefferson, in lecturing about "the Jews" within Holocaust history, rarely prompted his students to consider them as individuals with a wide variety of beliefs, practices, languages, origins, traditions, experiences, and attitudes. Likewise, he tended to depersonalize Jews; he rarely told stories about single Jews' experiences, infrequently shared survivor testimony, and only once discussed his own Jewish identity, thus missing opportunities to individualize, personalize, and perhaps help to "normalize" Jews in this history, that is, make them seem less foreign to the non-Jewish students in his class.

In Ms. Bess's class, by contrast, because each student was assigned to play one or two Jewish characters, Jews were highly normalized (over the course of the semester); the students came to see themselves as Jews when simulating and thus came to associate Jews and Jewishness with their own and their peers' attributes, diversities, normalcy. The historical content in Ms. Bess's simulation was also highly personalized, overlaid as it was with the personal lives of the students in the class. And because her students "experienced" 60 Jewish characters' decisions/fates, there was a remarkable balance achieved between Jews' being individualized on the one hand and collectively represented on the other. Unlike the plan of Mr. Jefferson's course, the structure of Ms. Bess's simulation enabled the students to see the threads of human experience within the fabric of communal atrocity.

Similar tensions played out in the representation of other groups within Holocaust history. Not only victims, but also victimizers, collaborators, resisters, bystanders, and rescuers were all individualized or collectively represented, normalized or exoticized, personalized or abstracted—that is, if their roles were included in the first place. (As may be recalled, the category of bystanders was structurally invisible in Ms. Bess's simulation.) As with the representation of Jews and other victim groups, each decision on these axes bore moral weight, inching students either toward or away from an ability to see themselves in those positions.

Representations of History

In terms of the third continuum, the examples of Mr. Dennis's and Mr. Jefferson's units illuminate the tensions involved in representing history. In Mr. Dennis's unit, the content, especially the Anne Frank reenactment, allowed the students to see history as based on contingency rather than as inevitable and as infused by individual decisions rather than dictated by larger societal forces. Mr. Jefferson, by contrast, tended to communicate Holocaust history as inevitable, the product of broad and sweeping sociopolitical and economic forces. It is not surprising that Elizabeth Miranda's religious casting of this history went unchallenged in Mr. Jefferson's room as her image of history as fated or destined found resonance in his style of teaching, his narrating events in succession as though no other possibilities existed. The idea of history embedded within the emplotment carries moral weight, then, in its implications for the efficacy of human agency amid larger forces.

The Three Continua Concluded

Indeed, all three of these continua cast Holocaust history in particular ways that resonate morally, influencing students' understandings of this history, of themselves, and of others as actors in history. Moreover, these continua are important not only for what they illuminate about Holocaust education, but also for their theoretical applicability to the teaching of other morally laden historical episodes. These features—the emplotment of the Holocaust, the image of actors within it, and the representation of history communicated—when phrased in terms of their more general concerns, contain pivotal questions for how teachers might think about representing all of their history units. The features point to questions that can be asked of any history curriculum, namely:

- What emplotment makes sense for this historical event or episode, and why?
- How ought the various groups of historical actors involved be represented?
- How am I representing history itself?

The information garnered to answer these questions determines, at least in part, a unit's moral terrain, and the opposite is also true. The moral answers to these questions determine, at least in part, a unit's informational coverage.

In the process of constructing their curricula, teachers necessarily answer these moral/informational questions, consciously or not. In constructing their units, teachers choose emplotments of the Holocaust, determining, for example, whether their coverage will end with the plight of Jewish refugees at the end of World War II, the dropping of the atomic bombs on Hiroshima and Nagasaki, the liberation of the concentration camps, or filmic representations of rescue and resistance. Teachers govern, at least in part, the representation of historical actors, too, whether, for example, victims will be valorized, bystanders will be overlooked, or rescuers will be overemphasized. Will perpetrators be understood primarily as "eliminationist anti-Semites" turned into "willing executioners" (Goldhagen, 1996), as opportunistic "neighbors" (Gross, 2001), or as "ordinary men" (Browning, 1992), ordinary human beings? Teachers make choices about how Novick's first and second sets of lessons will be addressed as well—the generalized ideas about human behavior and the more particular politicized parallels. Given that teachers inevitably make such curricular decisions, it seems clear to me that they need to be provided with adequate time and resources to make such decisions thoughtfully.

DISCUSSING LESSONS

Not only are lessons inevitable in Holocaust teaching, but students' interpretations of those lessons are similarly inevitable and need to be discussed. Without classroom discussion, how can teachers know if and when students are drawing (or imposing) distinctly objectionable lessons? Elizabeth Miranda, after all, did not express during class time her opinions that Jews were "fated" to die during the Holocaust. When Gordy did mention his vaguely anti-Semitic notions of the wealth of world Jewry in class, Mr. Dennis eloquently and soundly quashed them, or at least he thought he had. Mr. Dennis couldn't have known that a few weeks later during an interview, Gordy wouldn't even recall his teacher's strong remarks on the subject, adhering instead to the dispositions he inherited from his family.

I do not blame Mr. Dennis or Mr. Jefferson for not mining their students' thinking. Given the ratio of teachers to students in public schools, it should come as no surprise that teachers do not have the time to gauge individual student learning. Yet leaving the lessons implied rather than explicated, embedded rather than discussed, risks misleading our students morally and misinforming them simultaneously.

The inevitability of lessons, combined with the inevitability of students' and teachers' bringing to their classrooms their own values, ideas, and background influences, ought to push us, both teachers and students, to discuss openly the moral implications of the Holocaust: its lessons, its emplotment, and its embedded representations. And I believe we ought to discuss them in some detail, to probe not only the generalizations that masquerade as having widespread support, but also their specific political implications, their various interpretations, and even the sources of students' and teachers' clashing interpretations. What I am advocating recalls Gerald Graff's (1992) argument that we ought to be "teaching the conflicts." We should not let the illusion of moral consensus around the Holocaust dampen our debates over it.

The justifications for doing so are simple. In learning to compare, contrast, evaluate, and dissect our moral values, we stand to learn how to think critically, and in learning to think critically, we stand to gain morally (Simon, 2001). And through both processes, we come to know one another and ourselves more fully.

In this study, the discussion Mr. Dennis allowed his students to commandeer in reaction to the Anne Frank reenactment came closest to what I am recommending occur in classes. In that session, the students grappled with what might be called "metaquestions" about the Holocaust. They focused their attention on questions of representation and implication. They addressed, for example, Should Holocaust representations focus primarily on Jewish victims, and if so, why? If not, why not? In what ways is the Holocaust unique or universal in its implications? And how is the Holocaust meaningful personally? Unknowingly, Mr. Dennis's students were wrestling with some of Novick's (1999) central claims and proving the point that such discussions can be tremendously powerful learning experiences, opportunities that engage students' moral apparatuses, hone their critical thinking abilities, and deepen and complicate their interrelationships in healthy, if complex, ways.

I imagine that conversations like the one in Mr. Dennis's class could be exceedingly fruitful in most if not all Holocaust units. Suppose that the discussion could occur under the direction of a teacher who had tremendous background knowledge as well as the discussion-leading skills of Mr. Zee. Add to the picture students who had covered as much informational and moral terrain as had Ms. Bess's class and who had been cultivated in as trusting and inquiring a classroom climate as Mr. Dennis's. Students in that highly idealized context could, as did Mr. Dennis's, reveal, discuss, and negotiate deep conflicts of value that are both personally and societally meaningful. I can't help but fantasize about what Elizabeth Miranda might have gained from such a conversation or what Vince might have contributed.

My aim for such discussions would not be to build consensus around particular societal values; rather, I believe such discussions would allow individual students to see beyond the boundaries of their own visions. My hope is that the discussion in Mr. Dennis's class could serve as a model, not only of the kind of discussion that could occur about the Holocaust's so-called lessons—the "grand" question of what do we learn from all this—but also of the kind of discussion that could occur about other fraught moral questions that interlace all of Holocaust history, indeed all of history.

Teachers, too, could benefit from having such discussions among themselves as a way to prepare for the difficulties of leading these conversations in their own classrooms. The surprised reactions of the teachers I studied when they read a draft of my text suggest that, in the context of carefully designed professional development opportunities, such discussions could well aid them in considering their course and unit constructions as well as their moral roles in the classroom.

THE TEACHERS' REACTIONS

When Mr. Zee had read the chapter about his course, he was shocked. To him, the chapter was a "truth-telling," but the "truths" were hard for him to face in print. Reading his students' reactions and my observations caused him to reevaluate his teaching of Facing History and Ourselves, to stop and take stock of his expectations. In his first few years of teaching, he explained, he had overemphasized historical information and the dissemination of facts at the expense of building community and having a moral impact. While he was not disappointed to have excelled at these latter goals in the course I observed, he realized that his desire to "parent" these students had exacted a price in the intellectual growth he could have fostered. He explained to me that the Identity Projects had revealed to him how "emotionally needy" so many of his students were, and in response, he had chosen to create a classroom environment that would not threaten any of their academic insecurities. The chapter he read spurred him to consider whether he had moved too far in that direction.

Ms. Bess, too, while generally pleased with the account of her class, had never before considered some of the moral complexities embedded in her simulation. She had never thought about her representation of Jews or the concept of emplotment, for example. And though she was aware of some of the costs of simulating, she had never heard them articulated in such detail.

I bring up these teachers' reactions not because I wish to criticize what may seem to be their blindness, but rather because their reactions reflect the isolation of professionals built into the structure of public schools. In fact, I do not consider the teachers I studied to have been ignorant or negligent in their treatments of the Holocaust. On the contrary, I have tremendous respect for their accomplishments and struggles. These teachers simply hadn't had the chance to think through certain aspects of their curricula, nor had anyone observed their teaching in recent years or helped them consider these or related issues. Mr. Zee summarized a feeling common to all the teachers: "In all my years of teaching," he told me, "no one has looked this closely at my work" (personal communication, March 24, 1998). As successful, experienced professionals, these teachers were more commonly put in the position of training other teachers than in the position of reflecting on their own practices. Ironically, their isolation, a well-documented facet of the teaching profession as a whole, was exacerbated by their very status as experienced professionals.

To further the point, I can't help imagining how fruitful a conversation among the case study teachers would have been. There is no question in my mind that were these teachers to share their materials, activities, and course structures, or more profoundly, their fundamental philosophies of teaching and learning, moral education, and Holocaust history, all would inevitably question their own assumptions, deepen their thinking, and reflect on their own teaching. For now, this work stands in the place of those conversations; I hope, though, that in the future, it will catalyze them.

Teachers, even experienced ones, need to be afforded opportunities to observe one anothers' teaching, to discuss with researchers, administrators, and one another the moral dimensions of their work, in short to continue growing professionally. This model of teachers' sharing their wisdom, not only about their Holocaust units, but also about their teaching in general, constitutes the best option for state legislators, curriculum developers, school administrators, and teachers to embrace as a response to mandates and the malleability of curricular transformation. While structuring time for teachers to have such conversations could not ensure that a "one best system" of teaching the Holocaust would be found, developed, or agreed upon, the discussions would enable teachers to consider the range of options available to them, allowing them to make wiser curricular choices in view of their particular contexts and goals. Had the teachers in this study had opportunities to reflect on their own and one another's teaching, maybe they would have discussed their notions of emplotment, considered their representations of historical groups of actors, investigated the social psychological dimensions of bystanders' and perpetrators' behaviors more deeply, or more generally explored the moral impacts of their teaching styles and informational content on students.

The questions this research raises, in their applicability across the history curriculum, easily become unwieldy for any teacher to tackle, especially given the formidable time constraints of regular teaching loads. Although professional development opportunities are rarely time conserving, done well they can equip teachers by offering them the chance to share tools for the difficult work of considering moral terrain in the classroom carefully. I know that the conclusions at which I arrived in doing this research would have been impossible for me to discover alone. I benefited from reflecting on various models of Holocaust education and by discussing my thoughts and practices with a variety of professors, practitioners, and friends. By having such conversations with their peers and other professionals, teachers could similarly profit.

BALANCING ACTS

Justifying the professional development efforts I am recommending are the considerable complexities involved in teaching about the Holocaust. The portraits in this study affirm again and again that the teaching of the Holocaust, indeed of all morally laden history, is a fraught enterprise, laced with pedagogical pitfalls. As I see it, the best we can do as teachers is to strive toward balance in the competing pulls of Holocaust representation, recognizing that the tensions are intricate and, in some cases, interdependent.

To restate, those tensions include the pulls between tragic and redemptive, unique and universal, and insular or expanded emplotments; the pulls between individualized and collectivized, normalized and exoticized, personalized or depersonalized representations of victims, perpetrators, bystanders, and rescuers; and the pulls between chronological and thematic, broadly explained and specifically illustrated, climactic and quotidian, inevitable and contingent images of history.

Finding the balancing points for each of these tensions is exceedingly difficult to pull off with finesse, especially as these tensions are compounded by the balancing acts inherent in all history teaching, among them, to name but a few, the importance of balancing our needs as teachers to challenge our students intellectually and support them emotionally, our hopes to build community and at the same time foster individual achievement, our intentions to display openness on the issues to which there really are no right answers with our desires to inculcate in students firm moral judgments on the issues to which there are, balancing between what we can know and what we can't possibly know about history (Wineburg, 2001). The list is agonizingly long even only in its partial state.

And yet I am claiming that the tightropes are worth walking, and that the balancing, no matter how precarious, is worth striving for, for missteps in either direction beget troubling consequences. Both ends of these continua must be interlaced for complex understandings of this history to emerge. What is human agency, after all, if it is presented as functioning in a vacuum, stripped of larger social forces and constellations; and conversely, of what worth is an explanation of history that highlights major organizational and ideological constructs without attending to how such forces affect, constrict, and liberate individuals? Likewise, how can empathy be built between students and historical actors if victims are only collectively represented, never individualized? And yet how can group behavior or indeed totalitarianism be understood without significant attention being paid to collective experience? All the binaries, thus, are falsely dichotomized; the polarities are truly continua, where the ideas along them are fundamentally interconnected. The expertise of Mr. Zee, Ms. Bess, and Mr. Dennis attests that the balancing acts are neither easy to attain nor necessarily result from years of experience.

It may be a mistake, however, to presume that the poles of these tensions are equivalently weighted. One can make a compelling argument that for some of the tensions, faulting in one direction is preferable to faulting in the other. Of the U.S. Holocaust Memorial Museum Guidelines for teaching about the Holocaust, for example, the 10th recommends that teachers "translate statistics into people" (Parsons & Totten, 1994, p. 6). Specifically, the guideline is advocating the use of "first-person accounts and memoir literature" to "show that individual people" constituted the "sheer number of victims," a statistic that otherwise "challenges easy comprehension" (p. 6). Implied is the notion that in the tension between individualized and collectivized representations of victims, it is preferable to individualize, a choice that in most cases will tend toward normalization and personalization as well. Yet in chapter 2, I have critiqued just this aspect of Mr. Zee's course, arguing that the extremity of his individualization sacrificed his students' understanding of the Holocaust (even had he taught them that history). Why then might tipping in the direction of an individualistic representation of victimization be preferable to one that collectivizes?

The answer revolves around the potential long-term, moral impacts of Holocaust education; those representations that point students toward rescuer rather than toward victimizer or bystander behavior are obviously preferable. It may well be, for example, that the kind of engagement Mr. Zee fostered and the sense of community he built among his students through sheer force of personality will be more important in the long run than his students' having learned the statistics and even the historical events that make up the Holocaust. While I found troubling the survey data that his students thought they knew a lot about the Holocaust from his course without having learned much historical information, Mr. Zee may have actually predisposed his students to learning that information later in life. For all the failings of his course, after all, Mr. Zee had ignited his students' curiosities.

An important question to be asked in terms of Holocaust education, then, is not what the students experienced in the context of the class per se—not whether they felt engaged, gained a sense of community, learned historical information, or trusted their teacher, nor even what representations of the Holocaust with what moral messages they constructed—but what the classes' long-term effects might be. I have to ask myself, for example, of the teachers' classes, whose students I would want to move into the vacant apartment upstairs. Would I rather live beside someone who could define *Kristallnacht* on a survey or someone who would knock down my door if I were screaming for help? While I think it is crucial not to polarize the gaining of historical information and the acquisition of moral sensibilities, dichotomizing intellect and wisdom in the process, the answer is nonetheless clear. For the most part, Mr. Zee's students had come to consider themselves more fully moral agents through his teaching.

In the long run, Ms. Bess's students were most likely, I think, not to stereotype Jews in particular, and neither to diminish the import of the Holocaust nor trivialize its consequences. Her students were deeply touched by the simulation; the overwhelming majority seemed to have gained a sense of the enormity of this tragedy and how it affected individual Jewish lives. And yet whether they were more likely to look out for one another or for others, to be rescuers rather than bystanders, remains an open question. Although I strongly suspect that Ms. Bess's students' gained the deepest and most intimate knowledge of the Holocaust as a result of her teaching, a strong sense of community was sacrificed for their equally strong sense of excitement and engagement in the simulation. In her class, after all, the students competed with one another for "survival," and though they worked together in small groups on occasion, they hadn't learned one anothers' names by the end of the course. The simulation had compromised whatever potential existed for real camaraderie. While they may have felt a sense of community in that each shared in the intensity of the simulation, their sense of comfort in the classroom was certainly minimal. Moreover, Ms. Bess's students could not trust their teacher because of the role she played in the classroom; she had made no overtures inviting her students to confide in her or seek her advice when she was not simulating. And though her students most closely empathized with Jewish victims of the Holocaust, I can't help but wonder whether it wouldn't have been more useful, morally, for them to have identified with rescuers or to have more fully investigated the moral complexities of being victimizers and bystanders. I wish it could be assumed that by having identified with victims, students would automatically shun the role of victimizers. I am not convinced, though, that this sophisticated association necessarily occurs, nor that such learning translates into behavior.

Mr. Zee's, Ms. Bess's, and Mr. Dennis's students all showed moral impacts as the result of their Holocaust studies. In my opinion, though, of their students, it was Mr. Dennis's whose experience was most balanced. Note that I do not describe his as the best enactment of the Holocaust, only the one whose sacrifices seem most even handed and whose benefits seem most long term. Within the context of a strong sense of community in which student voice was valued, Mr. Dennis's students learned historical information in an engaging way and from a caring teacher whom they trusted deeply. These contextual factors helped shape the representation of the Holocaust that was enacted in his classroom; indeed, the openness and questioning he fostered among students allowed for the discussion of moral lessons and Holocaust representation that I advocate above.

Ultimately, the legacies of the Holocaust, its informational and moral dimensions, may be so complex as to require us to struggle with its implications, not only at the level of the event itself, but also in our teaching of it. In this regard, challenges such as those of Peter Novick and Deborah Lipstadt provide rich opportunities to discuss with one another and our students what it is we mean by "lessons," whether history bears them, whether the Holocaust in particular does, and, if the answer is affirmative, what those lessons ought to look like in the real world. To arrive at such sophisticated discussions and to engage such important questions necessitates careful balancing—in our thinking, in our preparation to teach, and ultimately, in our teaching. I close by reflecting on the lessons I learned from undertaking this study.

CONCLUDING THOUGHTS

When I began my study, I was much more confident about how to teach the Holocaust than I am now. I had a long list of assumptions about what good teaching of the Shoah would look like. Although I didn't express these ideas to those I enlisted in helping me find exemplary teachers, I "knew," for example, that I was seeking teachers who valued historical accuracy, who fostered student engagement, who believed in building community in the classroom. I wanted the class material on the Holocaust to forge connections between past and present while at the same time building a strong knowledge base in students about the distinctions. I wanted to see discussions about the impossible moral dilemmas that faced Holocaust victims and survivors, just as I wanted students to investigate why perpetrators, bystanders, and rescuers acted as they did. I also brought my own assumptions about the nature of learning, in particular that exposure does not equal understanding and that reflection is required for sophisticated learning. Finally, I knew that as a Jewish woman with some familial connections to this history, I had high personal stakes invested in what I would see. In short, I knew when I embarked on this study that what I sought was a tall order for any teacher, and I worried that I might be setting up for failure the teachers who participated. My own powerful commitments, after all, would dictate what I considered "good."

Instead, my foray into these teachers' classrooms changed the nature of the equations for me. While I still deem historical accuracy a "good" in and of itself, I no longer see it simplistically. Mr. Jefferson's representation of Jews, after all, was as historically accurate as Mr. Dennis's. To learn about Jews as a collective is no less historically accurate than to consider them as individuals; it is the moral dimensions of this choice that confound easy judgment. The same kind of tension is inherent in the problem of representing Jews positively, or as "normal" human beings despite the overwhelmingly negative history of Nazism and the Shoah, its dehumanization of Jews in propagandistic images or disembodied victims. And similarly, all the teachers' emplotments of the Holocaust can be seen as historically accurate. It is not inaccurate to cover the important concepts of rescue and resistance at the end of a Holocaust course, as did Mr. Zee. Nor is it inaccurate to end a Holocaust unit with the ending of World War II and the dropping of the atom bombs on Hiroshima and Nagasaki, as did Ms. Bess; what is at stake in all these examples are the moral messages embedded in the informational narratives, not their degrees of historical accuracy.

The same layers of complexity have come to be associated in my mind with all the judgment criteria I originally held. Indeed, the problems are inherent in representations of all morally laden history, from slavery to the Armenian genocide to the Vietnam War to the events of September 11. The moral dimensions of historical narratives render perplexing any act of representation.

As a result, I found myself in the course of my study stunned by the numerous complexities inherent in teaching about the Holocaust in particular and the precarious balancing acts involved in the teaching of history in general. It is thus with far more questions that I leave this study than those with which I began; the questions of how experienced high school teachers teach about the Holocaust, what moral lessons they convey implicitly and communicate explicitly, and what their impact on students is, have been joined by a host of others. And while I pose some recommendations in this book, I abstain from making broad generalizations about the teaching of this history.

One conviction, however, has stayed with me since the time I traveled to schools with Holocaust survivors: that the complexities involved in understanding the events of the Holocaust, its iconic status, its politicized usages and inevitable moral lessons, demand that we not pursue oversimplification in its teaching, no matter how seductive that urge. The Castlemont High School students, it might be remembered, were initially injured by just that allure.

References

Adelson, A., & Taverna, K. (Directors) (1989). *Lodz Ghetto* [Motion picture]. Jewish Heritage Project (Producer). Bethesda, MD: Atlas Video.

Alter, R. (1981). Deformations of the Holocaust. *Commentary, 71*, 48–54.

Ball, D. L., & Wilson, S. M. (1996). Integrity in teaching: Recognizing the fusion of the moral and intellectual. *American Education Research Journal, 33*(1), 155–192.

Barnouw, D. & Van der Stroom, G. (Eds.). (1989). *The diary of Anne Frank: The critical edition.* New York: Viking.

Bauer, Y. (1982). *A history of the Holocaust*. New York: Franklin Watts.

Bauer, Y. (2001). *Rethinking the Holocaust*. New Haven, CT: Yale University Press.

Bellah, R. N., Madsen, R., Sullivan, W. M., Swidler, A., & Tipton, S. M. (1985). *Habits of the heart: Individualism and commitment in American life*. Berkeley: University of California Press.

Ben-Peretz, M. (1990). *The teacher-curriculum encounter: Freeing teachers from the tyranny of texts*. Albany: State University of New York Press.

Berenbaum, M. (1990). *After tragedy and triumph: Essays in modern Jewish thought and the American experience*. New York: Cambridge University Press.

Bernstein, M. A. (1994). *Foregone conclusions: Against apocalyptic history*. Berkeley: University of California Press.

Bernstein, M. A. (1998). Homage to the extreme: The Shoah and the rhetoric of catastrophe. *Times Literary Supplement, 4953*, 6–8.

Bettelheim, B. (1960). *Surviving and other essays*. New York: Vintage Books.

Blair, J. (Director), & Frank, A. (Producer) (1995). *Anne Frank remembered* [Motion picture]. Columbia Tristar.

Bresheeth, H., Hood, S., & Jansz, L. (2002). *Introducing the Holocaust.* New York: Totem Books.

Brophy, J. (1993). Findings and issues: The cases viewed in context. In J. Brophy (Ed.), *Advances in research on teaching* (Vol. 4, pp. 219–232). Greenwich, CT: JAI Press.

Browning, C. R. (1992). *Ordinary men: Reserve Police Battalion 101 and the Final Solution in Poland.* New York: HarperCollins.

Cazden, C. B. (1988). *Classroom discourse: The language of teaching and learning.* Portsmouth, NH: Heinemann Educational Books.

Chazan, B. (1985). *Contemporary approaches to moral education: Analyzing alternative theories.* New York: Teachers College Press.

Clendinnen, I. (1999). *Reading the Holocaust*. Cambridge: Cambridge University Press.
Cohen, A. (1974). *Thinking the tremendum: Some theological implications of the death-camps*. New York: Leo Baeck.
Coles, R. (1986). *The moral life of children*. Boston: Houghton Mifflin.
Cuban, L. (1988). A fundamental puzzle of school reform. *Phi Delta Kappan, 69*(5), 340–344.
Cuban, L. (1990). Reforming again, again, and again. *Educational Researcher, 19*(1), 3–13.
Cuban, L. (1991). History of teaching in social studies. In J. Shaver (Ed.), *Handbook of research on social studies teaching and learning* (pp. 197–209). New York: Macmillan International.
Cuban, L. (1993). *How teachers taught: Constancy and change in American classrooms, 1890–1990*. New York: Teachers College Press.
Cuban, L. (2001). *How can I fix it? Finding solutions and managing dilemmas: An educator's road map*. New York: Teachers College Press.
Dawidowicz, L. S. (1992). How they teach the Holocaust. In N. Kozoday (Ed.), *What is the use of Jewish history?* (pp. 65–83). New York: Schocken Books.
Dawkins, J., & Jones, R., III, & Grasshoff, A., Director. (1981). *The wave* [Motion picture]. ABC Theatre for Young Americans.
Department of Education California. (1988). *History–social science framework*. Sacramento: Author.
Dewey, J. (1909). *Moral principles in education*. Carbondale: Southern Illinois University Press.
DJC Irving v. Penguin Books Ltd and Deborah Lipstadt (High Court of Justice, England, 1993).
Eichengreen, L. (1994). *From ashes to life: My memories of the Holocaust*. San Francisco: Mercury House.
Eisner, E. W. (1991). *The enlightened eye: Qualitative inquiry and the enhancement of educational practice*. New York: Macmillan.
Eisner, E. W., & Peshkin, A. (Eds.). (1990). *Qualitative inquiry in education: The continuing debate*. New York: Teachers College Press.
Elon, A. (1993). The politics of memory. *New York Review of Books, 40*, 3–5.
Epstein, T. (1998). Deconstructing differences in African-American and European-American adolescents' perspectives on U.S. history. *Curriculum Inquiry, 28*(4), 397–423.
Erickson, F., & Shultz, J. (1992). Students' experience of the curriculum. In P. Jackson (Ed.), *Handbook of research on curriculum: A project of the American Educational Research Association* (pp. 465–485). New York: Maxwell Macmillan International.
Evans, R. W. (1993). Ideology and the teaching of history: Purposes, practices, and student beliefs. In J. Brophy (Ed.), *Advances in research on teaching* (Vol. 4, pp. 179–218). Greenwich, CT: JAI Press.
Feinberg, S., & Totten, S. (2001). Preface. In S. Totten & S. Feinberg (Eds.), *Teaching and studying the Holocaust* (pp. xv–xvi). Boston: Allyn & Bacon.
Fine, M. (1993a). Collaborative innovations: Documentation of the Facing His-

tory and Ourselves Program at an Essential School. *Teachers College Record, 94*(4), 771–789.

Fine, M. (1993b). "You can't just say that the only ones who can speak are those who agree with your position": Political discourse in the classroom. *Harvard Educational Review, 63*(4), 412–433.

Fine, M. (1995). *Habits of mind.* San Francisco: Jossey-Bass.

Flanzbaum, H. (Ed.). (1999). *The Americanization of the Holocaust.* Baltimore: Johns Hopkins University Press.

Friedlander, H. (1972). *A critique of the treatment of the Holocaust in history books: Accompanied by an annotated bibliography.* New York: Anti-Defamation League of B'nai B'rith.

Friedlander, H. (1980). Toward a methodology of teaching about the Holocaust. *The Holocaust: Ideology, bureaucracy, and genocide.* New York: Kraus International Publications.

Friedlander, S. (Ed.). (1992). *Probing the limits of representation: Nazism and the "final solution."* Cambridge: Harvard University Press.

Frisch, M. (1989). American history and the structures of collective memory: A modest exercise in empirical iconography. *Journal of American History, 75*(4), 1130–1155.

Furman, H. (Ed.). (1983). *The Holocaust and genocide: A search for conscience.* New York: Anti-Defamation League of B'nai B'rith.

Gardner, H. (1999). *The disciplined mind.* New York: Penguin Books.

Gardner, R. (Director and Producer). (1985). *The courage to care* [Motion picture].

Geertz, C. (1973). *The interpretation of cultures.* New York: Basic Books.

Giroux, H., & Purpel, D. (1983). *The hidden curriculum and moral education.* Berkeley, CA: McCutchan.

Goldhagen, D. J. (1996). *Hitler's willing executioners: Ordinary Germans and the Holocaust.* New York: Knopf.

Goodlad, J. (1984). *A place called school: Prospects for the future.* New York: McGraw-Hill.

Goodrich, F., & Hackett, A. (1958). *The diary of Anne Frank.* New York: Dramatists Play Service.

Gourevitch, P. (1995, Feb 12). What they saw at the Holocaust Museum. *The New York Times Magazine,* p. 12.

Graff, G. (1992). *Beyond the culture wars: How teaching the conflicts can revitalize American education.* New York: Norton.

Grant, S. G. (2001). It's just the facts, or is it? The relationship between teachers' practices and students' understandings of history. *Theory and Research in Social Education, 29*(1), 65–108.

Green, G. (Writer), & Chomsky, M. J. (Director). (1978). *Holocaust* [Motion picture]. H. Brodkin (Producer), NBC Miniseries.

Greenbaum, B. A. (2001). *Bearing witness: Teaching about the Holocaust.* Portsmouth, NH: Heinemann.

Gross, J. (2001). *Neighbors.* Princeton, NJ: Princeton University Press.

Gutman, I., et al. (1990). Holocaust education, *Encyclopedia of the Holocaust* (Vol. 2). New York: Macmillan.

Gutman, I., & Schatzker, C. (1984). *A teacher's guide to the Holocaust and its significance.* Jerusalem: Historical Society of Israel.
Gutman, Y., & Schatzker, C. (1984). *The Holocaust and its significance.* Jerusalem: Zalman Shazar Center, Historical Society of Israel.
Hansen, D. T. (1993). The moral importance of the teacher's style. *Journal of Curriculum Studies, 25*(5), 397–421.
Hansen, D. T. (1995). *The call to teach.* New York: Teachers College Press.
Hansen, M. B. (Ed.). (1997). Schindler's List *is not Shoah: Second commandment, popular modernism, and public memory.* Bloomington: Indiana University Press.
Hayes, P. (Ed.). (1991). *Lessons and legacies: The meaning of the Holocaust in a changing world.* Chicago: Northwestern University Press.
Heller, C., & Hawkins, J. (1994). Teaching tolerance: Notes from the front line. *Teachers College Record, 95*(3), 337–368.
Hess, D. (2002). Teaching controversial public issues discussions: Learning from skilled teachers. *Theory and Research in Social Education, 30*(1), 10–41.
Hilberg, R. (1967). *The destruction of European Jews.* Chicago: Quadrangle Books.
Hudlin, R., & Toney, D. (Writers), Meza, E. (Director). (1994). *House Party 3* [Motion picture]. United States: New Line Cinema.
Jackson, P. W. (1968). *Life in classrooms.* New York: Holt, Rinehart and Winston.
Jackson, P. W. (Ed.). (1983). *The daily grind.* Berkeley, CA: McCutchan.
Jackson, P. W. (Ed.). (1992). *Handbook of research on curriculum: A project of the American Educational Research Association.* New York: Maxwell Macmillan International.
Jackson, P. W., Boostrom, R. E., & Hansen, D. T. (1993). *The moral life of schools.* San Francisco: Jossey-Bass.
Jick, L. (1981). The Holocaust: Its use and abuse in the American public. *Yad Vashem Studies, 19,* 303–318.
Jones, R. (1981). *No substitute for madness.* Covelo, CA: Island Press.
Kahne, J., Rodriguez, M., Smith, B., & Thiede, K. (2000). Developing citizens for democracy? Assessing opportunities to learn in Chicago's social studies classrooms. *Theory and Research in Social Education, 28*(3), 311–338.
Katz Bill. (1992). California State Assembly.
Kren, G., & Rappoport, L. (1994). *Holocaust and the crisis of human behavior.* New York: Holmes & Meier.
Ladson-Billings, G. (1995). Toward a critical race theory of education. *Teachers College Record, 97*(1), 47.
Langer, L. (1996). The alarmed vision: Social suffering and Holocaust atrocity. *Daedalus, 125*(1), 47–65.
Lanzmann, C. (Director), & Adelph, F. (Producer). (1985). *Shoah* [Motion picture]. France: Historia Films.
Laqueur, T. (1994). The Holocaust Museum. *The Threepenny Review,* 30–32.
Laughter at film brings Spielberg visit. (1994, April 13). *New York Times,* p. B11.
Levi, P. (1960). *Survival in Auschwitz.* New York: Orion Press.
Levi, P. (1989). *The drowned and the saved.* New York: Simon & Schuster.
Levstik, L. (1995). Narrative constructions: Cultural frames for history. *The Social Studies, 86*(3), 113–116.

Lightfoot, S. L. (1983). *The good high school.* New York: Basic Books.

Lipstadt, D. (1993). *Denying the Holocaust: The growing assault on truth and memory.* New York: Plume.

Lipstadt, D. (1995, March 6). Not facing history. *The New Republic, 212,* 26.

Loshitzky, Y. (1997). *Spielberg's Holocaust: Critical perspectives on* Schindler's List. Bloomington: Indiana University Press.

Margalit, A. (1994). The uses of the Holocaust. *New York Review of Books, 41*(4), 7–10.

Marker, G., & Mehlinger, H. (1992). Social studies. In P. Jackson (Ed.), *Handbook of research on curriculum* (pp. 830–850). New York: Maxwell Macmillan International.

Marrus, M. (1987). *The Holocaust in history.* New York: Penguin Books.

McKee, S. J. (1988). Impediments to implementing critical thinking. *Social Education, 52*(6), 444–446.

McLaughlin, M. (1994). *Urban sanctuaries: Neighborhood organizations in the lives and futures of inner-city youth.* San Francisco: Jossey-Bass.

Mehan, H. (1979). *Learning lessons: Social organization in the classroom.* Cambridge, MA: Harvard University Press.

Merriam, S. (1988). *Case study research in education: A qualitative approach.* San Francisco: Jossey-Bass.

Miles, M. B., & Huberman, A. M. (1984). *Qualitative data analysis: A sourcebook of new methods.* Beverly Hills, CA: Sage.

Milgram, S. (1974). *Obedience to authority.* New York: Harper & Row.

Noddings, N. (1984). *Caring: A feminine approach to ethics and moral education.* Berkeley: University of California Press.

Noddings, N. (1992). *The challenge to care in schools: An alternative approach to education.* New York: Teachers College Press.

Noddings, N. (1993). *Educating for intelligent belief or unbelief.* New York: Teachers College Press.

Novick, P. (1988). *That noble dream: The "objectivity question" and the American historical profession.* Cambridge, Eng.: Cambridge University Press.

Novick, P. (1999). *The Holocaust in American life.* Boston: Houghton Mifflin.

Nucci, L. (1989). Challenging conventional wisdom about morality: the domain approach to values education. In L. Nucci (Ed.), *Moral development and character education: A dialogue.* Berkeley, CA: McCutchan.

Nystrand, M., Gamoran, A., & Carbonara, W. (1998). *Towards an ecology of learning: The case of classroom discourse and its effects on writing in high school English and social studies.* Albany, NY: Center on English Learning & Achievement, University of Albany/ERIC Document Reproduction Service.

Oliner, S. P., & Oliner, P. M. (1988). *The altruistic personality: Rescuers of Jews in Nazi Europe.* New York: Free Press.

Ozick, C. (1996, October 6). Who owns Anne Frank? *New Yorker,* pp. 76–86.

Palmer, P. (1993). *To know as we are known: Education as a spiritual journey.* San Francisco: Harper.

Parr, S. R. (1982). *The moral of the story: Literature, values, and American education.* New York: Teachers College Press.

Parsons, W. S., & Totten, S. (1994). *Guidelines for teaching about the Holocaust.* Washington, DC: U.S. Holocaust Memorial Museum.

Pate, G. S. (1979). *The treatment of the Holocaust in United States history textbooks.* New York: Anti-Defamation League of B'nai B'rith.

Peshkin, A. (1986). *God's choice: The total world of a fundamentalist Christian school.* Chicago: University of Chicago Press.

Peshkin, A. (1988). In search of subjectivity—one's own. *Educational Researcher, 17*(7), 32–37.

Pesick, S. (1996). Writing history: Before and after portfolios. *The Quarterly of the National Writing Project and the Center for the Study of Literacy, 2,* 20–29.

Peters, W. (1987). *A class divided: Then and now.* New Haven, CT: Yale University Press.

Pope, D. C. (2001). *"Doing school."* New Haven, CT: Yale University Press.

Popkewitz, T. S., Tabatchnick, B. R., & Wehlage, G. (1982). *The myth of educational reform.* Madison: University of Wisconsin Press.

Portal, C. (Ed.). (1987). *The history curriculum for teachers.* Philadelphia: Falmer Press.

Purpel, D. E. (1989). *The moral and spiritual crisis in education.* Granby, MA: Bergin & Garvey.

Purpel, D. E., & Ryan, K. (1983). It comes with the territory: The inevitability of moral education in the schools. In H. Giroux & D. Purpel (Eds.), *The hidden curriculum and moral education* (pp. 267–275). Berkeley, CA: McCutchan.

Ravitch, D., & Finn, C. E., Jr. (1987). *What do our 17-year-olds know? A report of the first national assessment of history and literature.* New York: Harper & Row.

Rosenberg, A., & Bardosh, A. (1982–83). The problematic character of teaching the Holocaust. *Shoah: A Journal of Resources on the Holocaust, 3*(2–3), 3–7.

Rosenfeld, A. H. (1995). The Americanization of the Holocaust. *Commentary, 99*(6), 35–40.

Rosenthal, D. (1994, April 12). Spielberg hailed, Wison chided at Oakland school. *Los Angeles Times,* p. 1.

Schatzker, C. (1982). The Holocaust in Israeli education. *International Journal of Political Education, 5*(1), 75–81.

Schweber, S. (2003). Simulating survival. *Curriculum Inquiry, 33*(2), 139–188.

Segev, T. (1993). *The seventh million: The Israelis and the Holocaust.* New York: Hill & Wang.

Seidman, N. (1996). Elie Wiesel and the scandal of Jewish rage. *Jewish Social Studies, 3*(1), 1–19.

Seixas, P. (1993a). The community of inquiry as a basis for knowledge and learning: The case of history. *American Educational Research Journal, 30*(2), 305–324.

Seixas, P. (1993b). Historical understanding among adolescents in a multicultural setting. *Curriculum Inquiry, 23*(3), 301–327.

Seixas, P. (1994a). Confronting the moral frames of popular film: Young people respond to historical revisionism. *American Journal of Education, 102*(1), 261–285.

Seixas, P. (1994b). Students' understanding of historical significance. *Theory and Research in Social Education, 22*(3), 281–304.

Shaver, J. (Ed.). (1991). *Handbook of research on social studies teaching and learning.* New York: Macmillan International.
Short, G. (1995). The Holocaust in the national curriculum: A survey of teachers' attitudes and practices. *The Journal of Holocuast Education, 4*(2), 167–188.
Shulman, L. S. (1983). Autonomy and obligation: The remote control of teaching. In L. Shulman & G. Sykes (Eds.), *Handbook of teaching and policy* (pp. 484–504). New York: Longman.
Shulman, L. S. (1987). The wisdom of practice: Managing complexity in medicine and teaching. In D. C. Berliner & B. V. Rosenshine (Eds.), *Talks to teachers: A Festschrift for N. L. Gage* (pp. 369–386). New York: Random House.
Shulman, L. S. (1992). Toward a pedagogy of cases. In J. H. Shulman (Ed.), *Case methods in teacher education* (pp. 1–30). New York: Teachers College Press.
Shultz, L. H., Barr, D. J., & Selman, R. L. (2001). The value of a developmental approach to evaluating character development programmes: An outcome study of Facing History and Ourselves. *Journal of Moral Education, 30*(1), 3–27.
Simon, K. G. (2001). *Moral questions in the classroom: How to get kids to think deeply about real life and their schoolwork.* New Haven, CT: Yale University Press.
Sizer, T. R. (1984). *Horace's compromise: The dilemma of the American high school.* Boston: Houghton Mifflin.
Sockett, H. (1992). The moral aspects of the curriculum. In P. W. Jackson (Ed.), *Handbook of research on curriculum.* New York: Macmillan.
Spiegelman, A. (1986). *Maus.* New York: Pantheon Books.
Spielberg, S. D. (Director). (1993). *Schindler's list* [Motion picture]. K. Kennedy (Producer). United States: Amblin Productions.
Spolar, C. (1994, March 10). The kids who laughed 'till it hurt: Students' reaction to "Schindler's List" fires racial tensions. *Washington Post,* p. C1.
Stern-Strom, M. (1982). *Facing history and ourselves: The Holocaust and human behavior.* Watertown, MA: International Education.
Taylor, K. (1995). *Address unknown.* Cincinnati: Story Press.
Thornton, S. J. (1998, Summer). Curriculum consonance in United States history. *Journal of Curriculum and Supervision, 3*(4), 308–320.
Thornton, S. J. (1993). Toward the desirable in social studies teaching. In J. Brophy (Ed.), *Advances in research on teaching* (Vol. 4, pp. 157–218). London: JAI Press.
Tom, A. (1984). *Teaching as a moral craft.* New York: Longman.
Totten, S. (1988). The literature, art and film of the Holocaust. In I. Charny (Ed.), *Genocide: A critical bibliographic review* (pp. 209–240). New York: Mansell.
Totten, S. (2000). Diminishing the complexity and horror of the Holocaust: Using simulations in an attempt to convey historical experiences. *Social Education, 64*(3), 165–171.
Totten, S. (Ed.). (2001). *Teaching Holocaust literature.* Boston: Allyn & Bacon.
Totten, S., & Feinberg, S. (Ed.). (2001). *Teaching and studying the Holocaust.* Boston: Allyn & Bacon.
Trunk, I. (1972). *Judenrat: The Jewish councils in Eastern Europe under Nazi occupation.* New York: Macmillan Press.

Turkel, S. (1984). *The good war.* New York: New Press.

Tyack, D. (1988). Ways of seeing: An essay on the history of compulsory schooling. In R. M. Jaeger (Ed.), *Complementary methods for research in education* (pp. 24–58). Washington, DC: American Educational Research Association.

Tyack, D., & Cuban, L. (1995). *Tinkering toward utopia: A century of public school reform.* Cambridge, MA: Harvard University Press.

United States (1986). *"Expressing the sense of congress that public schools should be encouraged to include a study of the Holocaust in their history curriculums"*: H. Con. Res, 121.

VanSledright, B. (1992). Storytelling, imagination, and fanciful elaboration in children's historical reconstructions. *American Educational Research Journal, 29*(4), 837–859.

Wallace, L., & Tunberg, K. (Writers), Wyler, W. (Director) (1959). *Ben Hur* [Motion picture]. MGM Studios.

Weinstein, J. L. (1997). Lessons of history. *Thrust for Educational Leadership, 27,* 8–12.

Weissmann Klein, G. (1957). *All but my life.* New York: Noonday Press.

Weissmann Klein, G. (1995). *One survivor remembers* (K. Antholis, Director).

White, H. (1981). The value of narrativity in the representation of reality. In W. J. Mitchell (Ed.), *On narrative* (pp. 1–23). Chicago: University of Chicago Press.

White, H. (1992). Historical emplotment and the problem of truth. In S. Friedlander (Ed.), *Probing the limits of representation: Nazism and the "Final Solution"* (pp. 37–53). Cambridge, MA: Harvard University Press.

Wiesel, E. (1960). *Night.* New York: Bantam Books.

Wiesel, E. (1990). *From the kingdom of memory.* New York: Simon & Schuster.

Wiesenthal, S. (1977). *The sunflower.* New York: Schocken Books.

Wieser, P. (2001). Instructional issues/strategies in teaching the Holocaust. In S. Totten & S. Feinberg (Eds.), *Teaching and studying the Holocaust* (pp. 62–80). Boston: Allyn & Bacon.

Williams, J., & Perlman, I. (1993). *Schindler's list: Original motion picture soundtrack.* MCA.

Wilson, S. M., & Wineburg, S. S. (1991). Wrinkles in time and place: Using performance assessments to understand the knowledge of history teachers. *American Educational Research Journal, 30*(4), 729–769.

Wineberg, S. S. (1991). Historical problem solving: A study of the cognitive processes used in the evaluation of documentary and pictorial evidence. *Journal of Educational Psychology, 83*(1), 73–87.

Wineberg, S. S. (1993). Mr. Stinson's Vietnam: Moral ambiguity in the history classroom. In J. Kleinfeld (Ed.), *Teaching cases in cross-cultural education.* New York: Carnegie Corporation.

Wineburg, S. S. (1991). On the reading of historical texts: Notes on the breach between school and academy. *American Educational Research Journal, 28*(3), 495–519.

Wineburg, S. S. (2001). *Historical thinking and other unnatural acts: Charting the future of teaching the past.* Philadelphia: Temple University Press.

Wineburg, S. S., & Wilson, S. M. (1991). Subject-matter knowledge in the teaching of history. In J. Brophy (Ed.), *Advances in research on teaching* (Vol. 2, pp. 305–347). London: JAI Press.

Wouk, H., Wallace, E., (Writers), & Curtis, D. (Director). (1988). *War and remembrance* [Motion picture]. ABC Circle Films.

Yin, R. K. (1984). *Case study research: Design and methods.* Beverly Hills, CA: Sage.

Young, J. (1988). *Writing and rewriting the Holocaust: Narratives and the consequences of interpretation.* Bloomington: Indiana University Press.

Zimbardo, P. G. (1999). *The Stanford prison experiment* [slide-show]. Website: *http://www.prisonexp.org/.*

Zimbardo, P. G., Maslach, C., & Haney, C. (2000). Reflections on the Stanford prison experiment: Genesis, transformations, consequences. In T. Blass (Ed.), *Obedience to authority: Current perspectives on the Milgram paradigm* (pp. 193–237). Mahwah, NJ: Erlbaum.

Zwerin, R., Friedman Marcus, A., & Kramish, L. (1976). Gestapo: A learning experience about the Holocaust [Board game]. Denver, CO: A.R.E.

Index

About the Author

Simone Schweber is the Goodman Professor of Education and Jewish Studies at the University of Wisconsin–Madison, where she teaches courses on social studies teaching methods, religion and public education, and Holocaust history and memory. Before earning her doctorate from Stanford University's School of Education, shc taught elementary, middle, and high school students in Jewish schools and served as the coordinator for secondary education at the Holocaust Center of Northern California.